Contract Law in Australia

Contract Law in Australia

Eugene Clark
Lynden Griggs
George Cho
Arthur Hoyle

This book was originally published as a monograph in the International Encyclopaedia of Laws/Contracts.

General Editor: Roger Blanpain
Associate General Editor: Michele Colucci
Volume Editor: Jacques Herbots

Wolters Kluwer
Law & Business

Published by:
Kluwer Law International
PO Box 316
2400 AH Alphen aan den Rijn
The Netherlands
Website: www.kluwerlaw.com

Sold and distributed in North, Central and South America by:
Aspen Publishers, Inc.
7201 McKinney Circle
Frederick, MD 21704
United States of America
Email: customer.service@aspenpublishers.com

Sold and distributed in all other countries by:
Turpin Distribution Services Ltd.
Stratton Business Park
Pegasus Drive, Biggleswade
Bedfordshire SG18 8TQ
United Kingdom
Email: kluwerlaw@turpin-distribution.com

Printed on acid-free paper.

ISBN 978-90-411-5169-8

This title is available on www.kluwerlawonline.com

Printed and Bound by CPI Group (UK) Ltd, Croydon, CR0 4YY.

The Authors

Prof. Dr Eugene Clark is Distinguished Professor, China University of Political Science and Law. He is also Emeritus Professor of Law, University of Canberra. His first law degree was from Washburn University in the United States where he was admitted to practice before the Kansas and United States District Courts. He also holds a PhD in Law from the University of Tasmania and two Master's Degrees in Education. His former roles include: Pro Vice-Chancellor and Head of the Law School, University of Canberra; Executive Dean, Faculty of Law, Business and Arts, Charles Darwin University, Dean, Charlotte School of Law; Dean, Phoenix School of Law; and Head of Business Law, Griffith University.

He has published 20 books and over 100 journal articles, including: Managers and the Law (2nd eds.) (with Griggs et al.), and Australian Financial Institutions Law (1993, 2nd ed. 1996, with Blay) and Australian Marketing Law 1994, with Livermore). He is on the editorial boards of the Journal of Contemporary Issues in Business and Government, Journal of Law, Information and Science and International Journal of Technology, Policy and Law. Eugene was the general editor, author of the Introduction materials and new section on Future of Australian Contract Law. He also assisted co-authors with general updating of this title and also completed the Case Index.

Mr Lynden Griggs is a Senior Lecturer in Law at the University of Tasmania. He has an Honours and Masters degree in Law from the University of Tasmania. He is admitted as a barrister and solicitor of the Supreme Court of Tasmania and the Federal Courts of Australia. He is the Associate Editor of the *Competition and Consumer Law Journal* and is on the editorial board of the Australian and New Zealand Trade Practices Law Bulletin. His principal areas of interest are competition law, consumer law and property law. His principal areas of interest are consumer law, property law and sports law. He is currently researching the impact that electronic conveyancing will have on the Torrens system. He is a Fellow of the Higher Education Research and Development Society of Australasia. Lynden was the author of Part I, Chapters, 1, 2, and was co-author with Prof Cho of Part II. Lynden also completed the Index and assisted with final editing.

Prof. Dr George Cho, A.M. is Professor of Geographic Information Systems and the Law at the University of Canberra. He has an Honours Degree in Arts from the University of Malaya, a Masters Degree from the University of British Columbia and a PhD from the Australian National University (ANU). He also holds a Graduate Certificate in Higher Education from the University of Canberra and an LLB from the ANU and is admitted as a barrister and solicitor of the Supreme Court of the ACT and NSW and the High Court of Australia. He has published numerous books and journal articles on law and geography topics, including Australia: International Encyclopaedia of Laws: Commercial and Economic Law Supplement 45 series (October 2012) edited by Jules Stuyck, Alphen aan den Rijn, The Netherlands: Kluwer Law International with E. Clark, A. Hoyle & J. McLaren; The Malaysian Economy: Spatial Perspectives, Routledge Revivals first published in 1990 (2012). London: Routledge; Cyber Law in Australia (2010), Alpen aan den Rijn, The Netherlands: Kluwer Law International, with E. Clark, A. Hoyle & P. Hynes; International Encyclopaedia of Laws: Cyber Law, Supplement 24, Australia (2010), The Hague: Kluwer Law International, with E. Clark, A. Hoyle and P. Hynes. Geographic Information Science: Managing the Legal Issues (London: John Wiley & Sons, 2005); Cyber Law: Australia. International Encyclopaedia of Laws (with E. Clark and A. Hoyle), The Hague: Kluwer Law International 2004; E-Business Law and Management for the 21st Century (with E. Clark and A. Hoyle), Canberra: Info-Sys Law International Publications 2001; Marketers and the Law (with E. Clark and A. Hoyle), Sydney: Law Book Coy. Information Services 2000); Y2K: Avoiding the Legal Byte. A Guide for Managers and Legal Assessors (with E. Clark and A. Hoyle), Sydney: Prospect Publications 1999; Geographic Information Systems and the Law, London: John Wiley & Sons, 1998.

George was the author of Part I, Chapters 3 and 4, and co-author of Part II with Lynden Griggs.

The Authors

Mr Arthur Hoyle ASM is a Senior Lecturer in Law and Technology at the University of Canberra. He holds a bachelor's degree from the Australian National University, an LLB (Hons) and Master of Laws from the University of Canberra and a Graduate Diploma in Legal Practice. He is an admitted Barrister and Solicitor of the Supreme Court of the ACT and the High Court of Australia. He has over twenty years of government and legal related experience. He has published many conference papers and in several books including: Y2K: Avoiding the Legal Byte (Prospect Publishing 1999), An Introduction to Electronic Legal Research (three editions) (ILRT), Managers and the Law, 2nd edition (Thompson), E-Business Law and Management (Info Sys Law 2000). Cyber Law: Australia. International Encyclopaedia of Laws (with E. Clark and G.Cho), The Hague: Kluwer Law International 2004; Marketers and the Law (with E. Clark and G.Cho), Sydney: Law Book Coy. Information Services 2000); Y2K: Avoiding the Legal Byte. A Guide for Managers and Legal Assessors (with E. Clark and G.Cho), Sydney.

The Authors

Table of Contents

Table of Contents

List of Abbreviations

ABLR	Australian Business Law Review
AC	Appeal Cases
ACCC	Australian Competition and Consumer Commission
ACLC	Australian Company Law Cases
ACLR	Australian Company Law Reports
ACN	Australian Company Number
ACSR	Australian Corporate and Security Reports
ACTR	Australian Capital Territory Reports
AJR	Australian Jurist Reports
ALJ	Australian Law Journal
ALJR	Australian Law Journal Reports
All ER	All England Law Reports
ALR	Australian Law Reports
App	Cas Hare Appeal Cases
ATPR	Australian Trade Practices Reports
AUSTRAC	Australian Transactions Reports and Analysis Centre
ASC	Australian Securities Commission
Ch	Chancery
ClD	Chancery Division
CLR	Commonwealth Law Reports

List of Abbreviations

CoRep	Coke's Reports (UK)
CP	Common Pleas Division
DLR	Dominion Law Reports
Ex Ch	Exchequer Reports, Chancery Division
FCR	Federal Court Reports
FLR	Federal Law Reports
IPR	Intellectual Property Reports
JBFLP	Journal of Banking and Finance Law and Practice
JBL	Journal of Business Law
KB	Kings Bench
LIJ	Law Institute Journal
LJKB	Law Journal Reports Kings Bench Division
LR Exch	Law Reports Exchequer
LR HL	Law Reports House of Lords
LR PC	Privy Council Appeals
NSWLR	New South Wales Law Reports
NSWR	New South Wales Reports
NTR	Northern Territory Reports
OR	Ontario Reports
PC	British and Colonial Prize Cases
QB	Queens Bench Reports
QBD	Law Reports, Queens Bench Division
Qd R	Queensland Reports
QSR	Queensland State Reports
SALR	South Australian Law Reports
SASR	South Australian State Reports
SR (NSW)	State Reports (New South Wales)

SR (NSW)	EQ State Reports, New South Wales, Equity Division
St R (QD)	Queensland State Reports
Tas LR	Tasmanian Law Reports
TLR	Tasmanian Law Reports
TPA	Trade Practices Act
TPC	Trade Practices Commission
VLR	Victorian Law Reports
VR	Victorian Reports
WAR	Western Australia Reports
WALR	Western Australia Law Reports
WLR	Weekly Law Reports

List of Abbreviations

General Introduction

§1. General Background of the Country

I. Geography

1. Australia is an island continent situated in the Southern Hemisphere between the Indian Ocean and the South Pacific. Except for the coastal areas, much of Australia is dry and arid. Australia's nearest neighbours are Papua New Guinea and Indonesia to the north, New Zealand to the southeast and the Melanesian and Polynesian Islands to the east.

II. Cultural Composition

2. Although recent migrants are more likely to be from Asia, the majority of Australians continue to be of Anglo-Saxon origin, and the dominant culture, language, manners and customs remain similar to those found in other Anglo-Saxon countries such as England, Canada and the United States. Australia today is thus a multicultural country that is home to significant numbers of migrants from many other countries, including Italy, Greece, China and Vietnam. One of the most significant of Australia's minority groups are its approximately 200,000 indigenous inhabitants, the Aborigines, who continue to struggle for recognition and a rightful share of Australia's considerable wealth.

III. Political System

A. The Constitution and the Three Powers

3. The Australian political system is one of democratically elected governments – general elections must be held at least once every three years. The governmental framework in Australia draws on features from both the British parliamentary system and the American checks and balances system. Like the United States, Australia is a federation, comprised of a central government (the Commonwealth), six state governments and two territories. However, like Britain, Australia is a constitutional monarchy with allegiance to the Queen who maintains a representative at Commonwealth and state levels. Although generally regarded as a mere figurehead, the Queen's representative in the Australian Commonwealth Parliament, Sir John Kerr, in 1975 dismissed then Prime Minister Gough Whitlam and called for a general election. By virtue of the Australia Acts 1986, however, Australia terminated all British control over the former colonies, which would in any way be inconsistent with Australian sovereignty. As Australia approaches the next century, there is much debate about whether Australia should become a republic and have a president. Like Britain, government is formed by the majority party in the lower house of Parliament, the leader of which serves as Prime Minister assisted by a cabinet comprised of other members of Parliament drawn from both the House of Representatives (lower house) and Senate (upper house). Like the United States, membership in the House of Representatives is based upon proportion of population while the Senate is comprised of an equal number of senators (ten) from each state.

4. Australia became a federation in 1901 with the formation of the Australian Constitution,[1] which gives limited powers to the commonwealth government. These powers include: foreign policy, defence, immigrations, customs, currency, weights and measures, interstate commerce, foreign and financial corporations, post and telegraphic and telephonic communications.[2] All powers not specifically granted by the commonwealth constitution to the central government are reserved to the states. Thus, states continue to have power over such matters as education, justice, intrastate travel, and so on. If there is an inconsistency between state and commonwealth law, the commonwealth legislation prevails.[3] Since WWII the balance of political power has shifted markedly in favour of the federal government. This is especially so since 1942, when the Commonwealth government began collecting income tax revenue that was then re-apportioned to the states on an agreed formula. The commonwealth government, supported by the Australian High Court, has also used its 'external affairs' powers to commit Australia to various treaty obligations, which have enabled the Commonwealth government in turn to override any inconsistent state laws.[4]

B. Reform of the Constitution

5. The Australian Constitution can be amended only by a referendum that gains the approval of a majority of electors as a whole plus a majority of four of the six states. Despite numerous calls for reform, especially after the dismissal of Prime Minister Whitlam in 1975, Australia's Constitution has proven to be extremely difficult to amend, with the vast majority of referendums failing to gain the required vote. Voting in Australia is compulsory, with the eligible voting age being 18 years.

1. Commonwealth of Australia Constitution Act 1900 (Imp) 63 and 64 Vic, c 12 (Imp).
2. See Part V, s. 51 of the Australian Constitution.
3. Australian Constitution, s. 92.
4. See e.g., *Commonwealth of Australia v. State of Tasmania* (1983) 158 CLR 1, in which the commonwealth government relied on its obligations pursuant to a world heritage area designation to block the construction of a dam.

C. States and Territories

6. Australia has six states and two territories. The six states (and their capitals) are New South Wales (Sydney), Victoria (Melbourne), Queensland (Brisbane), South Australia (Adelaide), Western Australia (Perth) and Tasmania (Hobart). The Northern Territory (Darwin) and A.C.T. (Canberra) are the two territories. The state governments derive from the former British Colonies established by British Act of Parliament. However, today, all Australian states have their own constitutions and complete political independence from Britain. All states, except Queensland, have a bicameral legislature with an upper house serving some type of review function. Queensland employs a unicameral parliament.

D. Judicial Power

7. The highest court in Australia is the High Court, which consists of seven justices, though it is unusual for the court to sit en banc.[5] The High Court hears appeals from the state Supreme Courts, and is the final Court of Appeal in the Australian legal system. It also acts as the guardian and interpreter of the Australian Constitution. The High Court has original jurisdiction in a number of matters, such as indictable Commonwealth offences.

Also on the federal level is the Family Court of Australia, which governs marriage disputes as per the Family Law Act 1975 (Cth). The Federal Court of Australia was created by the *Federal Court of Australia Act 1976* and began to exercise its jurisdiction on 1 February 1977. The Federal Court of Australia has original jurisdiction in other federal matters, such as industrial law, patents, trademarks, bankruptcy and antitrust. The Federal Court sits in all capital cities as well as other locations from time to time throughout Australia.

The Federal Court's original jurisdiction is *conferred by over 150 statutes* of the Parliament. The Federal Court also has a broad range of appellate jurisdiction. When created the Court's jurisdiction comprised that formerly exercised in part by the High Court of Australia and the whole of the Australian Industrial Court and the Federal Court of Bankruptcy. It now hears appeals from decisions of single judges of the Court and from the *Federal Circuit Court of Australia* (previously the Federal Magistrates Court) in non-family law matters. The Court's jurisdiction covers almost all civil matters arising under Australian federal law and some summary and indictable criminal matters. It also has jurisdiction to hear and determine any matter arising under the Constitution through the operation of section 39B of the *Judiciary Act 1903*. The Court also exercises general appellate jurisdiction in criminal and civil matters on appeal from the Supreme Court of Norfolk Island. Especially significant to contract law is the fact that the Federal Court hears cases under Australia's Competition and Consumer Act 2010 (Cth) as well as a broad range of cases

5. Up until 1986 it was possible to have an appeal from a state Supreme Court to the Privy Council in England. This avenue of appeal ended with the passage of the Australia Act 1986 (Cth).

under the Corporations Act 2001 and Australian Securities and Investments Commission Act 2001. The Federal Court The shares first instance jurisdiction with the Supreme Courts of the States and Territories in the complex area of intellectual property (copyright, patents, trademarks, designs and circuit layouts).[6]

Appeal from the Federal Court is to the Full Court of the Federal Court and possibly to the High Court. Each of the states and territories has its own court system that is comprised of various administrative tribunals, inferior courts, a court of general jurisdiction and a Court of Appeal.

E. Political Parties

8. Australia today has two major political parties: the Labor Party, which on most matters is further to the political left than the more conservative Liberal-National Party coalition, which ruled Australia from the 1950s through the 1970s, and again during much of the past decade. During the 1980s, the Labor Party was in the majority, led for most of that time by Robert Hawke and by Paul Keating. From 1996 through 2007 Australia was led by the Liberal-National party coalition under the leadership of John Howard. Kevin Rudd was elected prime minister in 2007 and replaced in June 2010 by Julia Guillard, who became Australia's twenty-seventh prime minister and the first woman to win that position. In June of 2013, Mr Rudd's party returned him to power and he once again became Prime Minister. The 2013 election saw the return to government of the Liberal/National Party Coalition and the election of Tony Abbott as Australia's 28th Prime Minister.

Three other parties attract significant but small numbers. The Democratic party for a time had controlled the balance of power in the Federal Senate by agreeing to cast its votes with either Labor or Liberal in order to give them a majority. The Country National party represents agricultural interests and usually forms a coalition with the conservative Liberal party. The Green party and independents supported the Labor party and enabled it to retain power in the 2010 national elections.

IV. Population and Employment Statistics

9. Though occupying a land mass almost the size of the continental United States, much of Australia is sparsely populated desert. Most of the population of approximately 20 million dwell in the fertile coastal regions, and approximately half of the population resides in the seven capital cities. Of these capital cities, Sydney has approximately 4.6 million people, Melbourne 4.2 million, Brisbane 2.1 million, Perth 1.8 million and Adelaide 1.2 million people. Ironically, despite its large land mass and small population, Australia thus has a population density that makes it one of the most urbanized countries in the world.

6. http://www.fedcourt.gov.au/about/jurisdiction.

V. Economy

10. Australia is a developed country and rich in natural resources. Farming and mining continue to be major exports along with a rapidly growing service industry and minor manufacturing.

Australia's leading farm products are cattle, wheat and wool, followed by dairy products. Australia's major sources of economic activity include: agriculture (including forestry and fishing), mining and quarrying, manufacturing, tourism, and education and financial services (including insurance, real estate and business).[7]

Australia is the world's largest exporter of wool and a major exporter of sugar, beef and wheat, rice, eggs, cotton, potatoes and vegetables. Major mining exports are bauxite, industrial diamonds, lead, copper, gold, iron ore, manganese, silver, aluminium, zinc, and nickel.

Major service industries include: financial services, tourism, transport, communication, and education.

Manufacturing exports include: cars, processed foods, clothing, shoes, and household appliances.

Australia also has a significant fishing industry, exporting lobsters, abalone, oysters, prawns, scallops, salmon, and tuna.

Australia's major two-way trading partners are China followed by Japan. Approximately 70% of Australia's trade is conducted with APEC nation members.[8]

Australia has been an active player in the G-20 and internationally through its participation in WTO and other international organizations.[9] In addition it has multiple bilateral and other free-trade agreements with other countries.[10]

As an advanced economy, Australia has also been among the leading countries in its promotion of both e-government and e-commerce. It consequently has introduced and continues to work on providing the necessary legal infrastructure to promote these developments. This infrastructure includes the general promotion of e-government as well as legislation that permits electronic contracting, public key encryption infrastructure, reforms to privacy laws, significant protection of intellectual property rights, approved National Broadband Network and government encouragement of e-health, e-commerce, moves towards electronic conveyancing, growth in electronic banking, and more. Australia is also active in various international fora related to the promotion of paperless trade and is a signatory to international agreements such as the International Cybercrime Treaty,[11]

---

7. Economy Watch: available at www.economywatch.com/world_economy/australia/?page=full.
8. Department of Foreign Affairs and Trade: Composition of Trade Australia. www.dfat.gov.au/publications/stats-pubs/cot-cy-2010.pdf.
9. J.R. Wiseman, *Global Nation: Australia? Australia and the Politics of Globalisation* (Cambridge University Press 1998).
10. T. Ciro, B. Maacitelli & S. Muthaly, *Australia and the Global Economy* (Connor Court Publg. 2009).
11. See generally, B. Fitzgerald et al., *Internet and E-commerce Law, Business and Policy* (Thomson Reuters 2010); E-government Resource Centre: www.egov.vic.gov.au/focus-on-countries/australia/trends-and-issues-australia/e-government-australia.html.

VI. Social and Cultural Values

11. Australia has a mixed free enterprise economy and, as Australia has joined the world economy, it has significantly deregulated a number of industries, such as banking and aviation. Similar to many Western democracies, Australia has increasingly moved to a view of government as a guide for general policy, as opposed to a primary deliverer of services. This has led to significant outsourcing of traditional government activities to the private sector and to a blurring of public and private sector economic activity.

12. The social and cultural values that shape and form the foundation of Australia's legal system are found in the traditional freedoms of a free enterprise economy. These include private ownership of property and the right to make a profit from it, freedom of contract, commerce and industry to engage in any pursuit one chooses; freedom of association, whereby one is free to join with others in a commercial venture and freedom of labour, whereby one is free to contract to work in any position as mutually agreed between employer and employee. Australia's cultural values are increasingly shaped by a global economy, as trade barriers have come down, and Australian businesses have operated on an international scale. Economic and social values have also been impacted by Australia's rapid uptake of information technology, such as the Internet. The growth of electronic commerce has further accelerated Australia's more global outlook and presents significant challenges to existing commercial laws, which are premised in a world of paper commerce.

Introduction to the Law of Contracts

§1. Definition of Contract

13. A contract is a legally binding agreement between two or more people or companies (called 'the parties'). It is an agreement that the parties intend to be legally binding – or that they would have intended to be.

§2. Historical Background of the Law of Contracts

14. Prior to British settlement in 1788, Aboriginal customary law existed for over 40,000 years. However, the British settlers did not recognize Aboriginal customary law and regarded the Australian continent as land not owned by any prior group or government. It is only in the last few years that Australian governments, courts and society have recognized Aboriginal land ownership claims.[12]

15. The first government of the newly settled British colony of New South Wales was a military one. By 1823, however, the economic activity and the increasing arrival of free (as opposed to convict) settlers encouraged the British government to gradually grant a democratically representative form of government to the new colony. Thus, the New South Wales Act created a form of legislature appointed by the King. However, only the Governor could propose laws, and all laws had, as far as practical, to be consistent with the laws of England. By the Australian Courts Act of 1828 it was also made clear that English common law would also be applicable to the colony, as far as conditions allowed.

16. As settlement spread throughout the continent, representative government was demanded and conferred, as various colonies formed their own constitutions and established their own legislatures (New South Wales in 1842; Victoria in 1850; Tasmania and South Australia in 1856; Queensland in 1867 and Western Australia in 1870). In 1856 England passed the Colonial Laws Validity Act, which made it clear that the colonies were free to pass their own laws and were only subject to an English law specifically passed in regard to the colonies.

---

12. *Mabo v. Queensland (No. 2)* (1992) 175 CLR 1; 66 ALR 408. See also, F. Brennan, *The Implications of the Mabo Decision*, 65 *Reform* 1993. See also *Wik Peoples v. State of Queensland* (1996) 141 ALR 129 (held that native title was not extinguished by legislation that granted or authorized the granting of pastoral leases that did not confer on the grantee rights exclusive of indigenous peoples).

17. By 1900 Australia, driven by the need for a common defence and unified policies on such matters as immigration, customs and interstate commerce, formed a federation, the Commonwealth of Australia, which came into being on 1 January 1901. The federation was comprised of a national or Commonwealth government, situated in Canberra, and six states, i.e., the former colonies. Because the states had so recently won their independence from England, the founders of Australia's Constitution were adamant that the Commonwealth government should have limited power, with traditional state powers reserved to the states.

18. Since WWII the power of the Commonwealth government has grown steadily. In the commercial area particularly, there have been many that have advocated greater Commonwealth involvement and the need for harmonization of diverse, fragmentary and often conflicting state laws. Thus, aided by several key High Court constitutional interpretations and the cooperation of the states, the Commonwealth has continued to expand its role in the regulation of business. Examples include the *Trade Practices Act 1974* (Cth), the *Crimes Taxation Offences Act 1980* (Cth), the *Cash Transactions Reports Act 1988* (Cth), and the Proceeds of Crime Act 1987 (Cth). Finally, with the passage of the Australia Acts 1986, Australia proclaimed its legal independence from Great Britain and removed the last vestiges of doubt concerning the power of Great Britain to pass laws in regard to its former colonies.

19. While Australian contract law is derived from English common law, in recent times Australian High Court decisions have evolved an Australian common law, and statutory developments have resulted in significant changes and a distinctly modern Australian law of contract. Among the major statutory developments are the Sale of Goods Acts in each state, *Competition and Consumer Act 2010* (Cth) and a host of specific consumer legislation governing particular areas. With a modern international economy, Australia contract law has also been influenced by international treaties and bilateral or multilateral trade agreements (e.g., free-trade agreements between the United States and Australia) and by contract jurisprudence in leading countries, especially the United States.

§3. Classification of Contracts

20. There are various ways in which contracts may be classified. One is according to the degree of solemnity required. Thus, simple contracts are those that do not require any particular formalities. Other contracts, however, are required by law to meet various 'form' requirements in order to be legally enforced. These may be termed 'formal' contracts. Examples include contracts of guarantee, cheques, and insurance contracts, all of which must be evidenced in writing and signed by the person to be charged with obligations under the contact. Still other contracts must be under seal.

I. General versus Specialist Contracts

21. In Australia, the legal implications of the overwhelming majority of contracts are, in addition to the language of the parties in the contract itself, governed by ordinary case law and legislation. There are few categories of 'specialist' contracts. However, some specific areas of contracting are governed by specialist legislation. This includes contracts for consumer credit, landlord-tenant contracts and consumer contracts where the contract is governed by a special legislative regime that regulates the terms, conditions and other aspects of the contract.

II. Contracts for Goods versus Services

22. In the case of some legislative regimes, such as the Sale of Goods Act and Fair Trading Acts in Australian States and the Commonwealth *Competition and Consumer Act 2010*, a distinction is made between contracts for goods and those for services, with different provisions applying depending upon the characterization of the contract as one for goods or services. This is discussed in detail under Sale of Goods in Part II, Chapter 4.

III. Bilateral and Unilateral Contracts

23. A bilateral contract involves the mutual exchange of a promise for a promise to do a future act. In a unilateral contract, one party makes a promise in exchange for the other party doing an act. In a unilateral contract there is no bargaining or exchange of promises by the parties, as occurs in a bilateral contract. The essence of a unilateral contract is that one party's promise is conditioned on another party's performance of certain acts, and if the other party performs, the promising party is then bound.

IV. Express versus Implied Contracts

24. Some contracts are evidenced clearly from the express terms of the parties. In other cases, the terms may be implied, and it is a principle of contract law that that which is plainly or by necessity implied in the language of a contract is as much deemed to be a part of the contract as that which is expressed. The policy underlying this principle is that the law will presume to be part of the contract, that which the parties inadvertently omitted or that which was deemed to be so obvious to the parties that it was not included. Readers should also note that a major role of legislation such as the *Sale of Goods Acts* and *Competition and Consumer Act 2010* is to 'fill the gaps' where the parties have not expressly provided for those terms in the contract. In this way, the court plays a vital role in facilitating commerce, by implying into contracts acceptable commercial practices. A contract may also be implied from the conduct of the parties.

V. Legal versus Illegal Contracts

25. Parties to a contract are normally free to contract to do anything they wish, provided that the contract does not impose any obligations that are contrary to statutory laws, regulations or against public policy. An illegal contract is one that is prohibited in law because the formation of the contract, its performance or the object of the contract is against the law. The effect of an illegal contract varies. In general, an illegal contract is unenforceable. However, the courts tend to be averse to holding contracts to be unenforceable unless the illegality is clear and significant. Thus, a contract may be deemed enforceable notwithstanding a slight illegality. A court may also allow recovery of anything transferred, notwithstanding the illegality, where not to do so would result in a harsh forfeiture. In some jurisdictions the issue of enforceability of illegal contracts has been addressed by legislation. This is discussed in detail in Part I, Chapter 2.

VI. Void, Voidable and Unenforceable Contracts

26. In general, there are three classifications of contracts that are not binding:

- *Void*: If a contract is held to be void, the contract has never come into existence. For example, a contract is void if it is based on an illegal purpose or contrary to public policy; the classic example is a contract with a hit man. Such a contract will not be recognized by a court, and cannot be enforced by either party.
- *Voidable*: A contract is voidable if one of the parties has the option to terminate the contract. Contracts with a minor are examples of voidable contracts.
- *Unenforceable*: If a contract is unenforceable, neither party may enforce the other's obligations. For example, in some Australian jurisdictions, a contract is unenforceable if it violates the Statute of Frauds.

See Part I, Chapter 2 for a full discussion.

§4. CONTRACT AND TORTS

27. The obligation arising out of contract stems from promises made or implied between the parties to the contract. In contrast, a tort is a civil wrong arising as a matter of law. The commission of a tort may be by means of an intentional act (e.g., battery), negligence (breach of a duty of care) or by means of strict liability (use of dangerous explosives or statutory duty). Remedies in contract law are usually damages seeking to put the innocent party in the position it would have been had the contract been performed and not breached. In tort, the law seeks to place the party in the position the party would have been had the tort not been committed.

For much of the twentieth century, Australia had followed the US pattern that saw the expansion of tort law as the expanding remedy for civil law. In recent times, however, contract law has made a resurgence and expansion through promissory estoppel, an extended application of the doctrine of unconscionability, and restitution.[13]

§5. CONTRACT AND QUASI-CONTRACT

28. A quasi-contract involves a situation where the law finds there to be an obligation even though the technical requirements for a contract have not been fulfilled. A contract that is implied in law is also called a quasi-contract because it is not in fact a contract; rather, it is a means for the courts to remedy situations in which one party would be unjustly enriched were he or she not required to compensate the other. For example, an unconscious patient treated by a doctor at the scene of an accident has not agreed (either expressly or by implication) to pay the doctor for emergency services, but the patient would be unjustly enriched by the doctor's services were the patient not required to compensate the doctor.[14] Heavily influenced by the work of the late Professor Peter Birks, the whole area of quasi-contract has been the subject of much theorizing and debate. Birks[15] argued that the law of restitution is a separate branch of the law of obligations, distinct from tort and contract law and unified by a principle of unjust enrichment at the plaintiff's expense. Yet, other scholars such as Jackman point out that much of the law of restitution has concerned cases where neither the defendant has been enriched nor the plaintiff has suffered expense. Jackman posits three distinct categories of legal thought in this area: (1) reversal of non-voluntary transactions; (2) the fulfilment of non-contractual promises and (3) the protection of the private legal facilities of proprietary rights and fiduciary relationships.[16] This topic is discussed in detail in Part II, Chapter 13 of this title.

§6. CONTRACT AND THE LAW OF PROPERTY

29. Property law is concerned with various forms of ownership in real property (land) and personal property (moveable possessions, including intangibles such as intellectual property). Property rights are rights over the thing itself, whereas contract rights are against a particular person. Property rights may be created by means of contract, and thus there is some common ground between the two. However,

13. See generally, R. Balkin & J. Davis, *The Law of Torts* (3d ed., LexisNexis/Butterworths 2004).
14. Bryan, M., *Peter Birks and Unjust Enrichment in Australia*, Melb. U. L. Rev. 24 (2004): www.austlii.edu.au/au/journals/ MULR/2004/24.html; P. Birks, *Reviews and Notes: Meagher, Gummow and Lehane's Equity Doctrines and Remedies,* 4th ed. L. Q. Rev. 120, 344 (2001); P. Birks, *Equity, Conscience, and Unjust Enrichment*, Melb. U. L. Rev. 23, 1 (1991).
15. P. Birks, *Restitution: the Principle* (Federation Press 1992). See also S. Hedley, *The Empire Strikes Back? A Restatement of the Law of Unjust Enrichment*, Melb. U. L. Rev. 28, www.austlii.edu.au// cgi-bin/disp.pl/au/journals/MULR/2004/26.html?query=Unjust%20Enrichment; M. Bryan, *Peter Birks and Unjust Enrichment in Australia: An Essay*, U. Melb. L. Rev. 24: www.austlii.edu.au//cgi-bin/ disp.pl/au/journals/MULR/2004/24.html?query=Unjust%20Enrichment.
16. I.M. Jackman, *The Varieties of Restitution* (Federation Press 1998).

property rights may also be created by means of trust, wills, adverse possession and other means.

§7. Contract and Trust

29.1. A trust is a legal relationship where one person (the trustee) holds assets for the benefit of another person (the beneficiary). Common law trusts are established as a result of the right to contract with another person to create a trust. By virtue of an express contract, a 'trust indenture' creates a trust. Trusts may be created for various purposes. A trust may be revocable or irrevocable, depending upon the parties.

A trust may also be implied via the doctrine of resulting trust. A resulting trust will be found where the actions of the parties and the nature of the transaction imply an *intention* to create a trust. In many ways a resulting trust is similar to an express trust, as there must be intent. However, this intent is presumed rather than demonstrated through evidence. An example of a resulting trust is where an express trust does not have the required formalities, but it is clear the parties intended to form a trust.

In other circumstances, the law may create the fiction of a 'constructive trust', a trust imposed by the law as opposed to by agreement of the parties. A constructive trust is one type of trust that, instead of being set up expressly by a settler, arises by operation of law as a response to certain events. For example if someone steals money and uses it to buy a house, the law may impose a constructive trust that requires the thief to hold the property for the benefit of the victim of the theft.

§8. Good Faith and Fair Dealing

30. Although it has been considered, Australia has yet to adopt a definitive principle of good faith in contract law. In contrast to legal developments in Europe and the United States,[17] Australia does not require an explicit legal pre-requisite of good faith to form or carry out the obligations under a contract.[18]

§9. Style of Drafting

31. Reflecting its common law origins and history, the Australian style of contract drafting favours precision, structure and specificity. The underlying values of such an approach are to favour certainty and predictability and give maximum freedom of the parties to use contract as a form of private law-making. The best way to remain free from the constraints of the courts and individual interpretation of judges

---

17. M. Hoch, *Is Fair Dealing a Workable Concept for European Contract Law? Global Jurist Topics*, 1 www.bepress.com/gj/topics/vol5/iss1/art2/.
18. M. Harper, *Implied Duty of Good Faith in Australian Contract Law*, Murdoch U. Elec. J., 11 (September 2004); see e.g., *Burger King Corp v. Hungary Jacks Pty Ltd* (2001) NSWCA 187 at [165].

is to draft precisely and unambiguously so that little is left to the interpretation of the judges. This is in contrast to the civil law tradition of drafting in general terms and according to basic principles. In reality, there has in recent times been a convergence of the two systems with common law systems increasingly utilizing general principles such as unconscionability and civil law systems moving to greater specificity in legal drafting.[19]

§10. SOURCES OF THE LAW OF CONTRACTS

32. Other than the terms of the specific contract between the parties, there are two major sources of contract law in Australia: legislation and case law or the common law.

33. Legislation is comprised of the enacted laws of Commonwealth, state and territory parliaments. Examples of such enactments in the commercial law area include: *Australian Competition and Consumer Act 2010* (Cth); *Cheques Act 1986* (Cth), and Sale of Goods Acts and Fair Trading Acts that have been enacted in each Australian state and territory. Some legislation, such as the *Sale of Goods Act* in the various states, is enacted specifically for merchants, and incorporates many of the principles from the Law Merchant, especially as it evolved in England up to the nineteenth century. Legislation is also used to pass into law Australia's obligations under various international treaties, an example being the *Vienna Convention on the International Sale of Goods*, which has been passed into law in each Australian jurisdiction.

Traditionally, Australian Courts tended to take a literal approach to the interpretation of statutes. However, since the 1980s most of the states and the Commonwealth have amended their Acts Interpretation acts to require courts to interpret statutes in such a way as to carry out the purpose for which the legislation was passed. In ascertaining the legislative purpose, courts may have regard to extrinsic material, including: reports of royal commissions, law reform commissions and government inquiries, reports of parliamentary proceedings, explanatory memoranda, headings, marginal notes and end notes as printed by the government printer and so on.

34. Another major facet of legislation is delegated legislation – laws made not by Parliament, but by bodies whom Parliament has delegated the authority to make laws. Delegated legislation includes the regulations of various government departments and instrumentalities and by-laws of local governments.

35. Case law or common law includes the vast body of common law that originated from England, as well as law created by Australian judges, both in deciding new cases and in the interpretation of statutes made by Parliament. All jurisdictions have an Acts Interpretation Act that guides the Courts in this process. While Parliament, representing the electorate, is the supreme law making body in Australia,

19. L. Campbell, *Legal Drafting Styles: Fuzzy or Fussy?* Murdoch U. Elec. J. L, 3 (1996).

Australian courts are given the power to determine the constitutionality of legislation and interpret statutes of parliament as they apply to a particular case in controversy. In particular areas of the law, such as contract law and banking law,

Australian courts give considerable weight to business custom and practice. As a common law country, Australian courts follow a system of precedent that requires a court to follow the past decisions made by higher courts in similar cases. Although not binding on a court, Australian courts may, when there is not controlling Australian precedent, find persuasive the reported cases of other jurisdictions. In this regard, reported decisions from other common law countries such as the US, Canada and UK are particularly significant.

Part I. General Principles of the Law of Contract

Chapter 1. Formation

§1. Agreement and Quid Pro Quo (Reciprocity)

36. The law of contract is designed to answer the question, in what circumstances will a promise made by an individual be legally enforceable. In Australia, the requirements for a valid contract are six fold (the first three form the basis of a valid contract, the last three serve to vitiate what would otherwise be a valid contract. Chapter 1 will discuss the first three elements, Chapter 2, the latter three.

The six requirements are as follows:

(i) offer and acceptance;
(ii) an intention to create legal relations;
(iii) consideration;
(iv) capacity;
(v) consent; and
(vi) the contract is for a legal purpose.

I. Offer and Acceptance

37. As indicated by the above, it follows from the definition of contract law that there must be at least two parties. One of these parties must make the offer (the offeror); the other party must accept that offer (the offeree). An offer is generally seen as an act by one party by which it could be understood that that person is demonstrating an intention to be bound by the acceptance of the other party without any further discussion or negotiation.[20] Moreover, acceptance is merely an act by the offeree by which they demonstrate their intention to accept the terms stated by the offeror. In determining whether there is a valid offer and acceptance, the courts will take a global approach to determine whether the parties have reached a concluded contract.[21] However, in some situations the standard offer and acceptance approach will be inappropriate. In these cases courts may still find that contract has been concluded, even though it is not possible to analyse the activities of the parties from the

20. *Shearer v. Manly Warringah District Rugby League Football Club* (SC (NSW), 7 Nov. 1989).
21. *Brambles Holdings Ltd v. Bathurst City Council* [2001] NSWCA 61; 53 NSWLR 153.

basis of formal offer made by one party, which was accepted by the other party – in other words the contract will be inferred from the conduct or total circumstances surrounding the activities of the parties. For example, in *Clarke v. Dunraven*,[22] a yachtsman in a club regatta committed a breach of the rules and sank another yacht. Each of the participants in the regatta had agreed to abide by the club rules. One of these rules was that any damage caused by a breach would be compensable. The legal issue was whether the contract was only created between the club and each competitor, or whether there could be said to be a contract between each participant in the regatta. The House of Lords held that the entry into the race and the undertaking to be bound by the rules to the knowledge of each other was a sufficient basis to indicate that there was contractual liability on the part of one competitor to other competitors.

38. The following are rules governing the making of an offer:

(i) must be communicated;
(ii) can be made to a specific person or to the world;
(iii) may be revoked at any time prior to acceptance; and
(iv) must be distinguished from options and invitations to treat.

A. Communication

39. Obviously, the offer must be brought to the attention of the person to whom it is made before it can be accepted. In essence, undertaking something without knowing of the offer will not be deemed acceptance. Therefore, finding an item and returning it to the true owner without knowledge that there is a reward offered in respect of that item means that there will be no contract between the two, as the finding did not occur in relation to, or in any response to, an offer made by the person who lost the item. For example, in *R v. Clarke*[23] the plaintiff was not entitled to the monetary reward for information leading to the arrest of murderers – the information that he had provided was not in response to the promise of a reward of any such information. Although there is no Australian case on the issue, a modern application of the rule that an offer must be communicated relates to website terms and conditions. For such terms to be binding it would have to be evidenced that the terms were clear and unambiguous, fair and sufficiently brought to the attention of the website user.

40. An offer may be made to any specific person or brought to the notice of the world. An offer may be made to the entire world, and it may be accepted by any person who had notice of that offer. This is demonstrated in the seminal decision of *Carlill v. Carbolic Smoke Ball Co.* [24] The defendant promised GB 100 to any person who contracted influenza after using the product of the defendant. In seeking to deny the plaintiff's claim, the defendant alleged that the advertisement was not

22. [1897] AC 59.
23. (1927) 40 CLR 227.
24. [1893] 1 QB 256.

acceptable in contract law, as it was a putative offer (or an attempt to contract) to, or with, the world. This was not accepted by the court, which held that it was not a contract with the whole world, but rather it was an offer to the world – which could be accepted by any person who satisfied the requirements. The application of this case in Australia can be illustrated with the decision of *Mobil Oil Australia Ltd v. Lyndel Nominees Pty Ltd & Ors.*[25] In this case, it was alleged by Lyndel Nominees that at a Mobil dealers' breakfast, a number of statements were made by the Mobil representative indicating that if the franchisees operated at a certain level, their tenure on the service station site would be renewed. It was held that the statements were nothing more than an exhortation to perform better, and that it was said in the tone of 'corporate enthusiasm'. As such, it was distinguishable from *Carlill.* A similar conclusion was reached in the Victorian Supreme Court decision of *Mildura Office Equipment & Supplies Pty Ltd v. Canon Finance Australia Ltd*,[26] where it was argued by the plaintiff that a statement made by a Canon dealer that Canon photocopiers would be sold for a dollar at the expiry of a rental agreement (this statement made in the course of a five-minute comic skit at a Canon business dealers' conference) was a unilateral contract that was accepted by the plaintiff procuring a customer to enter into an arrangement of this nature. The Court held that the representations were too vague and uncertain and therefore could not amount to an offer that would form the basis of a contract. It is also recognized that where a term that is regarded as essential to a contract is not agreed upon, then the other terms that have been agreed will not constitute a binding contract.[27]

41. An offer may be revoked at any time prior to acceptance. Prior to acceptance, the offeror can revoke the offer. This was decided in the English decision of *Payne v. Cave.*[28] Similarly, an offer made to the world at large, such as through an advertisement, can generally be revoked in the same way. For example, an offer made by telephone may be revoked by telephone. Similarly, an offer made by mail may be revoked by mail. However, in an electronic era, the making and revocation of an offer becomes far more problematic. If the transaction is one to which electronic transactions legislation applies (e.g., *Electronic Transactions Act 1999* (Cth)), the time of communication will be the time when the email enters the recipients computer system. If however electronic means had not been designated as the method of communication, the communication will be made when the item comes to the attention of the recipient. Despite these legislative attempts, the principles surrounding offer and acceptance in an electronic area are still being affirmatively settled. The death of either party will also see an offer lapse.

25. (1998) 153 ALR 198.
26. [2006] FSC 42.
27. *Monarch Building Systems Pty Ltd v. Quinn Villages P/L* [2006] QCA 210 at [49]. See also, *Alford & Ors v. Ebbage & Ors* [2004] QCA 283; *Eastgate Properties P/L v. J Hutchinson P/L* [2005] QSC 196; *Bramble Holdings Ltd v. Bathurst City Council* (2001) 53 NSWLR 153.
28. (1789) 3 Term Rep 148; 100 ER 502.

B. An Offer Must Be Distinguished from an Invitation to Treat or an Option

42. An offer must be distinguished from:

(i) an invitation to treat (or invitation to bargain); and
(ii) an option.

An invitation to treat is an activity by which the person shows that he or she is willing to consider, though not necessarily to accept, offers made to purchase the goods or services that are the subject of an invitation to treat. A common example is items placed in a shop, with a price displayed. The law does not see this as an offer to sell at that price, rather a preparedness to negotiate.[29] This rule applies to items in a shop, most goods or services advertised on web sites, most tenders and auctions, as well as the classifieds in the newspapers. It is likely that the same rules will apply to electronic auctions.[30] However, automatic vending machines are not seen as an invitation to treat, rather they are seen as an offer.[31] However, an item advertised for sale at a particular price, and that sees an offer at that price rejected, may result in an individual or corporation being held liable for deceptive or misleading conduct.[32]

43. An offer must also be distinguished from an option which is a legal right to have for a specified period the right to buy or sell something on agreed terms. Options are commonly used in financial markets, where people will place an option to buy (call option), or an option to sell (put option) on a financial product, to be exercised at a future point in time. As to whether the option is to be considered as an irrevocable offer or a conditional contract will be determined by the construction of the agreement.[33] The resolution of this can be of practical importance because of the impact of capital gains tax.[34] If the option is to be exercised, it must be done unequivocally and in accordance with the terms specified.

C. Rules Governing Acceptance of an Offer

44. An offer can either be accepted or rejected. There are a number of rules that relate to the acceptance of an offer, these are as follows:

(i) the acceptance must relate to the offer;
(ii) acceptance must be unconditional;
(iii) the acceptance must be communicated;
(iv) if acceptance is mailed, it is effective from the time of posting;

29. *Pharmaceutical Society of Great Britain v. Boots Cash Chemists (Southern) Ltd* [1893] 1 QB 401.
30. A. Reynolds, *E-Auctions; Who will Protect the Consumer* 18 J. Contract L. 75 (2002).
31. *Thornton v. Shoe Lane Parking Ltd* [1971] 2 QB 163.
32. See provisions dealing with misleading conduct as found in the *Competition and Consumer Act 2010.*
33. *Hughes v. St Barbara Ltd* [2011] WASCA 234.
34. *Laybutt v. Amoco Pty Ltd* [1974] HCA 49; 174 CLR 57.

(v) any counteroffer will be a rejection of the original offer; and
(vi) the method of acceptance may be prescribed.

D. Acceptance Relates to the Offer

45. As previously noted, a person accepting an offer must do so in reliance on that offer and be aware that the offer exists. As noted, the return of a lost item out of civility, and without awareness that a reward exists for that item, does not amount to acceptance of an offer made by the reward.

E. Unconditional Acceptance

46. An acceptance must be completed and unqualified. The introduction of any new terms or the contradiction of any terms of the original offer will be seen as a rejection of the original offer and accordingly amount to a counteroffer. Disputes can arise in the area where a putative agreement is said to be 'subject to contract'. This was the case in the High Court decision of *Masters v. Cameron.*[35] In this situation, three possibilities exist:

(i) that the parties have reached finality in the terms but simply intend to have the agreement restated in more precise form – in this scenario, a contract exists on the agreed terms;
(ii) in a second scenario, the parties may well have agreed on the terms but may have performance conditional upon the execution of formal document. In this position a contract exists to bring about the formal contract; and
(iii) no contract exists, as the parties do not intend to make a concluded bargain until a formal arrangement is executed.

Finally, a request for additional information will not destroy the original offer – this not being seen as a counteroffer.[36]

F. Communication of Acceptance

47. Acceptance must be communicated to the offeror. The lack of this requirement led the New South Wales Court of Appeal in *ICTA Investments Pty Ltd & Anor v. GE Commercial Corporation (Australia) Pty Ltd & Anor*[37] to conclude that no contract existed in the circumstances of that case. ICTA owned a nightclub, and sought finance from GE through a broker to improve its lighting. The lighting was supplied, but subsequently ICTA decided that it did not wish to proceed with the purchase and returned the lighting. GE had paid, in the interim, the supplier directly

35. (1954) 91 CLR 353.
36. *Stevenson v. McLean* (1880) 5 QBD 346.
37. [2006] NSWCA 290.

for the lighting. It then continued to extract repayments from ICTA despite the appellant claiming that no contract was consummated. The New South Wales Court held that there was no contract. GE had never communicated acceptance of the offer to ICTA – paying the supplier directly was inadequate to convey acceptance to the other party.

48. The offeror cannot impose a requirement that the silence of the offeree will be deemed acceptance. For example, in the classic case of *Felthouse v. Bindley*[38] the plaintiff made an offer to buy a horse, indicating that 'If I hear no more about him, I consider the horse mine at that price.' It was held that there was no contract in place.

49. Communication of acceptance may be instantaneous (e.g., when items are purchased at a store); however, the legal problems generally arise when communication is not instantaneous. Difficulties arise in respect of communication of acceptance by way of fax, telex or email. If the method of communication is by telex it has been held that, where there is instantaneous communication, the acceptance is made when and where it is received.[39] It may well be the case that this rule would equally apply to communication by fax,[40] though the extension to email is still a matter of considerable debate. The issue will be whether the postal acceptance rules should apply (see *below*) or whether email (and, for that matter, acceptance by text phone messages) should be seen as equivalent to instantaneous communication.[41]

G. Postal Acceptance Rule

50. If mail is seen as the method of acceptance of a contract, then the postal delivery rule is that the contract is formed once the letter is posted. This is irrespective of whether the letter is ever received by the offeror.[42] The justification for this rule lies in the theory that the offeror had used the postal service as his or her agent for purposes of acceptance. Increasingly, contracts will be formed by other methods of communication. With advancements in modern telecommunications, the postal acceptance rule is rapidly becoming outdated and increasingly irrelevant. Australian cases related to the use of fax and other forms of modern communication have tended to regard these as equivalent to instant communications and thus the postal acceptance rule did not apply. [43] Moreover, as outline below, electronic transactions legislation has been passed in each Australian state which both recognises the validity and assists the enforceability of electronic contracts. This includes the adoption of various default rules as to what qualifies as communicating messages between

38. (1862) 11 CBNS 869; 142 ER 1037.
39. *Entores Ltd v. Miles Far East Corporation* [1955] 2 QB 327.
40. *Mendelson-Zeller Co Inc v. T&C Providers Pty Ltd* [1981] 1 NSWLR 366.
41. See Christensen, *Formation of Contracts by Email – Is it just the same as Post*, 1 Queensland U. Tech. L. & Just. J. 22 (2001); G. Hughes, *Shrinkwraps, Clingwraps and Webwraps: The Overseas Experience*, 79 L. Inst. J. 34 (2005).
42. *Adams v. Lindsell* (1818) 106 ER 250.
43. See generally *Brinkibon Ltd v. Stabag Stahl Und Stahlwarenhandelsgesellschaft mbH* [1982] 2 WLR 264.

different computers and computing systems. The use of the postal acceptance rule can be inferred where the offeror contemplated and intended that her or his offer would be accepted by such means. If this is not the case, then the general rule would apply that the contract is not completed until the acceptance of the offer is communicated to the offeror.[44]

H. Electronic Transaction Legislation

51. The Electronic Transactions Act 1999 was designed to ensure that contracting in Australia was electronically neutral. The *Electronic Transactions Amendment Act 2011* which received Royal Assent on 25 May 2011 amended the 1999 law to deal with important practical issues to reflect internationally recognised legal standards related to the enforceability of e-contracts in e-commerce and to prepare Australia to accede to the *UN Convention on the Use of Electronic Communications in International Contracts 2005*. The amendments took effect from 24 June 2011. Under the Electronic Transactions Legislation, the default rule for the determination of the time of dispatch of an electronic communication is when it leaves an information system under the control of the originator of the communication. This rule enables any delay, for example, by security measures or firewalls, to be taken into account in determining when a communication is received. The default rule for the determination of the time of receipt is when the electronic communication becomes 'capable of being retrieved' by the addressee at a designated electronic address or, if the communication is sent to another non-designated address then the time of receipt is when the message is 'capable of being received' and the addressee has become aware that the message has been sent to that address.

52. To accommodate the reality that many contracts in e-commerce deploy automatic message systems, section 15C of the Act (inserted in 2011) addresses the issue of automatic message systems in relation to the formation of contracts: a contract cannot be held to be invalid, void or unenforceable solely because no natural person reviewed or intervened in the making of the contract. Where a mistake is made because there is no opportunity for a person to inspect the automated communication, the Act provides in section 15D of the Act that a party may withdraw portions of a contract containing an error when the automatic message system does not give the opportunity to correct the error. This safeguard only applies when the person notifies the other party of the error as soon as possible and providing the person has not used or received any material benefit from the goods or services.

53. Finally, it is important to note that the Australian Act departs from and is wider than the 2005 Convention in that the Australian legislation covers transactions involving household, family and personal contracts. The UN convention in contrast excludes these types of contracts and is limited to business-to-business transactions. These types of contracts were included in Australian federal law as a

44. *Hinkley v. de Vries (No. 2)* [2006] NSWSC 1049.

result of the Competition and Consumer Act 2010 which provides protection for consumers.

54. Finally, even after the contract is formed, the performance of the contract and other contractual contingencies may require certain notices to be provided by the other party. If these notices are provided electronically, uncertainty may arise about when a notice sent by email is legally received and how that notice may be proved. At least one Australian court has held that in the circumstances of the particular case 'Any other conclusion would produce a capricious and commercially inconvenient result that might have wide-reaching and unintended consequences in modern day trade and commerce.' The provisions of the contact in question required that all notices: 'shall be in writing'; may be given to or served upon a party 'may be signed on behalf of the party giving the same by a director, manager, secretary or acting secretary of such party'. The NSW court held that the relevant notice, which was sent by email, satisfied these requirements because the mandatory requirement as to writing was satisfied and the two permissive requirements were also met by transmission of the email and inclusion of the sender's name and email address. To be totally safe and avoid this issue entirely one should use conventional means of notice, i.e., post. Where email is utilized, it is important for the parties to specify the rules by which they will determine 'when notice is received' and how that receipt can be evidenced.[45]

I. Counteroffer is a Rejection

55. Hyde v. Wrench[46] established that a counteroffer was a rejection of the original offer. Accordingly, if the offeree makes a counteroffer that is rejected by the original offeror, it is not possible for the offeree to then turn around and accept the original offer. That has been destroyed by the counteroffer.

J. Method of Acceptance May Be Prescribed

56. It is possible for the offeror to prescribe that only a certain method of acceptance is possible. However, if none is specified, the presumption will be that the method of acceptance will follow the form that the offer has been made. Accordingly, if the offer is made by telephone, there may well be a presumption that the acceptance should be by telephone. It is generally thought that if an instantaneous form of communication is used as the method of communication of the offer, then an equally responsive method should be used as the method of acceptance of the offer. That is, if the offer is by telegram, then acceptance should not be by post.[47]

---

45. *Reed Constructions Pty Limited v. Eire Contractors Pty Limited* [2009] NSWSC 678; *Bauen Constructions Pty Ltd v. Sky General Services Pty Ltd* [2012] NSWSC 1123.
46. (1840) 3 Beav 334; 49 ER 132.
47. *Quenerduaine v. Cole* (1883) 32 WR 185.

Acceptance of an offer may also be not required in a formal sense, *Carlill v. Carbolic Smoke Ball Co* (*supra*) representing an example of this – performance amounting to acceptance.

II. Intention to Create Legal Relations

57. After offer and acceptance has been established, the next requirement is that the parties intend to create legal relations. Formerly two presumptions assisted in this regard. One, if the matter is seen as a domestic or voluntary nature, then the initial premise is that the agreement will not be legally binding. By contrast, if the matter concerns business or commercial interests, then it will be presumed, at first instance, that the arrangement is to be legally binding. The consequence of this division can be demonstrated in the case of *Balfour v. Balfour*.[48] In this case, a husband promised that he would pay his wife GB 30 a month maintenance whilst they were obliged to live apart – the husband employed in what was then Ceylon, the wife residing in England. The English Court of Appeal held that the claim must fail, as the parties never intended to enter into legal relations. An Australian example of this is *Cohen v. Cohen*.[49] The plaintiff alleged that her ex-husband had promised to pay her a yearly dress allowance. After their separation, the wife sought arrears of this allowance. The High Court refused to endorse the claim. Contrast this decision with *Wakeling v. Ripley*.[50] The defendant persuaded the plaintiff (a Cambridge University lecturer) to move to Sydney in return for a promise that plaintiff could live in the defendant's house, and that when the defendant died the house would be left by bequest to the plaintiff. One year after moving to Sydney, personal relations between the plaintiff and defendant led to the house being sold and the defendant changing his will. The plaintiff was successful in arguing that there was an intent to create legal relations. This decision was supported in *McKeand v. Thomas* [51] where the New South Wales Supreme Court accepted that the seriousness to the promisee of undertaking the measures required by the contract is a relevant consideration in deciding whether the agreement was *intended* to be legally binding.

The status of these presumptions (that family arrangements do not create legal relations, and, conversely, that commercial arrangements do) must be questioned in light of the High Court decision in *Ermogenous v. Greek Orthodox Community*.[52] In this case, Archbishop Ermogenous was for twenty-three years the Archbishop of the Greek Orthodox Church in Australia. He was paid an agreed salary, and upon his resignation claimed to be entitled to unpaid annual and long service leave. It was argued that an arrangement between a minister of religion and a church was akin to a family arrangement and not intended to be legally binding. This was rejected by the High Court. There was no presumption that such agreements were not intended to be legally binding. Support for a wide reading of this decision (i.e., that it applies

48. [1919] 2 KB 571.
49. (192) 42 CLR 91.
50. (1951) 51 SR (NSW) 183.
51. [2006] NSWSC 1028.
52. (2002) 209 CLR 95.

generally, and not merely to agreements of a nature that were under examination in this case) can be seen in decisions such as *Re Dickson Catering Pty Ltd (in liq)*[53] and *Dowdell v. Knispel Fruit Juices Pty Ltd (trading as Nippys)*.[54] In this context, it is recognized that in considering whether a binding agreement has taken place, the courts do not search for the subjective intent of the parties. However, what the parties agreed upon is not irrelevant when considering what a reasonable bystander would have understood to be the concluded arrangement.[55] In deciding whether a binding contract comes into existence, the court will consider all the circumstances leading up to the date of the alleged contract, with the essential query to answer being 'did the parties intend that the consensus at which they arrived should constitute a binding contract'.[56]

58. Complexities arise in relation to business arrangements when the parties use so-called comfort letters. These are generally seen as a letter of expectation or purpose between the parties, but the legal issue is whether the letter of comfort will also be seen to be the creation of a legal relation. For example, in *Gate Gourmet Australia Pty Ltd (in liq) v. Gate Gourmet Holding AG*[57] a parent company indicated by way of comfort letter that it would provide the necessary financial support to enable the Australian entity to meet its obligations. It was held that this letter exhibited an intention to create legal relations, and that the parent company was thereby liable.

59. It will also be the case that in relations with government, the courts are more likely to find that no intent to create legal relations was ever made – the decision made on the basis that the arrangements reflected government policy, rather than government legal action.[58] A complex example of a clause in a commercial arrangement that was designed to ensure that no legal relations was created can be seen in the case of *Rose and Frank Co v. Crompton & Bros Ltd.*[59] The clause stated that: 'This arrangement is not entered into nor is this memorandum written, as a formal or legal agreement, and shall not be subject to legal jurisdiction in the law courts either of the United States or England, but it is only a definite expression and record of the purpose and intention of the parties concerned, to which they each honourably pledge themselves.' Not surprisingly, this clause was sufficient for a finding that there was no intent to create legal relations.

III. Consideration

60. Consideration is an essential component for simple contracts for Australia. Adopting the English requirement for consideration has seen the rejection of the

53. [2002] ACTSC 107.
54. [2003] FCA 851.
55. *Kovan Engineering (Aust) Pty Ltd v. Gold Peg International Pty Ltd* [2006] FCAFC 117 at [105].
56. *Air Great Lakes Pty Ltd v. KS Easter (Holdings) Pty Ltd* (1985) 2 NSWLR 309 at 326. See also *PRA Electrical Pty Ltd v. Perseverance Exploration Pty Ltd & Manly* [2006] VSC 432.
57. [2004] NSWSC 149.
58. *Australian Woollen Mills Pty Ltd v. Commonwealth* (1954) 92 CLR 424.
59. [1923] 2 KB 261.

enforceable promise without consideration – a feature of many legal systems based on the codification of the law by the French. By contrast to simple contracts, promises made by way of deed (discussed below) do not need to be supported by consideration. Many jurisdictions throughout the world do not require consideration as an essential ingredient in the successful formation of contracts. However, Australia has, in sourcing its law from England, adopted the requirement that consideration is necessary for the creation of a valid contract. As a concept, consideration is difficult to define, but an attempt was made in *Currie v. Misa*:[60] '[consisting] either in some right, interest, profit, or benefit accruing to one party or some forbearance, detriment, loss or responsibility given, suffered or undertaken by the other.' Another commonly cited definition is 'An act or forbearance of one party, or the promise thereof, is the price for which the promise of the other is bought, and the promise thus given for value is enforceable.'[61] An example may assist in understanding the distinction: if I was to promise to give you AUD 100, and nothing more was said – then the law whilst it may recognize a promise, it has not recognized a *legally enforceable* obligation (or promise). Two reasons can be given to support this: first, there was no intent to create legal relations, but also there was a lack of consideration by the recipient of the promise. In other words, the beneficiary of the promise has given nothing in return for the alleged obligation to pay. By contrast, if I promise to pay you AUD 100 in return for you mowing my lawns, then the obligation can be enforced, as consideration has been given by the recipient of the promise.

Consideration may be executed or executory, but it cannot be past. What this means is that a promise to pay today for something done in the past is unenforceable. For example, if you mow my lawns whilst I am on away on holiday, and I subsequently promise to pay you AUD 100, the consideration is past and unenforceable.

61. However, if the promised obligation is completed or undertaken in return for something presently on offer (please mow my lawns and I will give you AUD 100) then the consideration is executed and recoverable. If the promise of consideration is in the future, for example an obligation to pay thirty days hence in return for doing something now (please mow my lawns now, and I will pay you AUD 100 when I get paid next month) then the consideration is considered executory and also enforceable.

An example of the role of consideration can be seen in the case of *Pao On v. Lau Yiu Long*.[62] In this case, the defendants entered into the so-called main contract with the plaintiffs, whereby the plaintiffs would purchase a parcel of shares in a newly listed company. In this contract, the plaintiffs agreed, at the request of the defendants, not to sell the shares for a certain period of time after the purchase (so as not to deflate the share price). By way of subsidiary agreement, the defendants agreed to buy back part of the parcel of shares. The plaintiffs had some concerns with this transaction, and, at their initiative, the buyback agreement was cancelled prior to the

60. (1875) LR 10 EX 153 at 162.
61. *Dunlop v. Selfridge* [1915] AC 847.
62. [1980] AC 614.

completion of the main contract. The buyback agreement was replaced by an indemnity guaranteeing that the price of the shares would not fall below a certain value. When the shares did fall below a certain value, the plaintiffs sued the defendants under the indemnity. One defence put forward by the defendants was that there was no consideration for the indemnity, as the plaintiffs, pursuant to the main contract, were already under a legally enforceable obligation not to sell the parcel of shares. Whereas this defence was successful in the lower courts, the Privy Council considered that the promise not to sell the shares was consideration for the promise of the indemnity, as the act was done at the request of the defendant, and the parties understood that the act was to be remunerated. In effect, the plaintiffs' promise not to sell the parcel of shares was given at the defendants' request, with the defendants' indemnity given to honour this understanding.

62. Consideration must also be provided by the person who makes a promise.[63] For example, if I promise to pay your wife AUD 100 if you mow my lawn, your wife is unable to enforce the obligation. She has not provided any consideration for the promise. The result would be different if your wife had organized or arranged for you to mow my lawn. In this scenario, the wife will have provided consideration.

63. Australian law in relation to contracts also states that consideration does not need to be commercially adequate, provided that there has been no unconscionability, misleading or deceptive conduct, duress, undue influence or coercion in the process of forming the contract. The fact that, in economic terms, you get far more or less than the true value of the good or service is irrelevant to the law. In effect, freedom of contract prevails. For example, contractual arrangements relating to the lease of premises are enforceable despite 'peppercorn rents' only being paid for the leasehold interest. Thus, even though the commercial rent would be AUD 200/week, an agreement whereby the rent is only to be AUD 5/week or a 'peppercorn' is enforceable. The law is not concerned with the adequacy of the consideration.[64]

64. By contrast to the requirement that consideration need not be adequate, the law has however said that consideration must be sufficient. What this means is that if the obligation is performed due to:

(i) a moral obligation;
(ii) illusory promises;
(iii) an obligation imposed by law; or
(iv) arrangements with creditors and other third parties;

then the consideration will not be seen as sufficient. Some examples will assist in understanding this.

63. *Dunlop Pneumatic Tyre Co Ltd v. Selfridge Co Ltd* [1915] AC 847.
64. *Chappel & Co Ltd v. Nestle Co Ltd* [1960] AC 87.

A. *Moral Obligation*

65. An example of this can be provided in the well-known case of *Eastwood v. Kenyon.*[65] Sarah was the sole daughter and heir of one Sutcliffe. The plaintiff, the guardian of Sarah, voluntarily incurred expenses in her upbringing. Sarah agreed that she would reimburse the plaintiff, and when Sarah married the defendant, he also promised to reimburse the plaintiff. The plaintiff was unsuccessful in suing on this – there was only a moral obligation to pay, and not a legally enforceable obligation.

Further examples can be given of the offer of a dinner invitation, or a promise to give a lift to a certain location. If these are unsupported by consideration, then they are unenforceable. These matters could also be decided on the basis that there is no intent to create legal relations.

B. *Illusory Promises*

66. *White v. Blunt*[66] is an example of an illusory promise. The defendants promise not to 'bore his father' was seen as too vague or indefinite to form the basis of an enforceable promise.

C. *Obligations Imposed by Law*

67. The performance of a duty that a person is already required to undertake by reason of the law cannot form the basis of adequate consideration. Thus, in *Collins v. Godefory,*[67] a promise to pay someone to attend court, when this is already required by law, is an obligation to which there is not sufficient consideration. Therefore it is unenforceable. Similarly, consideration will be insufficient where the duty to perform the obligation is already imposed because of contract. Thus, in *Stilk v. Myrick,*[68] the promise by a ship's captain to distribute the wages of deserters to supplement the wages of the remaining crew was held unenforceable – the crew were already under a legal obligation to work for the required amount. However, more modern cases have indicated that if there is some practical benefit to the promisee, even though on a narrow interpretation there was no consideration, then the obligation can be enforced. Thus, in *Musumeci v. Winadell Pty Ltd,*[69] lessees of a shop in a mall negotiated for the reduction of rent by one third with the property owner. This was done when a competitor of the lessees was to open in the shopping mall. At a subsequent time, the property owner sought to recover rent in arrears, but was unsuccessful. There was a practical benefit to the property owner in the lessees' remaining as tenants in the shopping complex. The fact that the mall remained

65. (1840) 11 AD & EI 348.
66. (1853) 23 LJ Ex 36.
67. (1831) 1 B & Ad 950.
68. (1809) 2 Camp 317; 170 ER 1168.
69. (1994) 34 NSWLR 723.

occupied and that the plaintiff continued to exist as a vital tenant was held to be sufficient consideration for the promise to reduce the rent.

D. Arrangements with Creditors and Other Third Parties

68. Somewhat unusually, the law has suggested that where the existing duty is payment of a debt, payment of part of the debt, even at the instigation of the creditor, will not be adequate consideration to discharge the entire amount owing (established in *Pinnel*'s case;[70] *Foakes v. Beer*).[71] Thus, for example, if I owe you AUD 100 for mowing my lawn, and you suggest that I pay AUD 70 and forego the rest, the law will still allow you to pursue me for the remaining AUD 30. Perhaps not surprisingly, the law has sought to overcome the rigour of this doctrine by establishing exceptions, which allow part payment to validly occur where something is added to the smaller sum provided, where the smaller sum is given prior to its due date or in a different currency or at a different location. Other ways to avoid the inherent problems in this approach is to use promissory estoppel (see *below*), a formally completed deed of release or the defence of fraud on a minority, where the matter concerns creditors.

69. The performance of an existing contractual duty to a third party may also be enforceable in certain situations. This was decided in the case of *Shadwell v. Shadwell*,[72] where a promise by an uncle to a nephew of regular payments following the nephew's marriage to his then fiancée was held to be enforceable. The uncle argued that there was no consideration, as the nephew was legally bound to marry as he was engaged at the time (the law at that time could enforce a promise to marry). The court found in favour of the plaintiff, but it is a decision heavily criticized, and likely to be debated if a similar legal issue arose again.

Part payment of the debt will be adequate consideration where the payment is made to all creditors. Thus, if a debtor agrees to a composition with creditors, whereby they are all to agree to a certain percentage in the dollar as full payment of the amount owing (e.g., 50 cents to the dollar), then the payment of this will amount to complete discharge of the entire amount. The courts view it as a fraud if one of the creditors seeks to go beyond the agreement and recover the full amount owning. Today, arrangements of this nature are commonly settled pursuant to the legislative provisions of the *Bankruptcy Act 1966* (Cth).

E. Gratuitous Promises

70. As can be seen from the requirement of consideration and intent to create legal relations, a gratuitous promise is unenforceable. The legal basis on which this

70. (1602) 77 ER 237.
71. (1884) 9 App Cas 605.
72. (1860) 9 CBNS 159.

fails is either as a lack of consideration or the failure to create legal relations. This is the case even though there may be an offer and acceptance in the eyes of the law.

F. Natural Obligations

71. Natural obligations do not exist in the Australian legal system. Obligations based on conscience are merely moral obligations that are unsupportable in the legal system. However, as we will see in the discussion of promissory estoppel (and its effect on the law of consideration), the law has expanded the categories of enforceable promises where certain criteria are met.

G. Estoppel

72. Perhaps the most significant impact on the requirement of consideration is the law relating to estoppel. The decisions discussed earlier relating to the principle that part payment of a debt will not amount to adequate consideration led English and Australian courts to adopt the principle of promissory or, as it is sometimes called, equitable estoppel. What promissory estoppel achieves is to prevent an individual from going back on their promise not to enforce their contractual rights. The seminal decision establishing its place in English law was the English Kings Bench decision of *Central London Property Trust Ltd v. High Trees House Ltd.*[73] In this case, the defendant was the tenant of a block of flats. Due to the advent of the Second World War, the defendant was unable to let many of the units. Because of this reason, the plaintiff agreed to halve the rent. By the beginning of 1945, the defendant was able to let all units. The court held that the plaintiff was unable, by reason of estoppel, from claiming the full rent for the years 1940 to 1945. In Australia, promissory estoppel was accepted by the High Court in *Legione v. Hateley*[74] and expanded upon by the major decision of that same court in *Walton Stores Interstate Ltd v. Maher.*[75]

73. In *Walton Stores*, Maher was the property owner of land on which a shopping complex was to be constructed. Maher and Walton Stores had been in negotiations about Walton Stores leasing part of the shopping complex. Negotiations had continued for some months that saw a lease executed by Maher being sent to Walton Stores by way of exchange. Maher began to demolish the existing building and commenced the erection of the new store in line with the requirements of Walton Stores. At no stage between this time in November and January of the following year did Walton Stores give any indication that the lease was in any way unacceptable or that the transaction would not proceed. In December Walton stores became

73. [1947] KB 130.
74. (1983) 152 CLR 406.
75. (1988) 164 CLR 387.

aware of the demolition and construction work being undertaken by Maher. However, Walton Stores had decided to re-examine its retailing policy, and, having ascertained that there had been no formal exchange of the lease agreements (with this required by Australian conveyancing practice in that jurisdiction), instructed its solicitors to 'go slow' on finalizing the arrangements. In January Walton Stores notified Maher that it did not intend to proceed with the lease arrangements. By this time, the existing building had been demolished, and 40% of the new building constructed. As there was no formal contract in place or consideration provided for any agreement, it was argued that Maher could not recover any losses that it had incurred in proceeding to demolish the old building and construct a new building. The court found in favour of Maher despite the absence of any legal relationship or consideration between the parties. In so finding, this decision, and subsequent cases, established the requirements for promissory estoppel. They are as follows:

(i) an assumption of a particular legal relationship between the parties is unequivocally created;
(ii) the responsibilities for that assumption lie with the defendant;
(iii) there must be reliance, either by act or omission, on that assumption by the plaintiff;
(iv) the defendant must have intended the plaintiff to act, or not act, on the assumption;
(v) detriment will occur to the plaintiff if the assumption or expectation is not met; and
(vi) the defendant has given no indication that they will not act in a certain way.

Subsequent cases have, not surprisingly, used this doctrine to overcome the rigours of contract law – particularly those first three elements of offer and acceptance, intent to create legal relations and consideration. For example, in *Commonwealth of Australia v. Verwayen*,[76] an accident between two naval ships occurred in 1964. In 1984 the plaintiff began proceedings claiming damages for personal injury. The Commonwealth Government had given assurances that it would not contest liability. However, its defence indicated that it would rely on the limitation periods applicable (generally, in Australia, these are three years for tort actions). Some members of the High Court found that there was an estoppel that could be raised against the Government – in effect, it would be unconscionable for it to rely on the failure to pursue this matter within the timeframe as the assumption had been created by the Government, with this being relied upon be the plaintiff to his detriment.

74. Once an estoppel has been established, the courts have wide discretion to decide the appropriate remedy. The effect of this can be seen in the High Court decision of *Guimelli v. Guimelli*.[77] In this matter, the parents had agreed with their son, that, in exchange for his working without wages on the family property, the farm would be subdivided and he would be given an interest in the property. Due to the breakdown of the family relationship this did not occur, but the son was successful

76. (1990) 95 ALR 321.
77. (1999) 196 CLR 101.

in arguing that although there was no contract, an estoppel had been raised against the parents. The West Australian Full Court ordered that the farming property be held on trust for subdivision. However, the High Court, whilst still finding an estoppel, considered that the appropriate remedy, given the breakdown in the relations and the work put into the property by other members of the family, was that a monetary sum should be paid to the son representing the claim on the property.

IV. Modifications of the Contract

75. Subject to the terms of the contract, a contract can only be modified with the agreement of both parties. However, some contracts, such as standard form finance contracts and telecommunications contracts, will allow the contract to be modified or altered unilaterally. For example, the mortgagee bank pursuant to the mortgage contract will routinely be permitted to alter the fees, charges and interest rate payable on an agreement with a mortgagor. If a contract has been altered, it may operate to end the original contract and substitute a new, second contract, or it may leave the original contract in place (with alterations). Increasingly, standard form contracts of this nature are being questioned, particularly through legislative direction.[78]

§2. Formal and Evidential Requirements

I. Formal Requirements

76. In Australia, there are certain formal requirements that must be met in relation to certain types of contracts. The taxonomy of these types of contracts can be expressed as follows:

(i) contracts to be made by way of deed;
(ii) contracts to be reduced to writing; and
(iii) contracts required to be evidenced in writing.

A. Contracts by Way of Deed

77. As previously noted, an alleged contract without consideration is generally unenforceable. However, agreements without consideration will be enforceable where they are contained in a deed. These types of contracts obtain their capacity from the form in which they are expressed. The standard requirements are that the agreement be signed, sealed and delivered. The requirement of the signature is obvious, and delivery merely means the passage of the document to the other party or some person on their behalf (though this can be met if the other party indicates an intention to be bound by the document: *Bolton Metropolitan Borough Council v.*

78. For example, *Fair Trading Act 1999* (Vic) Part 2B.

Torkington).[79] Originally, sealing involved the affixing of wax of that person's coat of arms to the paper. Today, however, legislative requirements have provided for a deemed method of sealing. Compliance is obtained if the document is expressed to be by way of deed (e.g., *Conveyancing Act 1919* (NSW) section 38(3)).

B. Contracts That Must Be Reduced to Writing

78. There is a further category of contracts that must be reduced to writing. If these contracts are not in writing, they are void and unenforceable. The requirement for writing primarily comes from legislative provisions dealing with the type of contract. The list of these contracts that must be reduced to writing can be stated as follows:[80]

(i) bills of exchange and promissory notes;
(ii) cheques;
(iii) assignments of copyright;
(iv) contracts of marine insurance;
(v) acknowledgement of statute-barred debts;
(vi) submission to arbitration;
(vii) assignments of life insurance policies;
(viii) maintenance agreements;
(ix) contracts for the employment of seamen;
(x) contracts by deed;
(xi) real estate contracts;
(xii) transfer of shares in a company (this subject to modification); and
(xiii) consumer credit contracts.

C. Contracts Required to Be Evidenced in Writing

79. There is a further category of contracts that, to be enforceable, are required to be in writing. The genesis for this requirement can be found in the *Statute of Frauds* 1677 (Eng). The essence of this legislation was that unless the agreement between the parties was contained in some memorandum or note in writing, then, in respect of five classes of contracts, the contract would not be enforceable. The five categories of contracts were as follows:

(i) promise by the executor of a deceased estate to pay the debts of the deceased out of her or his own assets;
(ii) a contract of guarantee;
(iii) agreements made in consideration of marriage;
(iv) contract for the sale or disposition of an interest in land; and
(v) agreements not to be performed within one year from the making of that agreement.

---

79. [2004] 2 WLR 426.
80. Taken from P. Latimer (2006) *Business Law of Australia*, CCH, Sydney, 265.

80. Today, the Statute of Frauds has been substantially amended in most Australian jurisdictions. For the most part, the effect of the Statute of Frauds only applies in relation to a contract for the sale or disposition of an interest in land (e.g., *Conveyancing Act 1919* (NSW) section 54A(1); *Instruments Act 1958* (Vic)). However, in Western Australia and Tasmania any contract for the sale of goods in the value of AUD 20 and upwards must be evidenced in writing. Written evidence is unnecessary if there has been acceptance of the goods, part payment or part performance. For this reason, many cases discuss what is known as the doctrine of part performance. Other cases elaborate on what is mean by a sufficient note or memorandum in writing, and, finally, the practical impact of a lack of writing may be overcome by the use of restitutionary principles.

D. Part Performance

81. Three requirements are necessary for part performance to be established:

(i) First, the activities relied on must have been done in performance of the contract;
(ii) Second, activities must be unequivocally and in the own nature preferable to the alleged contract; and
(iii) Third, there must have been a change of position so that the plaintiff would be unfairly prejudiced if they were not able to rely on part performance.[81]

An example of the operation of this provision can be seen in the decision of *Carr v. McDonald's Australia Ltd.*[82] In this case, the plaintiff undertook year-long training as part of an agreement to be appointed to a McDonald's hamburger franchise. As part of the training, the plaintiff had undertaken a large amount of unpaid work over of the course of this year. Despite an absence of writing, this contract was enforceable in equity. However, the plaintiff was not liable to enforce a contract for any specific restaurant – there being no acts unequivocally referable to a specific location.

E. Note or Memorandum in Writing

82. Many cases have considered the extent to which the alleged contract must be supported by some note or memorandum in writing. First, cases have indicated that the memorandum can be located in more the one document,[83] however, all the material terms relating to the agreement must be in writing.[84] A signature must also

81. See *generally, Regent v. Millett* (1976) 133 CLR 679; the English requirements may be somewhat less, see *Steadman v. Steadman* [1976] AC 536.
82. (1994) 63 FCR 358.
83. *Harvey Edwards Dunlop & Co Ltd* (1927) 39 CLR 302.
84. *Ibid.*

appear to authenticate the document.[85] However, the existence of the signature has been loosely interpreted. It may appear in any part of the document, and need not be a signature as such, but merely recognition of acknowledgement by the person signing.[86] The destruction of a note or memorandum in writing that would otherwise prove the existence of such a document may be established orally.[87] Finally, as discussed above, Australia since 1999 has had Electronic Transactions Legislation which allows for true digital signatures, i.e., digital signature using secure cryptographic methods such as Public Key Infrastructure or XML code. The Electronic Transactions Act 1999 (Cth) and corresponding state and territory acts aim to remove legal impediments to electronic contracts. The Act adopts the following principles:

- Functional equivalence – as far as possible, paper based commerce and electronic commerce should be treated equally by the law; and
- Technology neutrality – the law should not discriminate between different forms of technology.

The Act broadly works by not making electronic transactions invalid for the purposes of Commonwealth and identical State Electronic Transactions laws, simply because they are electronic.

F. Restitutionary Principles

83. The final basis on which the lack of a note or memorandum in writing can be overcome is by the principles relating to restitution. Under this doctrine, courts may be willing to allow a plaintiff to recover where it would be unjust for the defendant to rely on the lack of the memorandum or note in writing. For example, in *Pavey and Matthews Pty Ltd v. Paul*[88] a builder of a house was entitled to recover for the material supplied and labour done in respect of the construction of the house – this despite the absence of any written contract. It would have been unjust to allow the defendant to retain the benefit of the constructed house and rely on the lack of writing to leave the builder unpaid for the work completed and materials used in the building of the dwelling.

G. Solemn Contracts

84. In the Australian legal system the only equivalent to the solemn contract as noted in Continental Europe is those categories of agreements made by deed (noted above).

---

85. There is of course considerable debate as to the effect of electronic signatures on this legislation. See S. Christensen & R. Low, *Moving the Statute of Frauds to the Digital Age*, 77 Austrl. L.J. 416 (2003).
86. *Gladstone v. Ball* (1862) 1 W & W (E) 277.
87. *Giasoumi v. Hutton* [1977] VR 294.
88. (1987) 162 CLR 221.

II. Evidential Requirement: Proof

85. If the contract is required to be in writing, the written evidence would obviously form the central basis on which the court will determine the terms and extent of the contract. If a contract is not one that is required to be in writing, the court will then be required to adjudicate between the whole evidence and other documentary information supplied to it to determine the ambit of the agreement. In essence, the courts will need to adjudicate as to whether the statements made, be they in writing or orally, were intended to form a term of contract or whether they were merely a representation made as part of the negotiating process. The following principles have been identified as relevant to that determination:[89]

(i) the more critical the alleged statement to the content of the agreement, the more likely that it will be seen as a contract term, rather than a representation;
(ii) the greater the time between the statement and the finalization of the agreement, the less likely that it will be a term;
(iii) whether any written contract was put in place after the alleged oral term – if the contract has been reduced to writing, it is more likely that statements made orally will not be seen as terms of the contract;
(iv) the precision of the statement; and
(v) whether the statement was made by a person with special expertise. If this was the case, the courts will be more likely to view the statement as a term of the contract rather than as a representation.

86. It should be noted that even if a whole statement is not deemed to be part of the contract, that there may be legal remedies available to the plaintiff. This could include misleading and deceptive conduct,[90] misrepresentation[91] or unconscionability.[92] However, the critical point to note for present purposes is that if the statement is not a term of contract, then there will be no possibility for either party to seek damages for breach of contract based on non-compliance with that term.

A. The Parol Evidence Rule

87. The courts generally apply what is known as the parol evidence rule when finalizing the terms of a contract. Under this doctrine, oral (or parol) evidence is not admissible to dispute the terms of a contract that has been concluded in writing. The theory behind this is that the parties, having placed the terms of the contract in writing, have decided that that would form the final statement and cover all the respective terms of their agreement. Obviously, one significant way in which the parol evidence rule can be overcome is to allege that the written document was never

89. Extracted from R.B. Vermeesch & K.E. Lindgren, *Business Law of Australia* 145 (LexisNexis Butterworths 2005).
90. See Misleading and Deceptive Conduct provisions of the *Competition and Consumer Act 2010*.
91. For example, fraudulent or innocent misrepresentation.
92. See Unconscionability Provisions under the *Competition and Consumer Act* discussed in the subsequent sections.

intended to encapsulate the entire terms of the alleged agreement between the parties – in this case the written and oral evidence can be put before the court to alleged that the entire agreement is to be found in the combination of the written and oral word.[93] It is also possible to use oral evidence to provide examples of trade or custom usage,[94] or where the common intention of the parties has not been adduced into written form. This allows for the doctrine of rectification to overcome these problems.[95] A second avenue by which the parol evidence rule can be overcome is to assert that the parties had, in addition to the principal contract, a collateral contract. In this context, a collateral contract is some agreement between the parties, promissory in nature and consistent with the main contract, and that is designed to be relied upon by one party to the contract. For example, in *Mendelssohn v. Normand Ltd* [96] a person parking their Rolls Royce at a car park specifically mentioned the presence of valuables in the car to the parking attendant. This latter promised to park and lock the car, and when the valuables were stolen, the owner of the car was able to recover on the basis that there was a collateral contract formed with the car park, which overrode the exclusion clauses (denying liability for any loss) printed on the car park ticket.

B. Function of the Notary

88. Unlike Continental Europe, the notary in Australia has no specific or formal role. If the parties resort to assistance with the drafting of contracts, the legal practitioner or solicitor will be the person used. However, there is no legal monopoly provided to the legal profession as regards the drafting of contracts, and in some transactions (e.g., real estate transactions in some jurisdictions), the contract may well be formed without the assistance of lawyers. Similarly, in many of the ongoing service-related contracts (such as a mobile phone contract or a pay television contract) the standard form contract is entered into without the assistance of the legal practitioner. If the legal practitioner is used in the formation of the contract, then their role will be to draft the terms, advise the client of the principles behind the transaction and ensure that registration requirements are attended to (e.g., lease agreements). Legal practitioners in Australia are regulated through the state-based law societies.

III. Burden of Proof

89. As with civil law generally in Australia, the burden of proof in contractual matters is based on the balance of probabilities. The plaintiff who is seeking to make her/his case will have the onus, on the balance of probabilities, of proving that the terms of the contract are as they allege. Often in contract matters, the defendant will

93. *Van Den Esschert v. Chappell* [1960] WAR 114.
94. *Hutton v. Warren* (1836) 1 M&W 466.
95. *NSW Medical Defence Union Ltd v. Transport Industries Insurance Co Ltd* (1986) 6 NSWLR 740.
96. [1970] 1 QB 177.

also be asserting a different course of events, and if this is the case, then the defendant will have the onus of proving their version of events. The defendant will also have the onus if they are asserting an affirmative defence, such as lack of capacity to contract.

90. Is there a distinction made between obligation of means and obligation of results?

Australia has no direct parallel to the Continental European distinction between obligation of means and obligations of results. However, certain terms are implied into contractual arrangements between the parties (see Chapter 3. The Contents of a Contract, for more detail). One such category is terms implied by law, and these can include the following:[97]

(i) a term imposed on a bailee to exercise reasonable care in the possession of goods;
(ii) a term imposed requiring the exercise of reasonable care; and
(iii) a term requiring reasonable performance in an employment contract.

§3. Liability and Negotiations

I. Pre-contractual Liability

91. The most common form of pre-contractual liability would emanate from misleading and deceptive conduct or unconscionable conduct of one party leading to allegations by the innocent party of a breach of Australia's Competition and Consumer Act 2010. Other pre-contractual liability may arise, as noted above based on as estoppel, and restitutionary principles. Absent any of the these special circumstances, being a party to a negotiation does not involve the making of a representation that an agreement will be formed, nor does it give rise to any sense of obligation that would be legally binding. It is only by the acceptance of a formal offer combined with consideration (or, in those limited circumstances where consideration is not required, such as a deed) that obligations arise, as this will involve the conclusion of a formal agreement. A formal agreement must be distinguished from that situation where the parties have essentially decided all relevant terms, but there is some critical aspect missing – such as the subject matter of the contract. In this case, there will be nothing more than an agreement to agree. This can be contrasted with a concluded contract, but that requires a third party (such as a valuer) to determine some aspect of the agreement (e.g., rent payable). In this situation, there will be a valid contract in place. Similarly, agreements to negotiate in good faith are generally nothing more than part of the pre-contractual process and nothing will follow if this is not perceived to be done.[98]

97. See Vermeesch & Lindgren, *supra* n. 74, at 150–151.
98. *Walford v. Miles* [1992] 2 WLR 174.

92. However, the courts may use extrinsic evidence to clarify the meaning of terms that are contained within a contract. This is somewhat different from the parol evidence rule (discussed earlier), as this relates to the identification of what the terms of the contract are. By contrast, extrinsic evidence can be used to understand the meaning or resolve any ambiguity of terms that have been identified to be within the contractual matrix. A range of circumstances have been identified where documentary evidence may be used to assist any understanding of the terms of the contract, and these can be stated as follows:[99]

(i) to identify the parties to the contract;
(ii) to identify the subject matter of the contract;
(iii) to identify the consideration;
(iv) to identify those circumstances when a term should be implied; and
(v) to establish the commercial circumstances surrounding the making of the contract.

93. By contrast, extrinsic evidence cannot be used where it relates to pre-contractual negotiations. Nevertheless, there is no general obligation of good faith in the contracting process or in the establishment of substantive contractual requirements. The role of good faith is, however, a matter of significant debate and further development is likely in the future.[100] For example, Victoria has introduced legislation that allows for the modification and voiding of unfair contractual terms.[101]

II. Breakdown of Negotiations

94. As indicated by what has previously been said, generally the breakdown of negotiations will not lead to any potential liability imposed on parties to the putative contract. However, as was seen in the decision of *Walton Stores v. Maher*,[102] liability may be imposed by way of doctrines other than breach of contract. For example, in this case it was held that the defendant was estopped from denying any obligation to the plaintiff following the plaintiff's reliance on a set of circumstances created by the defendant's behaviour. The other major exception is when pre-contractual conduct amounts to misleading and deceptive or unconscionable conduct which of itself may constitute a violation of the *Australian Competition and Consumer Law 2010* (Cth).

99. See Vermeesch & Lindgren, *supra* n. 74, at 162.
100. See I.B. Stewart, *Good Faith in Contractual Performance and in Negotiation* 72 ALJ 370 (1998).
101. See *Fair Trading Act 1999*, ss 32J–32K.
102. (1988) 164 CLR 387.

Chapter 2. Conditions of Substantive Validity

95. In this chapter a number of methods by which the substantive validity of the contract may be questioned will be discussed. For example, whilst the requirements of offer and acceptance, consideration and an intent to create legal relations may be established, the person seeking to contract may not have the capacity to contract. Alternatively, the person seeking to enforce the contract may be attempting to enforce it against a person who does not have the requisite capacity.

Another way in which the substantive validity of what would otherwise be a formal agreement will be brought into question is where there is some defect in the consent given by the parties. For example, there may be some mistake – common, mutual or unilateral – in the contracting process. In addition, there may have been some misrepresentation, improper pressure, gross disparity or unconscionability between the contracting parties. All of these under appropriate conditions may lead to a breakdown in the contract or in the courts' recognition of its substantive validity.

Furthermore, the problem may also occur where either the contract is initially impossible to perform or it is illegal for criminal or public policy reasons.

The final section of this chapter will then discuss the consequences of a lack of defective consent or lack of substantive validity. Whilst in many cases this will mean that the contract it unenforceable, in certain circumstances questions arise as to the retrospective effect of avoidance of the contract and the availability of damages.

§1. Capacity of the Parties

96. In Australia, discussions concerning the capacity to contract are generally divided into the following categories:

(i) minors;
(ii) the mentally ill;
(iii) the intoxicated;
(iv) married women;
(v) corporations;
(vi) bankrupts; and
(vii) prisoners.

I. Minors

97. In Australia, people over the age of 18 (and not subject to any other reason of incapacity) have full capacity to contract.[103] Perhaps unusually, minors are able to enforce a contract against the other party, yet this latter party will rarely be able to enforce the contract against the minor. The reason for this apparent anomaly

103. For example, *Age of Majority Act 1977* (Vic).

relates to the philosophy of the law that it should protect the minor from her or his own inexperience and vulnerability, and need not protect the party seeking to contract with the minor. Again, the law of restitution has provided a means by which a minor may be forced to disgorge a gain obtained through a void or voidable contract. Furthermore, the law of tort may also provide a means by which liability may attach to a minor – for example, conversion if they retain possession of goods supplied under a contract, or for fraud, if they misrepresent their age. The key however, is that the contract will be unenforceable.

II. Valid Contracts with Minors

98. There are two exceptions to the unenforceability of contract with minors. First, contracts for the supply of necessaries are regarded as enforceable; second, contracts involving employment, may also be considered enforceable. With the former contract, the critical aspect is to define what is meant by necessaries. Generally, necessaries are considered to be those items that are suitable to the life of that minor and that are required by him. An example may assist to understand this. In *Chaplin v. Leslie Frewin (Publishers) Ltd*,[104] the publication of the memoirs of the son of Charlie Chaplin was said to be very beneficial to the minor and therefore enforceable. Conversely, the supply of luxurious items of dress to a person already well endowed with clothing was held not to be a necessary.[105] An example of an enforceable employment contract can be seen in the decision of *Roberts v. Gray*,[106] where it was accepted by the court that a refusal by a billiards player (a minor) to go on a previously agreed joint venture tour was a matter that was of benefit to the minor and therefore a remedy in damages sounded because of the minor's refusal to travel.

III. Voidable Contracts

99. There is a category of contracts that remain binding on both parties, unless the minor repudiates those contracts prior to the age of 18, or within a reasonable time after turning 18. The contracts that pertain to this category include those that involve the acquisition of an interest in property of a permanent nature, or contracts that involve a continuing obligation. The operation of this can be seen in the English decision of *Steinberg v. Scala (Leeds) Ltd.*[107] A minor was allotted 500 shares in a company. She sought to repudiate the contract whilst still a minor, and to recover the money she had paid in respect of the initial allotment and first call. She was unsuccessful, as she had received the 500 shares and there had been no total failure of consideration in respect of the transaction.

---

104. [1966] Ch. 71.
105. *Nash v. Inman* [1908] 2 KB 1.
106. [1913] 1 KB 520.
107. [1923] 2 Ch. 452.

IV. Void Contracts with Minors

100. Within this category lie two types of contracts. The first is those contracts that are void until ratified. The second is those contracts that are void because of jurisdiction-specific legislation. With the former, ratification requires a positive, affirmative act by the minor. In many practical scenarios this will require ratification in writing. Legislation in Victoria,[108] New South Wales[109] and South Australia[110] also enlarges the common law principles concerning contracts, with Victoria in particular statutorily voiding any contract with a minor for the payment of money, for the payment of goods supplied (other than necessaries) and for accounts for non-necessaries.

V. The Mentally Ill

101. Given that a genuine offer and acceptance as well as intent to create legal relations is required for the formation of a valid contract, a mentally ill person will generally be unable to enter into a valid contract. The onus of establishing this will, however, be on the mentally disabled person, who must show that their genuine consent was overborne by the mental disability, and that the other party was, or should have been, aware of this condition.[111] The contract will be voidable at the option of the impaired individual.

VI. Intoxicated

102. This has the same test as for the mentally ill. The person intoxicated must show, once sober, that they were unable to understand what was occurring because of their intoxication, but also that the other party should at least have been aware of their condition. The contract is voidable, but if affirmed when sober is then incapable of being voided. For example, in *Mathews v. Baxter*[112] a person when drunk purchased a house at auction. He confirmed the contract when sober, but subsequently sought to withdraw on the grounds that he was affected by alcohol at the auction. The court ruled that whilst he may have had the opportunity to void the contract at an earlier stage, this had been lost by his subsequent sober ratification.

VII. Married Women

103. Statutory developments in 1857 in England, and subsequently adopted in all jurisdictions in Australia, now treat married women as being contractually liable

---

108. *Supreme Court Act 1986* (Vic).
109. *Minors (Property and Contracts) Act 1970* (NSW).
110. *The Minors' Contracts (Miscellaneous Provisions) Act 1979* (SA).
111. *Gibbons v. Wright* (1954) 91 CLR 423.
112. (1873) LR 8 Exch 132.

as if they are single.[113] Prior to this time, married women were held to lack contractual capacity, with the woman and her husband regarded as one legal person.

VIII. Corporations

104. In Australia, a corporation is for most purposes equated with a natural person.[114] This means that a corporation can contract and can sue, or be sued, on the basis of the contract. Obviously, however, the corporation does not have the capacity to sign as if it were a natural person – it must rely on agents to undertake these tasks. In a modern corporation, the directors, or those expressly authorized by the directors, will be empowered to enter into contracts on behalf of the corporation.[115] Furthermore, the corporation may sign documents by the use of the company seal and the affixing of two signatures (such as a director and secretary).[116] A statutory corporation, such as the Civil Aviation Safety Authority, established for the purpose of ensuring the safety of air navigation, may not have the capacity to enter into a binding contract where such a purported agreement was incompatible with this principle of safety.[117]

IX. Bankrupts

105. A bankrupt is able to contract. However, as title to the bankrupt's property vests in the trustee in bankruptcy, should the bankrupt be successfully sued, the other party will have no assets of the bankrupt against which they will be able to enforce any judgment. Contracts by the bankrupt in respect of any property acquired by the bankrupt after the date of bankruptcy will be valid against the trustee in bankruptcy if the other party dealing with the bankrupt was in good faith, the transaction was for valuable consideration and the transaction was completed prior to intervention by the trustee.[118]

X. Prisoners

106. Generally, prisoners will have full capacity to enter into contracts and to sue and be sued on those contracts. This follows the passage of legislation removing any disabilities on prisoners' transacting powers.[119]

---

113. For example *Marriage Act 1958* (Vic).
114. *Corporations Act 2001* (Cth) s. 124.
115. *Corporations Act 2001* (Cth) s. 126.
116. *Corporations Act 2001* (Cth) s. 128.
117. *Civil Aviation Safety Authority v. Sydney Heli-Scenic Pty Ltd* [2006] NSWCA 111 at [69], though in this case, the agreement did give rise to contractual obligations.
118. *Bankruptcy Act 1966* (Cth) s. 126.
119. For example, see *Felons (Civil Proceedings) Act 1981* (NSW).

§2. DEFECTS OF CONSENT

107. Consent of a contracting party may be vitiated in a number of ways where it can be claimed that the mutuality of minds – the matching of an offer by its acceptance – has not been met, by reason of mistake, misrepresentation, improper pressure, duress or unconscionability.

108. Mistakes in the contracting process can occur in a number of ways. First, the person may be mistaken as to what they are purchasing. For example, a person may see a puppy at a garage sale believing it to be a pedigree Cavalier King Charles Spaniel. After purchasing, the person may in fact find that it is not a Cavalier King Charles Spaniel, but a King Charles Spaniel (recognized as a completely different breed, though somewhat similar in appearance). The purchaser may well believe that they have been the victim of a mistake, but generally, and subject to an absence of misrepresentation, no remedy will be available to the purchaser. The law is not concerned with this. The principle of buyer beware remains fundamental. Nevertheless, the law does accept three categories of mistake:

(i) Common mistake (where both parties are mistaken. For example Purchaser (P) may agree to buy a pedigree dog from Vendor (V). Unbeknownst to both parties, however, the dog is not a pedigree, but a cross between a Cavalier King Charles Spaniel and a King Charles Spaniel).
(ii) Mutual mistake (where the parties misunderstand each other. For example, P may agree to buy a pedigree Cavalier King Charles Spaniel from V, whereas V believes he is selling a pedigree King Charles Spaniel).
(iii) Unilateral mistake (where one party is mistaken, and the other should reasonably have been aware of this – for example, P believes he is purchasing a Cavalier King Charles Spaniel, and V knows that P is a dog breeder of Cavaliers and that the puppy being purchased is in fact a King Charles Spaniel.

I. Mistake

A. Common Mistake

109. In addition to statutory developments that account for mistakes, for example in the use of automated contracting systems as discussed above, Australia also has a body of case law that provides judicial precedent covering various categories of mistake. The first of these is 'common mistake'. If mistake occurs, the contract will be void *ab initio.* However, it is necessary to establish that an essential component of the agreement was not in existence, despite the reasonably held belief of the parties that it was. For example, in the High Court decision of *McRae v. Commonwealth Disposal Commission,*[120] the respondents advertised a tender for the purchase of an oil tanker lying approximately 160 kilometres offshore. The appellant

120. (1951) 84 CLR 377.

was the successful tenderer. However, the oil tanker could not be located. The Commission argued that this was a case of mistake. This was not accepted by the High Court – the vendor had promised that the goods were in existence, when this was not the case. This case can be contrasted with the decision in *Couturier v. Hastie*,[121] where a cargo of corn in transit by ship was sold by the vendor to a purchaser. Unbeknownst to both parties, whilst in transit, the captain of the ship had already sold the corn, as delays had caused it to ferment. The Court held that there was no contract in existence. A somewhat controversial decision can be seen in the case of *Leaf v. International Galleries*.[122] Both the vendor and purchaser believed that the subject of sale was a Constable painted titled 'Salisbury Cathedral'. However, the picture was not a Constable. The Court found that there was no mistake. The subject of the contract was a painting title 'Salisbury Cathedral' and this had been sold. At common law, the contract is void and no damages are recoverable. Restitution may however be possible if money has been paid, or property transferred pursuant to the contract.

B. *Mutual Mistake*

110. The underlying ethos of mutual mistake is that no consensus can be located between the purchaser and the vendor. The purchaser believes they are buying one thing, the seller considers that they are selling a completely different thing. If found to exist, mutual mistake will operate to void the contract *ab initio*. In *Smith v. Hughes* [123] the vendor was selling oats to the purchaser. The purchaser wanted to buy old oats, the vendor only had new oats for sale. It was argued by the purchaser that this was a mutual mistake, and that accordingly there was no contract. The Court disagreed. There was consensus as to the sale of oats, merely a difference as to the age of the oats. Second, the test was to be looked at from the viewpoint of an objective person. If reasonably it could be thought that an agreement existed, then subjective differences on the part of one party would not be relevant. Contrast this decision with *Scriven Bros & Co v. Hindley & Co*.[124] The action concerned a claim by one party to recover the amounting owing by the defendants for the purchase of tow (course fibres) at an auction. The defendants had refused to pay because they believed that they were purchasing quality hemp. The defendant had inspected samples of hemp at the plaintiff's showrooms, and even though there were correct samples at the auction site, this had not been inspected by the defendants. Further evidence indicated that the bales of hemp and tow contained the same shipping label and that this had led to some confusion. It was held that there was no binding contract, as there was considerable ambiguity as to what was for sale and what was being purchased.

121. (1956) 5 HLCas 673; 10 ER 1065.
122. [1950] 2 KB 86.
123. (1871) LR 6 QB 597.
124. [1913] 3 KB 564.

C. Unilateral Mistake

111. Unilateral mistake occurs where one party is mistaken as to some fundamental aspect of the contract, and the other party has knowledge of this, or ought to be reasonably aware of this mistake. Theoretically this can be seen as a case where there has been no genuine offer and acceptance – the offer made by one party, being to the knowledge of the other party mistaken. The leading High Court decision on unilateral mistake is the case of *Taylor v. Johnson*.[125] In this case, Johnson entered into a contract to sell to Taylor 10 acres of land. The purchase price specified in the contract was AUD 15,000. Prior to the completion of the sale Johnson sought to rectify or rescind, alleging that she had intended the price to be AUD 15,000 per acre, rather than AUD 15,000 for the whole parcel. A mooted rezoning of the land would see the economic value of the land at approximately AUD 195,000. The High Court upheld the claim for rescission on the basis that Taylor was aware, or ought to have been aware, of the mistake by Johnson.

112. A second category of cases dealing with unilateral mistake concerns a situation where one party is mistaken as to the identity of the other. For example, in the classic decision in *Phillips v. Brooks Ltd*,[126] a rogue purchased a ring by fraudulently assuming the name of another. A cheque that was subsequently dishonoured paid for the ring. One issue before the court was whether there was a unilateral mistake, which would render the contract void *ab initio*. The Court said no, the shopkeeper intended to contract with the person that entered the shop, therefore there was no mistaken identity. This case can be contrasted with *Ingram v. Little*,[127] where the owners of a car intended to sell the car to a particular individual who had been identified by reference to a phone directory. The Court distinguished *Phillips v. Brooks Ltd* on the basis that the seller of the car intended to sell to a particular person, and not to any individual (unlike the shopkeeper). Having said this, however, the two cases are extraordinarily difficult to reconcile.

113. Mistake as to the nature of the document: *non est factum*

One final category of mistake deals with the situation where a person signs a document believing it to be something completely different from what it actually is. If this occurs, the person may be able to rely on the defence of *non est factum* (it is not my deed). This defence is rarely pleaded and difficult to establish. The person attempting to plead this defence will need to show that they are at a significant disadvantage, such as illiteracy, or that they are in a position where they could not have any understanding of the particular document.[128] An example of where the defence was successfully made is the decision in *PT Ltd v. Maradona Pty Ltd*.[129] An elderly lady, who was under the disability of a stroke, signed a document that was a guarantee of a loan of half a million dollars. It was held that when she had signed the

125. (1983) 151 CLR 422.
126. [1919] 2 KB 243.
127. [196] 1 QB 31.
128. *Petelin v. Cullen* (1975) 132 CLR 335.
129. (1992) 25 NSWLR 643.

document she did not have the capacity to understand what she was doing, and therefore the defence of *non est factum* succeeded. By contrast, an example of where the defence was not established can be seen in the case of *Saunders v. Anglia Building Society*.[130] A 78-year-old woman provided the deeds relating to her leasehold interest to her nephew in order for him to raise money on that interest. It was a condition of the provision of the deeds that she would be able to remain in occupation until her death. Fraudulent documents were then prepared, indicating that the property was being sold to the nephew. The documents were taken to the woman for signing, but she had broken her glasses and was unable to read them. The true effect of the documents was misrepresented to the elderly woman. The defendant then used the document and apparent ownership to mortgage the house for GB 2,000. The plaintiff's action alleging *non est factum* was unsuccessful. The ultimate object of the exercise was to raise money on the disposition of the interest. Given this fact, the transactions that were completed were not fundamentally different from what had been intended.

II. Misrepresentation

114. The general principle when contracting, particularly in the case of the purchase of goods, is that of *caveat emptor* (buyer beware). Furthermore, as seen above, when the contract has been reduced to a written document the Court will only consider the terms of that written document when examining and determining the common intent of the parties. However, the strictness of this principal has been ameliorated somewhat by the law regarding misrepresentation. There are now a number of areas where a person may be able to use the doctrine of misrepresentation to recover a loss incurred in the contracting process. The essential question in this area is the extent to which the law should intervene. As will be shown, statutory developments have largely supplemented the common law position, and to a significant extent have overcome the limitations contained within the common law.

115. Misrepresentation can be divided into four distinct categories:

(i) innocent misrepresentation;
(ii) fraudulent misrepresentation;
(iii) negligent misrepresentation; and
(iv) statutory misrepresentation.

At its heart, misrepresentations must refer to an existing or past fact or event, and be made by one party, either before or at the time of contracting. The essence of it is a representation that is untrue.

130. [1971] AC 1004.

A. Innocent Misrepresentation

116. As the name would suggest, innocent misrepresentation involves the situation where a person unintentionally misleads another as to a material term of a contract. Generally, an innocent misrepresentation, unless it involves some other contractual doctrine such as collateral contract or mistake, will not entitle the person misrepresented to a remedy for breach of contract. The general rule is that an innocent misrepresentation gives no cause of action. However, it may be possible to seek a range of remedies in appropriate circumstances. This may well include repudiation of the contract or rescission – though rescission will not be possible if the contract has been affirmed, if restitution is no longer possible or if a third party would be adversely affected by the operation of rescission. It was because of the very limited nature of the remedies available for innocent misrepresentation that subsequent developments have seen the enactment of statutory incursions into this area. Before considering this, however, it is necessary to consider fraudulent misrepresentation.

B. Fraudulent Misrepresentation

117. A fraudulent misrepresentation, as its name would suggest, involves the representation by one party to the contract to another, of a fact that that party knows to be false or is careless as to whether it is true or false. This is determined at the time the representation is made and the motive will be immaterial. If the representation relates to a material fact and the other contracting person relies on that misrepresentation to their detriment, damages may well lie as a remedy. In this context, the action lies in the tort of deceit, rather than in breach of contract. The person affected by the fraudulent misrepresentation may also seek to affirm (or not) the contract.

C. Negligent Misrepresentation

118. A further species of tortious action may lie for negligent misrepresentation. In this scenario, a duty of care is owed by one party to the other, and there has been a breach of that duty by the failure to take reasonable care in representing something to the other party. If this scenario does occur, the action, as noted will lie in tort.

D. Statutory Misrepresentation

119. The limitations of the common law concepts of innocent, fraudulent and negligent misrepresentation have led to a raft of statutory reforms to overcome these deficiencies. For example, in South Australia and the Australian Capital Territory (ACT) legislation has been introduced to expand the common law remedies.[131]

131. *Misrepresentation Act 1971* (SA); *Law Reform (Misrepresentation) Act 1977* (ACT).

However, the most significant change has been with the enactment of the *Trade Practices Act 1974* and its replacement legislation, the Australian Competition and Consumer Act 2010 (Cth). This piece of legislation dramatically altered the consumer and business landscape concerning misrepresentations in the contractual process. Specifically, section 18 of this legislation prohibits conduct in trade or commerce that is misleading or deceptive or likely to mislead or deceive. In addition to this, Chapter 3, Part 3-1 of the legislation (quoted below) prohibits a range of false or misleading representations. Since its enactment this legislation has been broadly read by the courts, and now gives rise to a vast case law as to what is misleading or deceptive. For example, a misrepresentation that may not be actionable at common law may now give rise to a remedy under the statute.[132] A remedial smorgasbord is provided under the legislation. Because of these reasons, actions for misrepresentation today will routinely begin with statutory misrepresentation. For this reason, it is appropriate to consider it in somewhat more detail.

E. Misleading and Deceptive Conduct

120. Section 18 of Schedule 2 of the *Competition and Consumer Act 2010*, (with Schedule 2 known as the Australian Consumer Law (ACL)) proscribes conduct by a person in trade or commerce that is misleading or deceptive or likely to mislead or deceive. It imposes strict liability, an intention to mislead not being necessary. While it may be considered the lynchpin of consumer protection, it has routinely been relied upon by businesses to protect their commercial interests.

121. The critical factor for present purposes is what conduct will be considered misleading or deceptive. Significantly, there is no requirement that the defendant have any idea or knowledge that their representations, or, in the language of the Act, conduct, would mislead or deceive. The fact that it does will establish liability independently of any belief on the part of the person making the representation. The plaintiff must however have relied upon the misleading and deceptive conduct, and the loss – though this is not necessary for a successful action; it just goes to the applicable remedy – must have been caused by the misleading conduct. An example of how this legislation can operate can be seen in the New South Wales Court of Appeal decision in *Metalcorp Recyclers Pty Ltd v. Metal Manufacturers Ltd.*[133] A supplier provided property to the vendor for resale. The vendor sold the items to the purchaser. The purchaser had been alerted that there was a possibility that the items had in fact been stolen. If this was the case, the vendor would not have any title to pass to the purchaser. Despite the vendor contacting the purchaser to discuss an unrelated issue, no mention was made by the buyer of their suspicions – the seller then went ahead and paid its supplier. It was subsequently shown that the property was stolen, with the buyer, understandably, refusing to pay for the items. In action by the vendor against the purchaser, it was held that the purchaser was liable for

132. See, for example, *SWF Hoists and Industrial Equipment Pty Ltd v. State Government Insurance Commission* (1990) ATPR 41-045.
133. [2003] NSWCA 213.

deceptive and misleading conduct. Critically, the parties had had a long-standing relationship of some ten years, and as part of that relationship, the vendor would normally have been notified of any concern with the delivery. When no mention was made of this, the vendor was entitled to think that there was no problem – the silence of the purchaser had been misleading and deceptive. There was a reasonable expectation of disclosure. Virtually every type of contractual relationship that is litigated today would have, at some stage, consideration of the potential of a misleading and deceptive conduct action under the Competition and Consumer Act. A wide range of remedies are available where the norm of conduct expected of business and established by this provision has not been met. Critically, for present purposes, the rewriting of contracts is a potential order.[134]

F. Specific Types of Misrepresentation Attracting Civil and Criminal Liability

122. Section 29, Chapter 3, Part 2-1, Division I contained in Schedule 2 of the Australian Competition and Consumer Law 2010 (Cth) supports section 18 by providing for both criminal (fines of AUD 1.1 million for a corporation and AUD 200,000 for a natural person) and civil (damages, injunctions and other orders) consequences where the standard set by this section is not met. In an expansive provision, the legislation covers a wide range of false representations in respect of both goods and services, and specifically targets the following: standard, quality, price, value, grade, composition, style, model and history. There is also coverage for a false representation that the goods are new, or that they have particular sponsorship, approval, performance characteristics, accessories, uses or benefits that they do not have. A false or misleading representation concerning the origin of goods will also be impugned, as will misleading representations concerning warranties or conditions.

III. Improper Pressure

123. The next part of this chapter considers those situations where a disadvantaged person in the contracting process will be given some relief. This will occur where some improper pressure has been applied to that party by the other party. In Australia, these categories are generally divided into two: duress (the common law test) and undue influence (developed from equity). The theory behind the application of these ideas is that where an agreement has been obtained by threats or other normatively inappropriate behaviour, then the essence of a free will voluntarily accepting an offer has been lost.

A. Duress

124. A contract made by a person under duress is voidable by that person. In this context, duress can be considered as the illegitimate pressure applied by one party

134. See generally the *Competition and Consumer Act.*

to the other. The legitimacy in the pressure may result from a range of means including physical, mental and economic. Furthermore, the duress may not be directly applied to the contracting party, but may be directed to family or friends of that person. Duress operates to make the contract voidable, as the consent of one party to the contract cannot be considered free and voluntary.

As examples, duress to the person was established where threats were made to an individual that he would be reported to the police if he did not sign certain documents.[135] By contrast, economic duress involves illegitimate pressure in the business or commercial process. It is this latter category that causes the most difficulty for the law, as driving a hard bargain is part and parcel of the commercial negotiating experience. The difficulty for the cases has been to ask when the hard bargain crosses the line of legitimate commercial tactics and becomes illegitimate duress on the other party. It has proved extremely difficult to establish economic duress through the cases. To succeed the person will need to show that when they were coerced they protested, that there was no opportunity to obtain independent legal advice and the unavailability of any other course of action.[136] Generally, overwhelming pressure in the business context, through the adoption of legitimate business methods will not be seen as economic duress – this despite the pressure that may be placed on the other contracting parties.[137] If duress is established, the contract is voidable.

B. Undue Influence

125. The limitations associated with duress led to the courts seeking to provide a wider range on which a person's consent to an agreement could be considered to have been overcome. The doctrine through which this was examined was to be found in the law relating to undue influence. As the name would suggest, the doctrine applies where influence or pressure is applied to the other party with the result that their consent to the transaction cannot be seen to be genuine. In this context, it is much broader than the common-law doctrine of duress, and resonates with its equitable genesis. Notwithstanding this, the concept has generally been limited to those situations where the parties are involved in a relationship of mutual confidence, or one party is vulnerable to the influence or expertise of the other. Having established that this relationship of trust and confidence exists between the parties and finding that the pressure applied was undue, the court can set aside the contract at the option of the party whose consent has been overcome. There are various categories that have been recognized as giving rise to this relationship of trust and confidence, and these include parent and child, solicitor and client and priest and parishioner.[138] A classic High Court case on the operation of this doctrine is *Johnson v. Buttress*.[139] In this case, Buttress, an elderly, illiterate person with little

135. *Seear v. Cohen* (1881) 45 LT 589.
136. See *Pao On v. Lau Yiu Long* [1980] AC 614.
137. *Crescendo Management Pty Ltd v. Westpac Banking Corporation* (1988) 19 NSWLR 40.
138. See Latimer, *supra* n. 65 at 355.
139. (1936) 56 CLR 113.

business experience, transferred ownership of his house to Johnson. Johnson was a relative of his wife and had provided some care and companionship to Buttress following the death of Buttress' wife. The transfer documents were signed in the office of Johnson's solicitor, with Buttress not receiving any independent legal advice. The Court held there was a relationship of confidence between the two parties, and that the presumption of undue influence had not been rebutted by the appellant.

IV. Gross Disparity

126. A final category that can see the substantive validity of a contract set aside can be demonstrated in those cases where there is gross disparity between the parties. In Australia, the doctrine that most fits this concept is that of unconscionability. Both the courts and legislation have provided a range of means by which a contract could be challenged because of unconscionability. The distinction between this doctrine and the previous two is that unconscionability considers the conduct of the stronger party, whereas undue influence and duress consider the quality of the consent given by the weaker party.

A. *Unconscionability in the Courts*

127. As grounds for intervention, the courts have long accepted that unconscionable conduct is the basis on which equity could intervene in the contractual process. However, given the emphasis placed by the courts on the notion of freedom of contract, the circumstances have been limited in which the courts have been prepared to establish unconscionability. The major contemporary Australian authority on this doctrine is *Commercial Bank v. Amadio.*[140] This High Court decision resulted in a holding that the bank was not entitled to retain the benefit of the guarantee given by the Amadios, as this guarantee had been given in circumstances where the Amadios were at a special disadvantage *vis-à-vis* the bank, and an unfair or unconscientious advantage had been taken of the respondents by the Commercial Bank. The circumstances that led to this finding included the absence of independent advice given to the Amadios, their lack of business acumen and their limited capacity to understand English. Significantly, it must be noted that a transaction that is merely a gross disadvantage to another is not enough to find liability – there must be a finding of disadvantage between the parties, and the unfair or unconscientious taking of advantage of that situation. If there is no knowledge of the special disability, there can be no finding of unconscionability.[141]

Case law examples provide illustrations of the factual matrix required for the invocation of the doctrine. Age, illiteracy, lack of assistance and infirmity have all been considered relevant.[142] Interestingly, the common law doctrine has arguably been extended in the recent High Court decision of *Garcia v. National Australia*

140. (1982) 151 CLR 447.
141. *Warburton v. Whiteley* (189) NSW ConvR 55-453.
142. *Bromley v. Ryan* (1956) 99 CLR 362.

Bank.[143] In this case, the wife, who was a physiotherapist who conducted her own business, was still able to void her signing of a guarantee to secure monies lent by the National Australia Bank to her husband's business. The court recognized that in the circumstances of this case, the lender would have appreciated that the wife relied on the trust and confidence of her husband, and that he may not have fully explained the transaction to her. Given that she obtained no financial benefit from the transaction, it was to be considered unconscionable – this despite the wife being a competent professional conducting her own business. The effect of unconscionable conduct is that the contract will be voidable at the option of the victim of the conduct.

B. Statutory Unconscionability

128. Again, common-law developments in this country have been significantly supplemented by statutory initiatives. The most broad-ranging of these can be found in sections 20-22 of the Australian Consumer Law (Schedule 2 of the *Competition and Consumer Act 2010*). The most broad-ranging[144] of these can be found in sections 51AA–51AC of the *Trade Practices Act 1974* and now have been consolidated under Australia's new Competition and Consumer Law.[145] On 6 December 2011, the Competition and Consumer Legislation Amendment Act 2011 (the Act) received Royal Assent. The Act provides *inter alia* for the amendment of the unconscionable conduct provisions of the Competition and Consumer Act 2010 (Cth) and the Australian Securities and Investments Commission Act 2001 (Cth) (ASIC Act) which:

- unify the current separate provisions relating to unconscionable conduct in respect to individuals and businesses so as to remove the risk that courts might accord different meanings to the two sets of provisions;
- introduce a statement of interpretative principles to assist the courts in applying the statutory prohibition of unconscionable conduct and clarify the meaning and scope of the provisions.

Provisions in respect to unconscionable conduct are now contained within the Australian Consumer Law which is Schedule 2 of the CCA. The Australian Consumer Law (Part 2-2 of Schedule 2 of the Competition and Consumer Act)contains the following three substantive provisions in respect to unconscionable conduct:

- Section 20 (formerly section 51AA of the TPA) prohibits conduct that is unconscionable within the meaning of the unwritten law of the States and Territories.
- Section 21 of the ACL (somewhat similar to former s51A of the TPA) prohibits unconscionable conduct in connection with the supply or acquisition of goods or services to or from a person other than a listed public company.

143. (1998) 194 CLR 395.
144. For jurisdiction specific legislation, see *Contracts Review Act 1980* (NSW).
145. These provisions are generally replicated in the state-based Fair Trading Acts, though in Tasmania, the introduction of the Australian Consumer Law saw the repeal of their Fair Trading legislation.

- Section 22 of the ACL lists a series of factors courts can take into account in determining whether conduct is unconscionable.

Almost identical provisions relating to unconscionable conduct in respect to the supply of financial services are set out in sections 12CA, 12CB and 12CC respectively of the ASIC Act.

The explanatory memorandum to the Act notes that the meaning of unconscionable conduct under each provision was intended to be the same and that the unification will avoid the risk that courts may have accorded different meanings to the two sets of provisions.

As a result, the factors to which a court may have regard when considering whether conduct is unconscionable will be the same for both business and consumer transactions.

With a view to clarifying the position for the courts, the Act adds statements to the following effect to section 21 of the Australian Consumer Law and section 12CB of the ASIC Act:

- the sections are not limited by the equitable or common law doctrines of unconscionable conduct;
- the sections are capable of applying to a system of conduct or pattern of behaviour whether or not a particular individual is identified as having been disadvantaged by the conduct or behaviour;
- in considering whether conduct to which a contract relates is unconscionable, the court's consideration of the contract is not limited to consideration of the circumstances relating to formation of the contract and may include consideration of the terms of the contract and the manner in which and the extent to which the contract is carried out;
- without limiting the factors to which the court may have regard, the new sections 22 and 12CC provide an extensive list of factors to which the court may have regard for the purpose of sections 21 and 12CB.

C. Section 20

129. This provision states that 'a person must not, in trade or commerce, engage in conduct that is unconscionable within the meaning of the unwritten law, from time to time, of the States and Territories'. In effect, this section extends the remedial provisions of the legislation to the type of scenario that was considered in *Commercial Bank v. Amadio.* These remedies can include injunctions, the rewriting of a contract and other non-punitive orders such as corrective advertisements. A particular instance of this provision can be seen in the case of *ACCC v. CG Berbatis Holdings Pty Ltd.*[146] Tenants of a shopping centre complex had begun legal proceedings against the property owner in respect of a number of financial matters. When the tenants wished to renew their leases, the owner refused to do so, unless the aforesaid legal action against it was dropped. The tenants who wished to sell their business needed a new lease to protect their goodwill, and reluctantly agreed to do as

146. (2003) 77 ALJR 926.

asked by the property owner. Without the new lease, no sale of the business could occur. No unconscionability was established (and the case is probably indicative of a narrower attitude to unconscionability than previously existed), as the property owner simply drove a hard bargain and was under no obligation to renew the lease in any event. There was no special disadvantage faced by the tenant.

D. Schedule 2, Australian Competition and Consumer Act (2010 (Cth) Section 21

130. This section defines unconscionable conduct related to the supply of goods or services that is prohibited by virtue of the Competition and Consumer Law. It is designed to provide some remedial protection to the situation of unconscionable conduct related to the supply of goods or services in both business-to-business and consumer transactions – i.e., goods supplied for household, domestic or personal use.

An example of the operation of this section can be seen in *ACCC v. Lux Pty Ltd.*[147] A vacuum cleaner salesperson was found to have engaged in unconscionable conduct when he indicated to a person who was on a disability pension and obviously suffered from some difficulties that her existing cleaner was about to 'blow up', and, when faced with the limited literacy of the individual, sought to fill out the application form (including financial information) for the purchaser. The salesperson's knowledge of these problems and his overbearing attitude led the Court to make a finding of unconscionable conduct. The remedies available for a breach of section 51AB include injunctions, non-punitive orders and other orders – such as the rewriting of contracts.

E. Schedule 2, Australian Competition and Consumer Act (2010 (Cth) Section 22

131. Section 22 of the ACL requires an assessment of whether conduct is unconscionable. In making this assessment, the court may have regard to a number of factors, the widest of which include whether the supplier acted in good faith, any risks to the consumer from the supplier's conduct, the relevant terms and conditions of the contract and the conduct of the parties in relying on the terms and conditions of the contract.

F. Conclusion on Unconscionability

132. The most significant development in the challenge to the substantive validity of the contracts in the past twenty years has been the rise of unconscionability. There are some who view this development with suspicion and as an attack on the freedom to contract. Others see it as a welcome balance to the contractual process, which is largely regulated through business and the adoption of standard form contracts. What the *ACCC v. Berbatis Holdings* decision demonstrates is that, arguably,

147. [2004] FCA 926.

the High Court has decided to place limits on any further expansion for the time being – preferring instead to allow the return of commercial certainty and the capacity to freely contract to become once again the dominant ideology behind contract law.

G. *Unfair Terms*

133. Another important provision of Australia's Competition and Consumer Law (2010) was the introduction of provisions relating to unfair terms in consumer contracts. The unfair contract terms laws apply to standard form consumer contracts entered into, varied, or renewed on or after 1 July 2010 (see sections 23-28 of the ACL).

There is a rebuttable presumption that a contract which is alleged to be a 'standard form' contract is in fact a standard form contract. Factors that a court will consider to determine this issue include whether the contract was prepared by one party, whether there was an opportunity to negotiate the contract terms, and whether one party had 'all or most of the bargaining power' in relation to the contract. In determining whether a term is unfair, a court must consider the contract as a whole, and the extent to which the term is 'transparent'; it may also consider other relevant matters. A 'transparent' term is a term expressed in reasonably plain language, which is legible, clearly presented, and readily available to the party affected by it. Note that the provisions regarding unfair contract terms contract terms are relevant as well to the enforceability of and terms of use regarding websites, especially where the terms and conditions of use are only accessible through a browse-wrap or clip-wrap arrangements which forces the user to go to another page or even scroll down to the very bottom of a page.[148]

§3. Other Conditions of Validity

I. Existing and Licit Cause

134. Subject to what is said below concerning illegality and unenforceable contracts, there is no Australian doctrine similar to the notion of existing and lawful cause as required in Continental Europe. This requirement of cause is a defining feature within those systems based on the French system, but generally is unseen in the common law countries.

II. Determined or Determinable, Possible or Licit Object

135. Despite the requirements for a valid contract being in the existence, such as offer and acceptance, consideration and an intention to create legal relations, the agreement may still lack substantive validity because it is in some way illegal or void. Obviously, the law is not going to uphold an agreement to commit a criminal

148. See e.g., *Specht_v._Netscape_Communications_Corp. Specht v. Netscape*, 306 F.3d 17 (2d Cir. 2002).

offence. However, in what other circumstances will the law decide that what would otherwise be an enforceable agreement is unenforceable?

III. Initial Impossibility

136. In Australia, contracts that are initially impossible will usually be considered under the doctrine of frustration (see Chapter 5). However, brief mention will be made here of its relevance to alleged agreements that are initially impossible to perform. For example, if a concert hall has been hired for the staging of an event, but at the time of agreement the hall has burnt down (this matter unknown to both parties) – it is then likely that both parties will be released from their obligations under the contract, as the agreement will be impossible to perform.[149]

IV. Illegality and Public Policy

137. Far more critical in Australian law in this area is those contracts that are either illegal by reason of statute, or illegal by reason of common law principles. Another category that shall be considered in the next part deals with unenforceable contracts that are rendered void by statute or rendered void at common law.

A. *Illegality at Statute*

138. The statute may expressly state that a person must not or shall not do something. For example, in the preceding discussion of the Australian Competition and Consumer law, the division starts: 'A person shall not … '. In this scenario, if a corporation does make an agreement that which would be in violation of this provision, the agreement will be illegal as formed and unenforceable. As an example of the operation of this principle, consider the case of *Re Mahmoud & Ispahani*.[150] In this matter, a statutory provision required that a person was not entitled to deal in linseed without the requisite authority. The defendant falsely told the plaintiff that he had such a license and contracted to purchase some linseed. Despite the mendacious behaviour of the defendant, the plaintiff was unable to enforce the agreement. As noted by the court, a contract with an unlicensed person was strictly prohibited. Similarly, in *Amadio Pty Ltd v. Henderson*[151] the contract of sale that was in breach of the relevant corporations' legislation was strictly unenforceable. In these two scenarios the contract was illegal as formed – despite the harsh consequences on the innocent party, the law was not able to recognize the validity of an agreement contrary to the express provisions of a statute. Furthermore, in *Haddin v.*

149. A similar thing occurred in *Taylor v. Caldwell* (1863) 3 B&S 826.
150. [1921] 2 KB 716.
151. (1998) 81 FCR 149.

Le Feuvre[152] a deed that purported to establish the business of milk vendor, but without meeting the registration requirements was illegal as formed.

139. In contrast to the above, the contract may be legal in formation, but illegal in performance. In these situations, it is more likely that the contract will be seen as enforceable. The law considers that it would be unjust or unconscionable to penalize the innocent party when the other party has illegally performed the contract. For example, we see in *St John Shipping Corporation v. Joseph Rank Ltd*[153] a shipowner still being able to recover contractual payments due under a freight agreement despite the fact that he overloaded the ship. Similarly, a person employed by an illegal enterprise, will still be entitled to workers' compensation when injured in that business.[154] It will only be where the illegality affects the very core of the contract that the illegality in performance will render the contract unenforceable. For example, in *Anderson Ltd v. Daniel*[155] a sale of artificial fertilizer was required to be accompanied by an invoice setting out the chemical composition of the product. When this was not done, the supplier was unable to enforce the contract as the illegal performance had rendered it unenforceable. Generally, a contract held to be illegal by reason of statutory illegality is unenforceable. The law of restitution, however, may provide a basis on which recovery can be had of items transferred or money paid pursuant to an illegal contract.

B. Illegal at Common Law

140. As indicated at the outset, the contract to commit a crime will be deemed illegal and unenforceable – the policy basis of this is patently clear, the law will not be involved in promoting illegal activities. An example of this can be seen in the English decision of *Alexander v. Rayson.*[156] In an attempt to reduce the rates payable on land (this amount determined by the market rent payable), the agreed rent was split between two agreements – one referring to the annual rent, the second referring to alleged services to be provided by the property owner. Not surprisingly, the court held that the agreements were merely an attempt to reduce the amount of taxes paid and were therefore illegal. Similarly, contracts that are seen to promote corruption in public life will also be challenged. This sees a person being unable to recover monies paid to an organization in return for a promise of knighthood.[157]

141. Far more nebulous than these situations are those contracts that are alleged to be illegal because of public policy, particularly sexual immorality. The cases demonstrate an eclectic and varying response to this question – with the courts indicating that this is to be judged by appropriate and relevant community standards at

152. [1969] 2 NSWR 32.
153. [1957] 1 QB 267.
154. *Barac (t/as Exotic Studios) v. Farnell* (1994) 125 ALR 241.
155. [1924] 1 KB 138.
156. [1936] 1 KB 169.
157. *Parkinson v. College of Ambulance Ltd* [1925] 2 KB 1.

the time in question. For example, the 1911 decision of *Upfill v. Wright*[158] prevented a property owner from recovering rent in arrears, when the premises were being tenanted by an individual for the purpose of secret meetings with her sexual partner. This can be contrasted with the 1983 decision of the New South Wales Court of Appeal in *Seidler v. Schallhofer*,[159] where the court was prepared to enforce a cohabitation agreement between an unmarried couple. With the recognition of de facto and same-sex couples now legislatively granted in a number of jurisdictions, the likelihood of these arrangements being deemed illegal in the present environment appear increasingly remote. Finally, contracts that are seen to prejudice the due administration of justice will also be illegal and unenforceable.[160] The most common illustration in this context is an agreement to stifle a prosecution. An example of this can be seen in the decision in *Keir v. Leeman*.[161] Various parties were charged with riot and assault following an attack on an officer of the court who was attempting to issue a warrant of execution in respect of a debt owed to A. Before trial, A agreed with two of the assailants that he would not give any evidence if they were prepared to pay the amount owing, plus costs. A provided no evidence, but was unable to enforce the agreement. Contracts illegal at common law are unenforceable.

V. Unenforceable Contracts

142. Finally, there is an additional category of contracts, which, whilst not illegal at common law, will be unenforceable as they will be considered void. These can include contracts rendered void by statute and contracts rendered void at common law.

A. *Contracts Rendered Void by Statute*

143. Certain agreements, whilst not illegal by statute, may well be rendered void by the operation of legislation. For example, gaming activities are strictly regulated by the states, and any agreement outside of these arrangements will be void. Similarly, under the *Competition and Consumer Act 1974*, implied terms of acceptable quality and fitness for purpose are incorporated into every type of consumer contract. Any agreement to exclude this will see that term in the contract rendered void.[162] The consequences of a contract rendered void by statute will depend on whether the offending provision can or cannot be severed from the remainder of the agreement. For example, if the offending provision is one ousting the operation of the *Competition and Consumer Act 1974*, then it is likely that this term will be excised, leaving the remainder of the agreement intact. However, should the statute

158. [1911] 1 KB 506.
159. [1983] 2 NSWLR 80.
160. See, for example, *A v. Hayden (No. 2)* (1984) 56 ALR 82.
161. (1846) 9 QB 371.
162. See relevant provisions of the *Competition and Consumer Act*.

render the entire agreement void, such as is likely with a gaming contract, then the whole transaction will be struck down.

B. Contracts Rendered Void at Common Law

144. There are three categories of contracts that are rendered void at common law:

(i) contracts ousting the jurisdiction of the courts;
(ii) contracts prejudicing the freedom of marriage; and
(iii) contracts in restraint of trade.

C. Contracts Ousting the Jurisdiction of the Courts

145. A fundamental tenet of Australian law is that the courts are accessible to all (though, given the cost of litigation, one might question the practical application of such a principle). For this reason, any attempt to prevent or forestall a party from utilizing the courts to enforce their rights is seen as unenforceable and void. Obviously, however, parties are entitled to insert arbitration clauses within the agreements – these will be considered valid provided they do not operate to oust the jurisdiction of the courts.[163]

D. Contracts Prejudicing the Freedom of Marriage

146. Arrangements, which in some manner seek to restrain the freedom of marriage, will be seen as unlawful. For example, a promise by one Peers to the following effect: ‘I do truly promise Mrs. Catherine Lowe that I will not marry with any person besides herself: if I do, I agree to pay to the said Catherine Lowe GB 2000 within three months next after I shall marry anybody else’ was held to be unenforceable.[164] Similarly, marriage brokerage contracts are unlawful.[165]

E. Contracts in Restraint of Trade

147. It is this area that has occupied the most attention. A restraint of trade contract is an agreement whereby the covenantor agrees with the covenantee that they (the covenantor) will in some way restrict themselves in the occupation, trade, location and/or time that they will work. For example, a purchase of a motor mechanic's business by another may see the purchaser requiring the vendor to sign a contract by which the vendor will agree not to open a competing business within a

163. *Scott v. Avery* (1856) 5 HL Cas 811; 10 ER 1121.
164. *Lowe v. Peers* (1768) 4 Burr 2225; 98 ER 160.
165. *Herman v. Charlesworth* [1905] 2 KB 123.

defined locality for a set period of time. By undertaking this, the purchaser is able to protect the value of the investment that they have made. As to whether this agreement is enforceable, the law seeks to balance on the one hand the ideology of freedom of contract encompassed by the agreement between the two parties, whilst at the same time recognizing that there is a public interest in ensuring that a person is not deprived of the right to earn a livelihood. The principles surrounding this doctrine were summarized in the decision of *Bacchus Marsh Concentrated Milk Co Ltd v. Joseph Nathan & Co Ltd*:[166]

(i) if freedom of contract is to prevail over freedom of trade, there must be sufficient legal justification;
(ii) there is no automatic right to be protected against competition;
(iii) if something is to be upheld it must be reasonable;
(iv) reasonableness is a question of law for the courts;
(v) the onus of providing that it is reasonable lies on the person asserting this; conversely, if the person alleges that it is unreasonable, then this person has that onus;
(vi) a covenantor can restrict him or herself, provided that it is reasonable;
(vii) on the sale of a business, a reasonable covenant is valid.

148. An example of the operation of this doctrine can be seen in the decision of *Coombes v. Bahama Palm Trading Pty Ltd*[167] The business sold was a restaurant. The covenant provided that the covenantor could not carry on ‘a business of the same nature as the business sold’. It was held that the opening of a take-away restaurant was in breach – the underlying nature of the business was the supply of food and drinks. Similarly, in *Peters (WA) Ltd v. Petersville Ltd*[168] the covenantor (the manufacturer of Pauls’ and Peters’ ice-cream nationally) agreed with the covenantee that they would not sell ice-cream in Western Australia (after selling the Western Australian ice-cream business) for an initial period of fifteen years, which could potentially extend up to double this time. The restriction also purported to prevent the sale of any type of ice-cream. It was held that this was an unreasonable restraint of trade. It operated to stifle competition, and was too long to be reasonable in the public interest. It was also unreasonable between the parties. Another example can be seen in the case of *Deacons (a firm) v. Bridge*.[169] A solicitor, while a partner of Deacons in Hong Kong, agreed that as part of the partnership that, should he leave the firm, that he would not act as a solicitor in Hong Kong for a period of five years for any client of the firm. Upon departing the partnership, the solicitor set up a sole practice and began to act for some of the Deacons clients. Deacons successfully sought an injunction. The clause was not unreasonable, despite Bridge not having any contact with 90% of the clients (the firm was established in various departments and Bridge was the head of the Intellectual Property department, and only dealt with those clients) – Deacons had been established as a single firm and the

---

166. (1919) 26 CLR 410 at 440–441.
167. (1991) ASC 56-0097.
168. (2001) 205 CLR 126.
169. [1984] 2 All ER 19.

remaining partners were entitled to protect the goodwill of the firm. The time restriction was reasonable, with the court noting that this agreement had been drafted by lawyers for the benefit of legal professionals.

149. As with contracts void at statute, a contract void at common law may well see the offending provision severed, rather than have the whole agreement struck down. The courts will look to enforce what parts of the agreement remain after the offending provision has been excised. It should also be noted that New South Wales has enacted state-specific legislation,[170] designed to overcome some of the uncertainties inherent in the common-law doctrine. Specifically, the legislation permits the covenantor to apply to the court for an order that the restraint be considered 'altogether invalid, or valid to such extent only (not exceeding the extent to which the restraint is against public policy) as the Court thinks fit'. Today it is recognized that the legislation permits the court to rewrite the terms of the offending clause to allow a modified and compliant version to be substituted for what was originally drafted. For example, in *Wright v. Gasweld Pty Ltd*[171] it was held that the trial judge was entitled to reduce an unlimited time prohibition to four years and to restrict the limitation on contact from one on all customers to one on specific customers. In essence, the legislation as presently interpreted appears to provide greater remedial flexibility than what the common law currently provides.

§4. The Consequences of a Defect of Consent or a Lack of Substantive Validity

150. If the first three elements of a putative contract are not established, then no contract exists at all. Unless the parties have some other basis on which to invoke the jurisdiction of the court (legislative, such as the Australian Competition and Consumer Act 2010 (Cth), or case law orientated, such as estoppel or restitutionary principles), then there will be no jurisdiction on which the court will have the option of even considering the matter. However, if these three elements are made (offer and acceptance, consideration and intention to create legal relations), then the issue becomes one of substantive validity. Do the contracting parties have the requisite capacity (are they a minor, mentally ill, intoxicated, etc.) and if not, has their consent been overborne by undue influence, duress, or did one party engage in a misrepresentation or was there some form of mistake in the contracting process. Assuming none of these occur, then the final aspect of substantive validity is the extent to which the contract may be illegal or void because of statute or common law. The central question that therefore arises in respect of the conditions of substantive validity is what the consequences are if there is a failure to comply with some aspect? In what circumstances will the contract be void, voidable or unenforceable? When will problems be able to be overcome by severance of the offending aspect? In addition, will damages be available? Table 2.1 is designed to elucidate the answer to those questions – with more detail on the remedial aspects of contract law to be found in Chapter 6.

170. *Restraint of Trade Act 1976* (NSW).
171. (1991) 22 NSWLR 317.

151. *Table 2.1*

		Valid	*Void*	*Voidable*
Capacity of the Parties	Minors	Provided it is for necessaries or beneficial employment.	Otherwise, most will be void unless ratified.	Certain categories of minors' contracts are voidable – e.g., contracts of a continuing nature.
	Mentally disabled			At option of person affected.
	Intoxicated			At option of person affected.
	Bankrupt	Can be valid, but bankrupt will have no assets against which judgment can be made if a dispute arises.		Can contract in respect of after acquired property after going bankrupt, but trustee in bankruptcy can avoid the contract.
	Corporation	Has capacity of a natural person.		
Mistake			Void *ab initio,* though occasionally equitable principles will mitigate the harshness in application.	

	Valid	*Void*	*Voidable*
Misrepresentation			In limited circumstances the contract may be avoided by the representee. Because of the inadequacy of the common law remedies, statutory remedies may now be available under the *Australian Competition and Consumer Act 2010.*
Duress			Voidable at option of coerced party.
Undue influence			Voidable at option of contracting party effected.
Unconscionability		There is significant remedial flexibility under the Competition and Consumer Act to cover both void and voidable scenarios.	There is significant remedial flexibility under the *Australian Competition and Consumer Act 2010* to cover both void and voidable scenarios. At common law the contract is voidable.
Illegality in formation		The contract is completely unenforceable.	

	Valid	*Void*	*Voidable*
Unfair Contract terms		There is significant remedial flexibility under the Competition and Consumer Act to cover both void and voidable scenarios.	There is significant remedial flexibility under the Competition and Consumer Act to cover both void and voidable scenarios.
Illegality in performance	If the illegality is incidental to the contract, the contract is likely to remain enforceable.	If the illegality is not incidental, the contract will be unenforceable.	
Statutory illegality		These will be void.	
Common law illegality		These will be void.	
Statute may make contract void.		Generally, the contract will be void, though severance may be possible.	
Common law may indicate that the contract should be void.		Generally, the contract will be void, though severance may be possible.	

Chapter 3. The Contents of a Contract

§1. The Different Clauses

152. The *terms* of a contract give efficacy to the intentions of the parties. These terms can either be express or implied. Express terms are relatively easier to handle because these are the ones that the parties have actually discussed and decided to include in the contract. Implied terms, however, are a bit more difficult as these are sometimes interpreted by the courts or imposed by relevant legislation.

153. The *terms* of a contract are the starting points of reference to ascertain the respective obligations of the parties to the contract, such as their agreed obligations and responsibilities, what is to be delivered, price and other specifications. As the focal point of the contract, care must be taken to ensure that the terms reflect the intentions of the parties to the contract as these terms are binding on the signatories.

154. Hence, in determining whether something has become a term of the contract, whether it has been breached and, if so, what remedies might be appropriate, the courts will examine four elements:

- ascertain what the parties actually said and agreed;
- determine whether they intended those statements to be contractually binding;
- determine the level of importance the parties intended to attach to those statements; and
- provide an appropriate and adequate remedy in the event of any breach.

155. Where there is a written contract, and one that appears whole and complete on its face, a court will presume that the words contain the entire contract and are not to be varied by any oral terms. So where a contract is partly written and partly oral, there is a difficult task of deciding what parts of the oral statements are to be included in the contract. In such cases, courts will then rely on the intentions of the parties. However, where the oral agreement is reduced to writing, then the written agreement constitutes the whole contract. Written terms will generally be preferred to oral terms when construing a contract. (See a discussion of the parol evidence rule and written contracts in Chapter 1. Formation, §2. Formal and Evidential Requirements *above*.)

156. *L'Estrange v. Graucob (F) Ltd*[172] provides the rule that once a party has signed a document, knowing that it contains contractual terms, in the absence of fraud, that person is bound by those terms, irrespective of whether they have read them or not. The approach taken in this case was approved by the High Court in *Toll (FGCT) Pty Ltd v. Alphapharm Pty Ltd.*[173]

As a general rule, parties are bound by all terms contained in a document that they sign, regardless of whether they have read them or understood them. There are some

172. [1934] 2 KB 394.
173. (2004) 219 CLR 165.

exceptions to this general rule including misrepresentation, mistake (*non est factum*) and certain statutory exceptions.

157. However, such a rule can be burdensome and can raise other difficulties because of the lack of specificity. In *Interfoto Picture Library Ltd v. Stiletto Visual Programmes Ltd*,[174] an advertising agency received an invoice for almost GB 4,000 because it was late in returning photographs that it was examining with a view to purchase from the photo library. The total money owed was calculated on the basis of the contractual terms included in the invoice that was sent together with the photographs. The terms stated that the photographs had to be returned by a certain date or else daily charges would begin to apply. The court held that the terms were onerous and had not been drawn to the attention of the borrower.

158. One of the means of overcoming some of the problems that have surfaced in the cases above is to use *standard form contracts* with uniform terms and conditions to be displayed on all documents. This practice is the norm for commercial contracts that involve transport of goods, hire of cars and shipping, and avoids confusion as to what the terms are.

I. Representations versus Terms of the Contract

159. In negotiations leading up to a contract, it is likely that both parties say things intended to influence the other party's decision about whether to contract. Such things might be written or spoken or even both, but they do not necessarily become part of the resulting contractual obligation. Some of these are labelled mere representations or non-contractual representations, and hence have no contractual significance unless they are materially misleading, which gives rise to an actionable misrepresentation. Determining whether such statements made during negotiations are part of the contract is not easy and depends on the intentions of the parties.

160. Terms in contracts must be distinguished from statements and representations such as:

- puffery (mere puff) or sales talk;
- an invitation to treat, such as those found in sales brochures and catalogues;
- a statement or opinion of law;
- a representation of intention;
- an independent or collateral contract.

161. These must be further differentiated between a term of a contract and a mere *representation*. For example, in the purchase of a computer system, a buyer relied on the promises of a salesperson that the system could do certain things. When the system was unable to perform such things, a court found that there was no requirement in the contract that it do so.[175] To form part of the contract, both

174. [1988] 1 All ER 348.
175. *Christopher Hill Ltd v. Ashington Piggeries Ltd* [1969] AC 441.

parties must have intended that the statements of the salesperson should form part of the contract. Here, the salesperson's promises could be interpreted as mere representations or sales talk.

162. Some sub-rules have developed that assist in determining the intention of the parties. These include the timing and placement of the statements that are made in relation to the writing of the contract, and the skill of the person making the statement. In the first place, any representation made during early negotiations but not repeated later is unlikely to form part of the contract. Likewise, a representation made after the formation of the contract will unlikely form part of the contract.

163. In *Routledge v. McKay*,[176] during the course of negotiating the sale of his motorcycle, the defendant told the plaintiff that it was a 1942 model. Seven days later, the parties entered into a written contract of sale. It made no mention of the year of manufacture. The plaintiff later discovered that the motorcycle was a 1930 model. He sued for damages but failed. The interval between the negotiations and the final agreement, coupled with the failure to include the motorcycle's age in the written contract, indicated that the parties had not intended the statement to be anything other than a mere representation – made to induce the contract but not intended to have any contractual effect. Accordingly, it had not become a term and there was no breach. The rule is that where following pre-contractual negotiations, the agreement is reduced to writing and the oral statement upon which the innocent party seeks to rely is omitted from the document, the indication is that the parties did not intend the statement to be contractual in nature.

164. The next issue concerns the skill of the person making the statement. Where the person making the representation is in a position to know the truth of the statement, a court will be more willing to infer an intention that the statement forms part of the contract. In *Dick Bentley Productions Ltd v. Harold Smith Motors Ltd*[177] the defendant told Dick Bentley that a new engine and gearbox had been fitted to the car offered for sale, and that since then it had only been driven 20,000 miles. That was not in fact true, but the defendant believed that it was. The car had in fact travelled 100,000 miles. When Dick Bentley discovered the truth, he sued. It was held that the misleading statement had been incorporated into the contract as a term and Bentley was entitled to damages. The dealer had special knowledge and skill and the statement was made in such a way that both parties should have realized that the buyer would rely on it. Hence, even if the person making the statement does not claim to have personal knowledge of the accuracy of the statement, if the person is in a better position to ascertain it's accuracy than the innocent party, the court will more readily infer that it was intended to be promissory.

165. A statement will thus be a term of a contract if it is intended to be promissory in nature. In *Smythe v. Thomas*[178] statements were made in the context of an

176. [1954] 1 All ER 855.
177. [1965] 1 WLR 623.
178. [2007] NSWSC 844.

eBay 'online auction' that the item to be sole, a 1944 Wirraway Australian Warbird aircraft, would be able to be flown from Albury to South Australia and would have a current airworthiness certificate on completion of the 100 hour inspection, were held to be promissory in nature and treated as part of the contract of sale.

Where the maker of the statement cannot be regarded as warranting or guaranteeing the truth of the statement, it will not be a term of the contract, and will not have contractual force.[179]

166. The statement will be a representation only.[180] In *Hospital Products Ltd v. United States Surgical Corporation*[181]. A distributorship agreement between Blackman and USSC was discussed in restaurant a month prior to agreement being reached. In that discussion Blackmann agreed among other things to promote USSC products in Australia and not to deal in or promote any products in competition. Later correspondence confirming the agreement did not include statements made by Blackman at the restaurant. Hospital Products an entity with links to Blackman was later substituted as the Australian distributor. Hospital Products began supplying existing customers of USSC with products in direct competition. The issues before the High Court was whether the oral statements made at the restaurant formed express terms of the distributorship agreement. The High Court by a majority of 4:1 held that those statements formed part of the express terms of the distributorship agreement, and were breached by the conduct of HPI and Blackman. The statements were promissory and formed express terms of the contract between the parties.

167. The importance of making the distinction between representations and terms lies in the remedies available. Subject to statute, a representation does not give rise to a right to damages at common law unless it was fraudulently or negligently made, whereas the breach of a term gives rise to a right to damages in all cases. In addition, damages for fraud or negligence are recovered on tortious principles and may not be as beneficial as damages recovered on a contractual basis.

II. Collateral Contracts and Collateral Warranties

168. The distinction, discussed above, between the terms of the contract and mere representations suggests that when the latter is not incorporated into a contract, it confers no contractual rights, and if it proves to be incorrect, there is no breach of contract. In between these extremes is the case where some statements that are clearly intended to have contractual significance have not been included as terms of the contract. Courts will treat such statements as collateral contracts, sometimes called collateral warranties.

169. Courts have come to recognize that sometimes a statement is not a term of the contract but it was seriously made, and that without it the main contract would

179. See for example *Wyllie v. Tarrison Pty Ltd* [2007] NSWSC 184.
180. *Australian National Nominees Pty Ltd v. GPC No 11 Pty Ltd* [2004] NSWSC 773.
181. (1984) 156 CLR 41.

probably not have come into being. In such cases, the promise is collateral to the main contract, and, if the necessary pre-conditions are fulfilled, it may be enforceable as a contract in its own right.[182]

170. Thus, there are two types of collateral contract. The first is a contract that is entered into between the parties to the main contract. This is a more common type of contract, and it is usually supported by consideration in the form of entry into the main contract. The second is a contract between parties only one of whom is a party to the main contract. This may arise, say, when a finance company provides financing for the main contract. The collateral contract is with the person who conducted the negotiations that led to entry into the main contract with the finance company.

171. Of critical importance here for distinguishing a collateral contract from mere representation is that the statements made should be *promissory* and not merely *representational.* A clear distinction is given in *J J Savage & Sons Pty Ltd v. Blakney*,[183] where Blakney entered into a contract to buy a motor cruiser from Savage. During negotiations Blakney inquired about motors, and Savage's written reply set out details of three engines that it believed would satisfy Blakney's requirements. The resulting contract contained an itemized specification and quotation, but contained no reference to the speed of the motor. The boat, when delivered, could not attain a certain speed. Blakney sued for breach of term or, alternatively, for breach of collateral contract. However, Blakney failed in his bid because only statements made as firm promises can give rise to collateral contracts. No firm promise had been given here, and, accordingly, no collateral contract had arisen. The joint judgment of the High Court in this case suggests that the following must be satisfied before a statement will give rise to a collateral contract:

- a statement is made to induce entry into the contract;
- the statement is relied upon; and
- the statement relied upon was promissory in nature.

172. In Australia, an alleged collateral contract cannot be inconsistent with the terms of the main contract. That is, it cannot vary or contradict the terms of the main contract in any way. This is because the contracts coexist and are equally enforceable. If they are inconsistent, there would of necessity be a breach of one, and this would create an unworkable situation.[184] In *Hoyt's Pty Ltd v. Spencer*[185] the High Court's justification for not allowing a collateral contract to have force if it is inconsistent with the terms of the main contract was explained by Knox CJ that 'The reason for this conclusion is that the alleged consideration for the collateral contract is the assumption by the purchaser of the obligations specified in the main contract, which obligations are immediately varied or abrogated by the collateral contract.'

182. per Moulton, L.J. in *Helibut Symons & Co v. Buckleton* [1913] AC 30 at 47.
183. (1970) 119 CLR 435.
184. See *Hoyts Pty Ltd v. Spencer* (1919) 27 CLR 133.
185. (1927) 27 CLR 133, 139-40.

While this principle has yet to be overruled the main criticism is that it does not give effect to the actual intention of the parties.

It was previously established that a collateral contract is one in which the consideration for a promisor's promise is the promisee's entry into the main contract.[186]

173. The breach of a collateral contract only entitles the innocent party to damages. Specific performance of the main contract cannot be awarded, nor may the innocent party repudiate the main contract. The measure of damages is equivalent to the diminished value of the main contract.

A. Ascertaining Express Terms

174. As terms are critical to the operation of a contract, the expectation of the parties is one of strict performance. Without such terms the parties would probably not have entered into the contract in the first place. Some other terms are ancillary to the contract's main purpose and do not get to the heart of it. If there is a breach, the party not at fault will get something less than bargained for, but will not get something substantially less. For these reasons, terms may be classified either as conditions or warranties depending on how essential they are.

175. Hence, a *condition* is any term (either express or implied) that is of major importance to the contract, while a *warranty* is a minor term of the contract. The distinction lies in the fact that a breach of condition entitles the affected party either simply to reject the contract or to reject the contract and sue for damages. The breach of warranty only confers a right to sue for damages. Conditions are major terms of the contract, breaches of which render performance of the contract something substantially different from what was agreed.

176. In *Tramways Advertising Pty Ltd v. Luna Park (NSW) Ltd*[187] the New South Wales Supreme Court held that the test for a condition is whether or not it is essential or vital to the contract.

177. In *Associated Newspapers Ltd v. Bancks*[188] a newspaper company contracted to produce a cartoon on the first page of its newspaper, but failed to do so due to technical reasons. The owner of the cartoon regarded the contract as being at an end. It was held that the requirement to publish on the front page was a condition, and therefore Bancks was within his right to do so.

178. A warranty is a minor term of the contract, a breach of which renders the contract different but not substantially different. In general, a breach of warranty can be compensated for by damages, and this is the only remedy available for such a

186. *De Lassalle v. Guildford* [1901] 2 KB 215.
187. (1938) 38 SR (NSW) 632.
188. (1951) 83 CLR 322.

breach. This is because the contract can still be performed in substance, and damages will compensate the innocent party for any loss or inconvenience.

179. Furthermore, a warranty is normally provided by any vendor, usually stating that the product is fit for the purpose for which it was sold. Warranties are subsidiary to the main purpose of the contract. A breach of the contract would not bring the contract to an end, but the injured party is required to perform their obligations under the contract, with the right to sue for damages for loss suffered as a result of the breach of warranty.

180. In making the distinction between conditions and warranties, it seems that the division is binary, in the sense of relative importance of the terms – major and minor respectively. However, there may be situations in which a term may be capable of being breached in both major and minor ways. This is the *innominate term* or an intermediate term that is capable of being breached in both a major and minor way. The remedy available for the breach of an innominate term will depend on the effect of the particular breach complained of. A major breach will entitle the innocent party to terminate the contract and/or seek damages; a minor breach will only permit an action for damages.

181. Hong Kong Fir Shipping Co Ltd v. Kawasaki Kisen Kaisha Ltd[189] is the leading case that established the rules with respect to innominate terms. The defendants chartered a ship for twenty-four months from the plaintiffs. The contract required the plaintiffs to provide a ship that was 'in every way fitted for ordinary cargo service'. Despite this, the engine-room staff was incompetent, and the ship's machinery was ancient. Twenty weeks of sailing were lost due to engine trouble. The defendants repudiated the charter. The plaintiffs sued for breach of contract, and claimed damages for wrongful repudiation

It was held that the ship owners were clearly in breach of their obligation to provide a seaworthy vessel. Seaworthiness was not a condition of the charter party, so a breach did not automatically entitle the charterer to repudiate. Furthermore, the delays caused by the breakdowns and repairs, taken in the context of the overall period of the charter, were not so great as to frustrate the commercial purpose of the charter party. Accordingly, the defendants should not have repudiated; they should have sought damages to compensate them for the lost time. The plaintiffs were entitled to damages for wrongful repudiation.[190]

182. Furthermore, the mere use of the word 'condition' when describing a term will not necessarily impute its construction as a condition in the legal sense. This view has been approved by the Privy Council in *ANZ Banking Group Ltd v. Beneficial Finance Corp.*[191] Note also the terms condition precedent and condition subsequent. A contract is said to be subject to a condition precedent if it is not to be binding unless some specified event takes place. A contract is said to be subject to

189. [1962] 2 QB 26.
190. per Diplock, L.J. at 71–72.
191. (1982) 44 ALR 241; (1983) 57 ALJR 352 per Diplock, L.J. at 246–247; at 355.

a condition subsequent if its terms provide that it will terminate on the occurrence of a specified event.

B. Implied Terms

183. *Implied terms* are those that are imported in order that the contract be continued in operation in the face of an apparent breach. Implied terms are those that are not agreed to by the parties explicitly at the time of the agreement, but that the courts and legislators have decided to import on behalf of the parties. Courts are reluctant to imply terms into a contract as they believe that it is not their task to make the contract for the parties, but only to interpret what the parties have actually agreed.

184. Sometimes certain obvious terms were intended by both parties, but through inadvertence or bad drafting have not been included in the formal agreement. In such cases, the courts may find that the terms should be given effect through implication in order to implement what the parties intended.

185. Implied terms, however, are subject to strict criteria. There is a general duty of cooperation in every contract, including to act in accordance with the objectives of the contract, and to act with due care and skill. There is also the duty on parties claiming detriment to mitigate loss through taking whatever action is deemed necessary to reduce losses.

186. Terms may be implied into a contract in one of three ways:

(i) by trade usage or custom (terms implied by custom);
(ii) by law (terms implied in law); and
(iii) by the courts, in cases other than 1. and 2. above, because of the presumed intention of the parties.

187. *Term implied by custom* arises where there is an established practice or custom in a particular trade, industry, market or members of an identified group. The High Court had to consider whether a particular custom existed in the insurance industry. In *Con-Stan Industries of Australia Pty Ltd v. Norwich Winterthur Insurance (Australia) Ltd*[192] the High Court discussed situations where trade usage or custom can be used to justify implying a term into a contract. One situation is where custom or usage justifies implying a term into a contract as a question of fact. Another situation is where there is evidence to show that the custom relied on is so well-known and acquiesced in that everyone making the contract in the circumstances can be reasonably presumed to have implied that term in their contract. In the instant case the insured paid a premium to a broker who should have passed on the payment to the underwriter. The broker failed to do so and the insured was sued

192. (1986) 160 CLR 226.

by the underwriter for payment of the premium. The High Court had to consider whether was a custom in the insurance industry where the underwriter could only look to the broker for payment of the premium or alternatively that the payment by the insured to the broker was a sufficient discharge of the insured's obligation to pay the underwriter. The High Court held that there was insufficient evidence of either of the customs alleged. The underwriter was therefore entitled to recover the premium from the insured.

188. A third situation is where a term will not be implied if it is contrary to the express terms of the agreement. This is illustrated in *Summers v. Commonwealth.*[193] Summers contracted to supply the Commonwealth with marble for Australia House. The contract provided that each block should be of a specified size. Summers delivered blocks larger than that size and they were rejected; He sued for the price and gave evidence of a trade usage that, he said, allowed him to deliver blocks large enough to produce blocks of a specified size. Summers failed in his case because Issacs J pointed out that it was quite clear that no implication based on trade usage can ever be made 'where there is a written clause which is inconsistent with it'.

189. A fourth situation is where a person can be bound by a custom of which he/she is totally unaware, if the custom is 'so notorious' that he/she should have been aware of it. A final proposition is that terms will not be implied if the custom or trade usage on which they depend offends against any statutory provision.

190. Terms implied by statute merely codify the common law so that most of these are terms implied in the sale of goods, commercial code and the special cases related to consumer contracts and consumer protection legislation. Clear examples include those provisions in the Sale of Goods Acts and the Competition and Consumer Act 2010 (Cth).[193a]

191. Caslec Industries Pty Ltd v. Windover Data Systems Pty Ltd,[194] involves the case of the installation of an expensive computer system. While the maintenance agreement was a standard form written agreement capable of little ambiguity, the software agreement, however, was partly written and partly oral. Caslec bought its own hardware directly from a different supplier, and Windover installed the software in the computer before delivery to Caslec. After installation, all appeared

193. (1986) 160 CLR 226.

193a. This Act replaces the Trade Practices Act 1974 (Cth). This new Act is the most significant development in contract law since 2010. The Australian Consumer Law (ACL) 2010 is contained in Schedule 2 of the main Act. that automatically give customers rights relating to merchantability and fitness with respect to any goods they acquire. Thus, in every contract of sale of goods there is an *implied warranty* relating to ownership of the goods being sold, fitness of goods for the purpose for which it is sold, general 'merchantability' of goods, 'quiet possession' of goods (i.e., that the buyer will get legal ownership of the goods free of any encumbrance, and that the goods conform to the description or sample. Such practices have since been extended to loans, leases or hire of goods and to the supply of services.

194. Federal Court of Australia, No. G627/90 13.8.90 unreported.

according to the specifications and Caslec paid Windover. However, a fault was subsequently discovered in that the system did not produce the expected invoices. Caslec called upon Windover to fix the problem under contract but this was refused.

The court held that Windover had contractual obligations to rectify faults in the software, and also that they had an implied obligation under Schedule 2 section 60 of the Competition and Consumer Act 2010 (Cth) to deliver a product that was fit for the purpose for which it was sold and with a guarantee as to due care and skill. The court awarded damages of almost AUD 100,000 for the breach.

192. Terms implied by the court will be found where it is obvious that the parties intended them to be included but, for some reason, failed to include them in their express agreement. The court will use an objective test to ascertain the parties' presumed intentions.

193. In *Scanlan's New Neon Ltd v. Tooheys Ltd;* and *Caldwell Neon Electric Signs Ltd*[195,196] the plaintiffs manufactured and installed neon advertising signs. They agreed to install signs on the defendants' premises, and the defendants agreed to pay rent for a specified term of years. Before that term elapsed, legislation made it illegal to illuminate exterior advertising signs because of the war with Japan. The defendants fell into arrears, the plaintiffs sued and the defendants pleaded that the contracts contained an implied condition that they were to be discharged if the signs could not be illuminated. The argument was unanimously rejected. It was highly unlikely that both parties would have agreed to the inclusion of such a clause if the question had been raised during negotiations. Accordingly, it was not proper to include it as an implied term.

In some classes of contracts courts have imposed obligations on one or both parties even though such obligations were not expressly agreed upon by the parties. The terms implied by the courts were not because they reflected the presumed intention of the parties but because the courts have taken the view, on policy grounds, that such terms should be implied.[197]

194. The Australian position is laid down by the Privy Council in *BP Refinery (Westernport) Pty Ltd v. Shire of Hastings*,[198] where the court held that five criteria must be satisfied before a term could be implied into a contract. Accordingly the 'five tier test' suggests that it must be:

(i) reasonable and equitable for the parties;
(ii) necessary to give 'business efficacy' to the contract, so that no term will be implied if the contract is effective without it;
(iii) so obvious that it goes without saying;
(iv) capable of clear expression; and

195. (1943) 67 CLR 169.
196. per Latham, L.J. at 197.
197. See *Liverpool City Council v. Irwin* [1977] AC 239; *Australis Media Holdings Pty Ltd v. Telstra Corporation Ltd* (1998) 43 NSWLR 104.
198. (1977) 180 CLR 266; 16 ALR 363 at 365.

(v) expressed in ways that do not contradict any express term of the contract.

195. The term implied into the agreement for reasons of business efficacy is intended to reflect the presumed intention of the parties, the term must be both reasonable and equitable. If the term were unreasonable or inequitable, a person could not be regarded as intending the term to form part of the contract. If the term is necessary for the purpose of giving business efficacy to the transaction, it will generally be a term that is so obvious that it goes without saying. But this is not necessarily the case in some circumstances. In *Codelfa Construction Pty Ltd v. State Rail Authority of New South Wales*[199] while His Honour Justice Mason conceded that the term sought to be implied may have been necessary for the purpose of business efficacy, in the circumstances of the case, His Honour held that it was not a term that was so obvious that it went without saying.

196. In practice, the difficulty with most implied terms is that they are only mentioned when the parties are in dispute, and, ironically, at a time when it will be virtually impossible to agree either as to the existence of the terms or as to their meaning. Being emotional and upset at this stage is unhelpful to the parties. The broad warning therefore is to define as carefully as possible, expressly and in writing, as many issues as possible, and to exclude all other terms. It is also important that both parties read carefully all 'boilerplate clauses' (standard clauses) that are typically appended at the end of a contract, but that ironically are reproduced in very small type. The courts will construe these first before proceeding to imply any term into the agreement. Standard boilerplate clauses tend to be the least read and yet the most harmful to parties of a contract, especially when disagreements arise.

197. A more difficult issue is where the term is purportedly introduced into the earlier contract after its formation and perhaps in some instances even performance. Whether such a term may be incorporated as a result of previous dealings was considered in *Henry Kendall & Sons v. William Lillico & Sons Ltd.*[200] The parties in this case entered into contracts for the sale of meal for feeding to pheasants and partridges. It was business practice to conclude contracts orally with the seller forwarding a sale note to the buyer later that day or the next. The sale note contained a clause under which the buyer undertook responsibility for any latent defect in the product. This practice of contracting took place three to four times a month over three years. The issue was determined by the House of Lords that held that the terms had become part of the contracts of sale. In the circumstances it was reasonable to hold that when the buyer placed an order, it did so on the basis and with the knowledge that an acceptance of the order would be on the terms and conditions set out in the sale note.

In certain circumstances the incorporation by a prior course of dealings may be possible only if the party has actual knowledge of the terms from the judgment of *Lord Devlin in McCutcheon v. David MacBrayne Ltd.*[201] It may be noted that is

199. (1982) 149 CLR 337 at 355-6.
200. [1969] 2 AC 31.
201. [1964] 1 WLR 125.

view is contradicted by the later case of *Henry Kendall & Sons v. William Lillico & Sons Ltd* discussed above.[202]

198. It is an implied term of all contracts that each party agrees to do all things necessary to enable the other party to have the benefit of the contract.[203] This is generally referred to as the duty of cooperation, a term implied as a matter of law in the sense that it is implied in contracts generally, and not because of the facts of a particular case might warrant that implication. Notions of good faith, fair dealing, and reasonableness have become increasingly important in a variety of different legal contexts, not all of them relating to issues of contract law.[204]

199. The notions of good faith, fair dealing and reasonableness may be traced to the suggestion by *Priestley JA in Renard Constructions (ME) Pty Ltd v. Minister for Public Works*,[205] a decision that remains influential. However, this case has produced uncertainty about the basis on which the term was being implied. Good faith implied as a matter of fact, a matter of law, or some hybrid implication of both fact and law continue to be a matter of debate. In the instant case Priestly JA at 291 justified the finding on the basis of business efficacy grounds and that there was no real different between these types of implication.

The High Court has not engaged in the good faith debate although an opportunity presented itself in *Royal Botanic Gardens and Domain Trust v. South Sydney City Council.*[206] The majority whilst acknowledging the debate in various Australian jurisdictions did not consider it an appropriate occasion to determine these issues (at 301).

200. In *Burger King Corporation v. Hungry Jack's Pty Ltd.*[207] The NSW Court of Appeal held that a term of good faith and reasonableness should be implied and, on the facts of the case had been breached by Burger King. One of the reasons for its breach was its failure to comply with this term when purporting to terminate the lease. Following this case the decision has been cited as authority for the proposition that a duty of good faith and reasonableness will be implied in all commercial contracts. One instance when this proposition was tested is in *Vodafone Pacific Ltd v. Mobile Innovations Ltd*[208] and again the NSW Court of Appeal held that the Agreement was a commercial contract and should be implied into it an obligation to act in good faith.

202. [1969] 2 AC 31.
203. *Butt v. McDonald* (1896) 7 QLJ 68; affirmed by the High Court in *Peters (WA) Ltd v. Petersville Ltd* (2001) 75 ALJR 1385.
204. *In Gibson v. Parkes District Hospital* (1991) 26 NSWLR 9 for example, the duty to act in good faith was held by the NSW Supreme Court to apply to obligation of a workers' compensation insurer and employer in processing a worker's compensation claim.
205. (1992) 26 NSWLR 234.
206. (2002) 186 ALR 289.
207. [2001] NSWCA 187.
208. [2004] NSWCA 15.

C. Standard Terms and Exemption Clauses

201. An *exemption clause* is a term of the contract that has been inserted to exclude or limit the liability of one or the other of the parties. Such a clause can protect the party from the consequences of both breach of contract and tortious conduct, such as negligence, that is committed while performing the contract. There are two forms of exemption clauses: excluding terms and limiting terms.

202. An *excluding term* (exclusion clause) is one that completely excludes one party's liability. This means that the other party agrees that in the event of the breach of contract or if some tort is committed, he/she will not hold the party liable. While a *limiting term* (limiting clause) is much the same nature, it does not exclude liability entirely. Here the term merely limits it to a particular fixed or determinable monetary amount. If the person inserting the clause (the 'proferens') commits a breach of contract or a tort, he/she will not be liable for the full consequences of that act or omission, but only for a lesser, pre-stated, maximum monetary amount.

203. Exemption clauses can be found in all forms of contract – written, partly written/partly oral and oral. However, the problems associated with such terms have mainly arisen where they have been incorporated into written, standard form contracts. Standard form contracts are usually drafted by the party in a superior bargaining position, indicating the terms under which it is prepared to deal. Such contracts are sometimes known as *contracts of adhesion* – because the party in an inferior bargaining position must adhere to what is being demanded by the other party – there is no room for negotiation.

204. The potential for abuse and injustice are readily apparent from such contracts. Courts view such a term circumspectly, and demand clear proof that it has become a term of the contract; and is wide enough to cover the breach complained of.

205. To be considered a term of the contract, the exclusion clause must have been brought to the notice of the party against whom it is to be used. Thus, in the absence of appropriate notice, the exemption clause will be ineffective.

206. There are two types of notice – actual and constructive. *Actual notice* is when the existence and contents of the clause are actually brought to the attention of the person against whom it is to be used. The person inserting the clause specifically brings it to the attention of the other party. Alternatively, it may simply involve the other party reading it in the document. In both cases the other party will become aware of the existence and contents of the clause, and he/she is said to have actual notice of it.

207. *Constructive notice* occurs where the other party has not actually become aware of the existence and contents of the clause, but the proferens has done all that is reasonably necessary to bring it to the attention of any party. Constructive notice only applies where the other party should have read the exemption clause – because it was contained in something that clearly affected the contract, for example, a 'condition of entry' notice displayed on a sign over the entrance to commercial premises such as car parking stations and retail outlets.

208. Actual notice of the exemption clause is required for non-contractual documents, whereas if a document is contractual in nature, constructive notice may suffice. Whether a document is contractual or not will depend on the view of the general public or on whether the person who receives it knows whether it is contractual or contains terms that govern his/her dealings with the proferens. Examples of non-contractual documents include tickets, vouchers, receipts and claim checks, where it seems that a reasonable person might not feel obliged to read the document. So if there is an exemption clause, a proferens must show that the clause was actually brought to the attention of the other party, that is, that the other party had actual notice of it.

209. In *Causer v. Browne*[209] a plaintiff's husband left one of her frocks with the defendant dry-cleaners. When he collected it a week later, the dress was stained and some of the threads had been pulled out. The plaintiff sued. The defendants sought to escape liability by relying on the clauses printed on the docket that they had given to the husband. Those clauses purportedly exempted the dry-cleaners from liability for any loss of, or damage to, articles left for cleaning. The court held that the defendants were liable and could not rely on the exemption clauses. A reasonable person would not assume the dry-cleaning docket was contractual; it appeared to be a mere receipt. There had been no actual notice and, therefore, no effective notice.

210. Whether one has taken 'reasonable steps' to bring an exemption clause to the other party's attention is always a question of fact. If there is any doubt about whether the steps taken were sufficient, the other party will be given the benefit of that doubt, and the exemption clause will not preclude a successful action.

211. In *Thornton v. Shoe Lane Parking Ltd*,[210] Thornton drove his car to the entrance of the defendant's automated parking station, received a ticket from a machine and drove in. The ticket referred to 'conditions of issue' displayed on the premises. Those conditions exempted the defendant from liability for personal injury that customers suffered on their premises. Thornton was injured and sued. The company pleaded the exemption clause. At trial it admitted that it had not done what was reasonably sufficient to give Thornton notice of the exemption clause before he contracted, but it argued that he was still bound by it because he either 'knew or believed' from the face of the ticket that it had been issued subject to conditions. It was held that as there was no evidence Thornton had ever been aware of either the conditions generally or the exemption clause in particular, he was not bound by it. The court held therefore that he was entitled to recover for losses incurred.

---

209. [1952] VLR 1.
210. [1971] 2 QB 163.

212. The 'reasonable steps' in the giving of the notice also include a time element. The clause must be brought to the attention of the other party before or at the time of the contract. So any exemption clause brought to the attention of the other party after the contract has been entered into will not be effective to exclude liability. This is because any additional clause added after the contract is an additional term and will be a variation to the original contract. As there is no consideration given for this additional clause it is ineffective.

213. *Olley v. Marlborough Court*[211] is the classic illustration of the principles above. The Olleys arrived at the defendant's hotel, paid for a week in advance and went up to the room allocated to them. On one of the walls was a notice to the effect that 'the proprietors will not hold themselves responsible for articles lost or stolen unless handed to the manageress for safe custody'. A little later, the wife closed the room's self-locking door, went downstairs and hung the key on the board at the reception office. In her absence, the key was taken by a third party who opened the room and stole her furs. She sued. The hotel relied on the notice to escape liability. The court found the hotel liable because the contract was completed at the reception desk before the Olleys went up to their room and no subsequent notice could affect their rights.

214. An exclusion clause that is included in a signed document will bind the person signing it (see *L'Estrange v. Graucob Ltd*[212] discussed previously). There are three exceptions to the rule governing signatures on documents. The first is those documents that appear to have no contractual effect. The second is where the contents of the document or their effect are misrepresented. And the third is a plea of *non est factum* (this is not my deed).

215. In *D J Hill & Co Pty Ltd v. Walter H Wright Pty Ltd*[213] the contract of carriage was orally concluded over the telephone. Upon delivery of the machinery, Wright's employee gave two documents to Hill's employee for signature and they were signed. One of these documents appeared to be a receipt for delivery of the goods, and contained a clause excluding Wright's liability for any loss of, or damage to, goods carried. Wright sought to rely on that clause to escape liability. Hill sued when the machinery was delivered in damaged condition. The court held that Wright was liable and could not rely on the exclusion clause, as it had not been brought to Hill's notice. The signature by Hill's employee was immaterial, as the signature was not intended to operate as the acceptance of a contractual term.[214,215] A similar reasoning was given in *Le Mans Grand Prix Circuits Pty Ltd v. Iliadis.*

216. However, where a person seeks to escape liability by relying on an exemption clause but misrepresents the clause or its effect, the clause's full protection will

211. [1949] 1 KB 532.
212. [1934] 2 KB 394.
213. [1971] VR 749.
214. per Winneke, C.J. at 753.
215. [1998] 4 VR 649.

be lost and its effect will be restricted to what it was misrepresented to be. This will also apply where the misrepresentation was made by a person's servant or agent.[216]

217. In rare circumstances a person may escape liability by pleading *non est factum*. Such pleas are common where people were unable to read but had deeds read to them and the 'reading' did not correctly state what was in the writing. Hence, if the document signed was radically different in character or effect from what the signer thought he or she was signing, or the signer was not careless in signing without checking the contents, the plea could succeed. The case of *Gallie v. Lee*[217] is such an example. In Australia, the High Court has approved and applied the reasoning in *Gallie v. Lee* in the case of *Peterlin v. Cullen.*[218]

D. *Penalty Clauses*

218. A penalty clause may have the same effect as a liquidated damages clause, in that it provides a genuine pre-estimate of the actual loss that is expected in the event of a breach of contract. Sometimes, however, what may appear to be a liquidated damages clause bears no relationship to the probable loss. Such penalty clauses are designed as a means of threatening the other party into performing the contract, by making it too expensive to commit a breach. For this reason, courts will deem such penalty clauses invalid. This penalty is irrecoverable because it would be unconscionable or contrary to public policy to enforce the term in the contract. A penalty is described as a sum fixed *in terrorem* (in fear), to penalize the defendant rather than to compensate the plaintiff.

219. This rule against penalties renders void a clause that requires payment of a sum that is extravagant or unconscionable, having regard to the greatest loss that could be suffered by the plaintiff following the breach of contract to which the sum relates. If a clause is classed as a penalty, the plaintiff will not be entitled to recover the sum specified in the clause, but must instead rely on an action for damages for the breach of contract.

220. Courts accept liquidated damages clauses as a bona fide means of reducing unnecessary litigation, but seldom uphold penalty clauses. Where a clause is deemed as a penalty, it is disregarded and the courts substitute their own determination of what amount of damages is appropriate. Normally, such an action will benefit the defendant, since a penalty clause invariably stipulates an amount greater than any possible loss. But in extraordinary circumstances – where losses exceed all expectations – it could benefit the plaintiff.

221. Whether the sum stipulated in a contract is liquidated damages or a penalty depends on the intention of the parties at the time of contracting. The intention is

---

216. *Curtis v. Chemical Cleaning & Dyeing Co* [1951] 1 KB 805.
217. [1969] 2 Ch. 17.
218. (1975) 132 CLR 355.

ascertained objectively by examining the clause in the light of all the surrounding circumstances. In *Dunlop Pneumatic Tyre Co Ltd v. New Garage & Motor Co Ltd* [1915] AC 79 a contract contained a clause stipulating that liquidated damages of GB 5 were payable in respect of each breach the defendants committed. The court held that Dunlop was entitled to the amount claimed when the defendants breached this clause. The clause was not a penalty but a bona fide attempt to estimate the likely loss flowing from the breach. The principles laid down here have been approved and applied by the High Court in Australia.[219]

222. Note also that the practice of resale price maintenance (RPM) engaged in by *Dunlop* is now prohibited by section 48 Part VIII of the Competition and Consumer Act 2010 (Cth). But the rule outlined in *Dunlop* is not equivalent to a statutory provision, as the application is a matter of substance to be determined by reference to the particular facts of the case. (For a discussion of this, see Part II, Chapter 4 Sale of Goods *below*).

E. Arbitration Clauses

223. Arbitration clauses can be, and have been, inserted into contracts and are deemed valid and enforceable, with the proviso that their effect is not to substitute arbitration for the jurisdiction of the court. Indeed, arbitration must be tried first, and if that fails then resorting to the courts of law is possible. Thus, there can be clauses that make arbitration a condition precedent to court jurisdiction, and these are valid, so long as arbitration does not take the place of the court.

224. In *Scott v. Avery*[220] a marine insurance contract provided that claims were to be determined by a committee, and that any dispute concerning their amount had to be referred to arbitration. It also provided that no party 'could maintain any action at law or suit in equity on his policy until the matter has been decided by the arbitrators'. A court held the clause to be valid. The requirement for arbitration did not oust the court's jurisdiction; it merely made arbitration a condition precedent to jurisdiction arising.

225. Arbitration clauses included in a contract will remain binding after termination of a contract.[221]

226. In Australia, commercial arbitration is governed by uniform state and territory *Commercial Arbitration Acts*.[222] These acts all provide (in section 55) that the

219. See, *for example, O'Dea v. Allstates Leasing System (WA) Pty Ltd* (1983) 152 CLR 359; *AMEV-UDC Finance Ltd v. Austin* (1986) 162 CLR 1970; and *Esanda Finance Corp Ltd v. Plessnig* (1989) 166 CLR 131.
220. (1856) 5 HLC 811; 10 ER 1121.
221. See *Codelfa Construction Pty Ltd v. State Rail Authority of NSW* (1982) 149 CLR 337.
222. NSW 1984; Vic 1984; SA 1986; Qld 1990; WA 1985; Tas 1986; ACT 1986; and NT 1985.

types of clauses found in *Scott v. Avery* 'shall not operate to prevent legal proceedings being brought or maintained' until arbitration has been attempted. Furthermore, section 53 of these acts also provides that if court proceedings are brought in defiance of the arbitration requirement, either party may apply to have the proceedings stayed until arbitration has been attempted.

§2. Interpretation

227. Construction is the process by which courts will determine the meaning and legal effect of the terms in a contract. Courts step in because disputes over the construction of terms arise because the parties themselves did not foresee all of the events that could affect performance of their contract.

228. In construing a contract a court aims to give effect to the parties' intention. Such intentions are interpreted objectively by using the natural or ordinary meaning of the words used. Where the plain and ordinary meaning of the terms of a contract yield non-commercial, unreasonable or absurd results, or where the words bear more than one possible meaning, the courts will take an interpretation that would produce a reasonable commercial result, as this would probably be what the parties had intended.

229. In *Australian Broadcasting Commission v. Australasian Performing Right Association Ltd*,[223] the court said that 'if the language is open to two construction, that will be preferred which will avoid consequences which appear to be capricious, unreasonable, inconvenient or unjust, even though the construction adopted is not the most obvious, or the most grammatically accurate'.

230. In other cases, a court will carefully examine a clause to restrict its effect. Hence, where the notice requirements have been satisfied and exemption clauses properly incorporated into the contract as a term, courts will still examine an exclusion clause carefully to determine its effect. If the clause may be restricted in any way, the courts will do so, and the benefit of any bad drafting be given to the person against whom the clause is being used. This 'reading down' in interpretation is extremely important because of the resultant adverse effects on the party at the receiving end of the limitation.

231. The *contra proferentem* (against the one bringing forth) rule states that any ambiguities in the clause will be construed against the person relying on it. This rule is used where the clause is ambiguous or where other rules of interpretation are insufficient to resolve any conflict in meaning, in which case the clause should be read against the party who wrote it. That is, the preferred interpretation will be the one that helps the party who drafted it the least. The reason behind this rule is to encourage the drafter of a contract to be as clear and explicit as possible and to take into account as many foreseeable situations as possible.

223. (1973) 129 CLR 99 at 108.

232. This rule reflects the court's dislike of standard form take-it-or-leave-it contracts – standard form contracts where there is a perceived display of uneven bargaining positions of the respective parties. To ensure balance, the court will apply *contra proferentem* using a strict approach and at times striking the terms in favour of the other party. *Contra proferentem* also places the cost of losses on the party who was in the best position to avoid the harm – usually the party who drafted the contract. Insurance contracts are a good example of this because the insurance company is the party that is completely in control of the terms of the contract, and is generally in a better position to, for example, avoid contractual forfeiture.

233. In *Alex Kay Pty Ltd v. General Motors Acceptance Corp and Hartford Fire Insurance Co*[224] a court held that all ambiguities are construed against the person who inserts the clause and the meaning least helpful to it was the one to be preferred.

234. A further concept associated with the insertion of clauses is that of a fundamental term to a contract and the potential of a breach of this term. The idea here is that each contract may contain some critical obligation, the non-performance of which would result in no performance of the contract as a whole. This term then becomes 'fundamental' to the contract and its breach is equivalent to non-performance of the contract. The definition is given by Lord Diplock at 849 in *Photo Production Ltd v. Securicor Ltd*,[225] where he said 'the failure by one party to perform a primary obligation [which] has the effect of depriving the other party of substantially the whole benefit which it was the intention of the parties that he should obtain from the contract'.

235. A party in fundamental breach, therefore, is deemed to have repudiated their obligation under the contract (by not performing as required), and this permits the innocent party to accept that repudiation and, thereby, bring the contract to an end.[226] The House of Lords case of *Photo Production* noted above also accepted the fact that there was no general rule that exemption clauses could not protect a party in fundamental breach. In effect, one had to look at the words of the clause on a case-by-case basis and decide whether, on the narrowest of constructions, they actually were excluded from liability for the breach that had occurred.

236. In Australia, two major High Court decisions in the area are *City of Sydney Council v. West*[227] and *Thomas National Transport (Melbourne) Pty Ltd v. May and Baker (Australia) Ltd.*[228] In *City of Sydney* Windeyer J at 503 said that 'much depends in every case upon the precise meaning of the words that the parties used

224. [1963] VR 458.
225. [1980] AC 827 at 849.
226. See *Laurinda Pty Ltd v. Capalaba Park Shopping Centre Pty Ltd* (1989) 166 CLR 623.
227. (1965) 114 CLR 481.
228. (1966) 115 CLR 353.

read in their context and circumstances; for the question, as I see it, is one of interpretation. It is not for a court to say that persons may not contract out of [their] obligations … or put new limits on their power to do so'.

237. It follows, therefore, that if words are broad enough to exempt liability for fundamental breach, then a court would hold accordingly. If it cannot, then there can be no exemption from liability. In *Nisshio Iwai Australia Ltd v. Malaysian International Shipping Corp Berhad*,[229] the court at 227 said that:

> in determining whether an exemption clause should be construed so as to apply to an event that defeated the main object of the contract, much must depend upon the nature of the events that the clause identifies as giving rise to the exemption from liability. If the happening of a stipulated event will always result in the defeat of the main object of the contract there will be no scope for holding that … the exemption clause is not applicable to that event.

§3. Conditional Contracts

238. A promise to hold an offer open is binding at common law if consideration has been given in return for that promise. The agreement between the parties is described as an option. An *option* is an agreement between an option holder and a grantor, under which the option holder is entitled to enter into a contract with the grantor on specified terms, either at a specified time or within a specified period. The option holder is then free to choose whether to exercise the option at that time or within that period.

239. In *Goldsborough, Mort & Co Ltd v. Quinn*[230] the grantor gave the option holder an option to purchase certain land at a specified price at any time within one week of the agreement, in return for the sum of five shillings paid to the grantor. The grantor's attempt to repudiate the offer before acceptance was held to be ineffective. The option holder exercised the option within the specified period and was able to force the grantor to sell the land as agreed. The view here is that the option to purchase the property was a contract for the sale of that property, conditional upon the option being exercised within the specified period. Such a view has since been endorsed in *Carter v. Hyde*;[231] and *Laybutt v. Amoco Australia Pty Ltd.*[232]

229. (1989) 167 CLR 219 at 227.
230. (1910) 10 CLR 674.
231. (1923) 33 CLR 115.
232. (1974) 132 CLR 57.

Chapter 4. Privity of Contract

§1. The Rule of Privity of Contract

240. The privity of contract rule is a legal doctrine that only an original party to a contract may sue or be sued on it. Third parties who are affected in the execution of the contract may not take action against a party with which they have no contractual relationship. While doctrine of privity denies rights to third parties it also prevents a third party from being liable under any contract to which he/she is not a party. Accordingly, a third party beneficiary cannot demand that a contract be performed. This view of the law has been succinctly put by Windeyer J in *Coulls v. Bagot's Executor & Trustee Co Ltd.*[233]

241. In this case Coulls granted to a company the right to quarry stone from his property in return for the payment of certain royalties. The agreement headed 'Agreement between Arthur Leopold Coulls and O'Neil Construction Proprietary Limited', was signed by Coulls and his wife Doris as well as O'Neil on behalf of the company. After stipulating the royalties payable, the agreement provided that Arthur Coulls 'authorized' the company to pay all moneys connected with the agreement to Doris Coulls and himself 'as joint tenants'. When Arthur Coulls died, his executor sought directions from the court as to whether the company was entitled or bound to pay the royalties to Doris Coulls. A majority of the High Court held that the company owned no contractual obligation to Doris Coulls because she was not a party to the agreement. The principal indication of this was that the contract expressly purported to be made between Arthur Coulls and the company. Moreover, the company made no express promise to pay royalties to Doris Coulls, and it was not possible to imply such a promise.

242. The privity rule has been criticized and is subject to significant exceptions as it may be circumvented in various ways and has been substantially abrogated in some jurisdictions. Note also that this rule is distinct from the doctrine of consideration that says that in order to sue on a promise, the plaintiff must also have given consideration in return for that promise as well as also being the promisee. The plaintiff, must therefore have been a party to the contract.

243. Thus, in *Trident General Insurance Co Ltd v. McNiece Bros Pty Ltd*,[234] Trident entered into an insurance contract with A Ltd Coy. To cover against liability for renovations being carried out by McNiece, Trident refused a claim on the grounds that an injured crane driver was not a party to the contract and had given no consideration. The court held by a 4:3 majority that Trident was bound to indemnify McNiece under the insurance policy with A Ltd Coy. This reasoning was subsequently approved in *Federal Commissioner of Taxation v. Orica.*[235]

233. (1967) 119 CLR 460 at 494.
234. (1988) 165 CLR 107.
235. (1998) 194 CLR 500 at 542.

I. Limitations to Rule

244. Limitations or exceptions to the rule can arise by means of agency, trusts, 'three party' collateral contracts, assignments and statute. Thus, a typology for the circumstances under which the privity doctrine may be circumvented may include the following:

- where the promisee is seen as having made a contract as agent of a beneficiary-third party;
- where the promisee may hold rights under the contract on trust for the beneficiary-third party;
- where the beneficiary-third party is entitled to assert an estoppel against the promisor;
- where the beneficiary-third party is entitled to claim damages for misleading or deceptive conduct; and
- where the beneficiary-third party is entitled to claim damages in tort.

245. These various ways of circumventing the privity doctrine are discussed at length in Part I – General principles of Contract as well as in Part II Specific contract under Agency, Trusts, and in the general law of tort, estoppel and misleading or deceptive conduct.

246. An *agent* is a person who has the power to enter into a contract on behalf of another person. The privity rule can be circumvented if a person promised a benefit under a contract can show that one of the contracting parties entered into the contract as his or her agent. This method of circumventing the privity rule has been used most often in relation to the limitation of liability clauses in contracts of carriage. Such clauses are sometimes referred to as *Himalaya clauses* after *Adler v. Dickson (The Himalaya).*[236] Such a clause typically extends the exclusion or limitation of liability to cover employees, agents and sub-contractors of the carrier who load and unload the goods.

247. The *trust* may be used as a means of alleviating some injustice occasioned by the application of the privity rule. The argument here is that a contractual right is a form of property – a chose in action, which, like any other form of property, can be held by a trustee on trust for a beneficiary. Where such an intention may be discerned, then it follows that while the beneficiary is not made a party to the contract, the trust creates an obligation on the part of the promisee to enforce the promise on behalf of the beneficiary. The beneficiary can rightly enforce the promise by compelling performance of the promise.

248. The difficulty here is when the courts will be prepared to imply or infer an intention to create a trust. In some instances courts have insisted on a clear expression of intention to create a trust, and hence have been unwilling to infer such an intention. In others, the courts have been prepared to infer a trust from the fact that

236. [1955] 1 QB 158.

a contract was made for the benefit of a third party. Such arguments have been made in the various opinions of the justices in *Trident v. McNiece*.[237]

249. Three-party collateral contracts arise as a result of promises made in a main contract between two parties and one of these parties then enters into a further promise with a third party. Such a situation leaves one of the parties outside of the subsequent contract but yet potentially able to sue in the event of a breach of contract.

250. In *Shanklin Pier Ltd v. Detel Products Ltd*,[238] Detel, was the manufacturer of paint products that promised Shanklin Pier that its paint would last for between seven and ten years if Shanklin used it on its pier. On the faith of promise, Shanklin Pier directed its contractors to use Detel's paint. The paint was found to be unsuitable for it lasted only three months. Shanklin was not a party to the contract under which the paint was bought and, therefore, it could not sue for breach of the implied condition that the paint was suitable for the purpose. However, it could sue for breach of the collateral agreement under which, in exchange for Detel's assurance about the paint, it had instructed its contractors to use that paint in preference to something else. As a result it could recover damages, indirectly, through the collateral agreement.

251. An *assignment* is an arrangement where one party to a contract transfers all or some of the benefits that that party would have received under the contract to a third party. This assignment now means that the third party has acquired the rights arising under the contract and the right to sue to enforce them. This power to assign is derived from equity and hence is restricted to the assignment of 'rights'. There is no formality involved other than that the assignor and assignee have intended to assign. No notice of such an assignment is needed, although if it is not, the assignee may lose the benefit of the assignment to either the assignor or to some third party.[239]

252. Statute. For statutory provisions concerning the privity rule and third parties see §5 *below*.

A. Third Parties and the Contract

253. As noted, a third party cannot force a promisor to hand over the benefits promised, nor can he/she be made subject to liabilities or restrictions under the contract.

254. In *Dunlop Pneumatic Tyre Co Ltd v. Selfridge & Co Ltd*[240] Dunlop entered into a contract to sell car tyres to Dew & Co. The contract specified that the latter

---

237. (1988) 165 CLR 107.
238. [1951] 2 KB 854.
239. See *Roxburghe v. Cox* (1991) 17 Ch. D 520.
240. [1915] AC 847.

could not resell the tyres for less than the list prices except to trade customers and that, if it sold them to trade customers, it would do so only on their promise to observe list prices when reselling. Selfridge & Co a retailer, bought tyres from Dew & Co. It agreed not to resell for less than list prices but then did so. Dunlop sued. But its actions failed. The undertaking was between Selfridge & Co and Dew & Co Dunlop was a stranger to the contract, and hence, could not enforce it.

Dunlop also argued that Dew & Co had entered into the contract as their agents. It was held that, even if that were the case, Dunlop could still not enforce it because no consideration had moved from it to Selfridge in exchange for the promise[241] on the principles that a stranger to the contract cannot sue on it, and a stranger to the consideration cannot sue on the contract.

255. The privity doctrine prevents a third party from enforcing the contract but it does not prevent a contract from conferring a benefit on a third party.

B. Contract for the Benefit of a Third Party

256. The common law position is that even if the third party is specifically intended to benefit from a contract, he/she cannot sue to enforce that benefit. However, the original parties to the contract can sue. Thus, if a promisor fails to honour a promise, there is nothing that the third party can do.[242]

William Tweddle was engaged to Guy's daughter. Guy and Tweddle's father agreed that they would each pay William GB 100 to provide for the young couple after their marriage. They further agreed that William could sue for the money. When Guy died, he had not paid the promised sum. William sued the executor, Atkinson. The action failed because William was 'a stranger to the consideration' and, not having paid for the promise, could not enforce it. The fact that Guy's promise had not been made to him would also have debarred him on the grounds of privity of contract.

257. While the original parties to the contract may sue, the performance of an existing contractual duty to a third party may be enforceable in specific circumstances as in the case of *Shadwell v. Shadwell*.[243] An uncle wrote to his nephew who was engaged to be married with the promise 'to assist you in starting … I will pay to you GB 150 during my life or until you annual income … shall amount to 600 guineas'. The annuity fell into arrears, the uncle died and the plaintiff sued the executors. The nephew recovered the moneys even though he had merely carried out an already existing contract to marry.

258. Where the promise is made for the benefit of a third party as well as an intended beneficiary together; there is no third party to the contract. There is,

241. per Viscount Haldane LC at 853.
242. *Tweddle v. Atkinson* (1861) 1 B&S 393; 121 ER 762.
243. (1860) 9 CBNS 159.

instead, a promisor and joint promisees. In this case, the beneficiary is not a stranger to the contract; he/she is party to it and is entitled to enforce it as a party.[244]

259. The law has suggested that where the existing duty is payment of a debt; payment of part of the debt, even moving from the creditor, will not be adequate consideration to discharge the entire amount owing as established in *Pinnel's case*[245] and *Foakes v. Beer.*[246]

§2. Transfer of Contractual Rights

260. The privity doctrine also prevents a contract from imposing a legal burden on a third party. A contract between a manufacturer of goods and a wholesale cannot restrict the terms on which the goods may be sold by a retailer who purchases the goods from the wholesaler, for example, the retail price sold. The contract between the manufacturer and the wholesaler cannot impose obligations on a retailer.[247] In any case, any restriction relating to the price at which the goods can be resold will infringe the Competition and Consumer Act 2010 (Cth) section 48 and Part VIII relating to resale price maintenance noted above.

261. The apparent transfer of contractual rights may also occur through Agency as in the relationship between an Agent and Third Party. In normal instances an agent will not be liable to the third party. The contract would have been made on behalf of the principal and it is this person that is responsible. Likewise, a third party cannot rely on apparent authority where they have knowledge that the authority of the agent is restricted.

262. An agent will be liable to a third party for breach of a warrant of authority where the agent suggests that he or she has the authority to act on behalf of a principal, but in fact does not have such authority.[248] For further details see a discussion in Part II, Chapter 1. Agency *supra.*

§3. The Special Case of a 'Sub-Contract'

263. Where the contract contains an exemption clause, especially in cases of a sub-contract, to exclude or limit one party's liability for the consequences of any breach, the modern trend is that it excludes not only that party's liability but also the liability of anyone acting through or under that party. That is, it is also designed to protect servants or agents who may be called on to perform some service under the contract and who, in the course of that service, could damage the property or

244. See *Coulls v. Bagot's Executor & Trustee Co Ltd* (1967) 119 CLR 460.
245. (1602) 77 ER 237.
246. (1884) 9 App Cas 605 see elsewhere in Part I, Ch. 1 under Consideration.
247. See *Dunlop Pneumatic Tyre Co Ltd v. Selfridge & Co Ltd* [1915] AC 847 discussed above.
248. *Black v. Smallwood* (1966) 117 CLR 52.

interests of the other party. The result acts such that the servant or agent is not generally protected by the exemption clause.

264. In *Wilson v. Darling Island Stevedoring & Lighterage Co Ltd*[249] a plaintiff's goods shipped to Sydney were damaged through the negligence of the defendant stevedoring company hired by a carrier to unload and store them. The bill of lading between the shipper and the carrier included a clause that:

> the carrier has no responsibility whatsoever for the goods … subsequent to the discharge from the vessel. Goods in the custody of the carrier or his agents or servants before loading and after discharge … are in such custody at the sole risk of the owners of the goods and the carrier shall not be liable for loss or damage arising or resulting from any cause whatsoever.

The plaintiffs sued the stevedores as the carrier's agents. The High Court held that the exemption clause protected the carrier but not the stevedoring company. It had not been a party to the contract and thus could not take the benefit of any of its terms.[250]

265. While the United Kingdom courts took the same attitude as in the *Wilson* case above[251] the omission was rectified with the use of use of third party clauses popularly known as 'Himalaya clauses' after the decision in *Adler v. Dickson*[252] – so named after the case involving the liner *Himalaya.*

266. Later cases where the inclusion clause was approved and applied included *New Zealand Shipping Co Ltd v. A M Satterthwaite & Co Ltd* (The Eurymedon);[253] and approved in the High Court of Australia case of *Port Jackson Stevedoring Pty Ltd v. Salmond and Spraggon (Aust) Pty Ltd* (The New York Star).[254]

§4. Remedies Available to the Promisee

267. Where a promisee sues a promisor to enforce a contractual promise to confer a benefit on a third party, the remedies available may be insufficient to ensure that the third party obtains the promised benefit. Sometimes substantial damages may be available while in other cases specific performance may be decreed by the courts. In some instances specific performance may be unavailable and it is also doubtful if the promisee may be entitled to recover substantial damages. These are vexed questions for which no answers are readily available.

249. (1956) 95 CLR 43.
250. per Fullagar, J. at 67.
251. *Scruttons Ltd v. Midland Silicones Ltd* [1962] AC 466.
252. [1955] 1 QB 158.
253. [1975] AC 154.
254. (1980) 144 CLR 300.

268. In general, if a non-performance of the promise causes no particular harm to the promisee, then the promisee will only be entitled to nominal damages – per *Trident v. McNiece*;[255] and *Beswick v. Beswick*.[256]

Peter Beswick, a coal merchant of advancing age, contracted to sell his business to his nephew John, who undertook to pay him GB 6 10s a week for as long as he lived and, if he survived him, to pay Peter's widow GB 5 a week for the balance of her life. When Peter died, John paid the widow one instalment only and then refused to pay any more. The widow sued John for the unpaid arrears and for specific performance of future payments.

The widow succeeded in obtaining an order for specific performance. The remedy was thought to be appropriate here because of the peculiar circumstances of the case – as she had not been a part to the original contract and hence could not sue in her personal capacity; and she was restricted to an action as administrator. As administrator she would have only been entitled to nominal damages because the estate did not suffer as a result of John's default. A just result was thus to order specific performance of the promise.

269. However, where the promisee holds the relevant contractual rights on trust for the third party beneficiary, then it appears that the promisee can recover all that the third party could have recovered if the contract had been made with the third party.[257]

270. Specific performance is a useful remedy for the enforcement of a promise made for the benefit of a third party. This remedy might be sought by the promisee and, if granted, will result in the third party obtaining the promised benefit. But this will only be granted where damages are inadequate.[258]

271. However, there may be situations where even such a remedy is inappropriate, for example, where the contract involves the performance of personal services that may require the supervision of courts.[259]

§5. Statutory Provisions

272. In some Australian jurisdictions, parliament has enacted legislation to give intended third party beneficiaries direct rights against a defaulting promisor.

273. Section 48 of the *Insurance Contracts Act* 1984 (Cth), provides an example of a departure from the common law. Here it is provided that where cover is extended to a third party under a contract of general insurance, the third party may,

255. (1988) 165 CLR 107 at 118, 158.
256. [1968] AC 58.
257. *Coulls v. Bagot's Executor and Trustee Co Ltd* (1967) 119 CLR 460 at 501; and *Trident v. McNiece* (1988) 165 CLR 107 at 118 discussed above.
258. *Trident v. McNiece* (1988) 165 CLR 107.
259. See *Jackson v. Horizon Holidays Ltd* [1975] 3 All ER 92.

if necessary, sue the insurer direct on that contract. Note the specificity of this provision.

274. However, in other jurisdictions the provisions are wider and more general. Section 11 of the *Property Law Act* 1969 (WA), section 55 *Property Law Act* 1974 (Qld); and section 56 *Law of Property Act* 2000 (NT) are almost identical in providing general rights of direct action to third parties.

275. Elsewhere, the *Contracts (Privity) Act* 1982 (NZ) and the *Contracts (Rights of Third Parties)* Act 1999 (UK) are devoted entirely to this question of third party rights.

276. The third party can personally enforce, as of right, a promise made between others even though he/she was not a party to the contract containing the promise. The sole requirement is that the third party must have 'accepted' the promise. Acceptance is defined in the statute and it is not necessary for the third party to have provided consideration for the promise but he/she must fulfil any duty imposed by its terms in order to take advantage of its benefits.

277. An example of the application in Western Australia is *Westralian Farmers Co-operative Ltd v. Southern Meat Packers Ltd.*[260] Westralian Farmers were livestock agents acting for King in the sale of cattle to Southern Meat Packers. The contract of sale provided that Southern Meat Packers were to make payment for the cattle not to King but direct to Westralian Farmers – King's agents, and not party to the contract. Southern Meat Packers paid King direct and Westralian Farmers sued.

Westralian Farmers suit was successful. Even though King were not a party to the contract of sale, the clause regarding payment did confer a direct benefit on them within the meaning of section 11(2) of *Property Law Act* 1969 (WA). Consequently, Westralian Farmers could enforce that aspect of the contract even though they were not a party to it.

§6. *Actio Pauliana*

278. This legal doctrine of *Actio pauliana*, of Roman law heritage, is not available in any Australian jurisdiction. The principle relates to fraudulent conveyancing of property with the express purpose of putting it beyond the reach of a known creditor. In such a case the creditor may bring a lawsuit to void the transfer. However, if the transfer was made without knowledge of the claim (or before a debt has matured), for other legitimate reasons, and/or in the normal course of business, then the creditor's attempt obtain a judgment setting aside the conveyance will probably fail.[261]

260. [1981] WAR 241.
261. See *Fenhalls v. Ebrahim 1956(4)* SA 723(N).

279. The doctrine of privity of contract has been abrogated by statute in Western Australia, Queensland and the Northern Territory. In the federal jurisdiction the Commonwealth Government has abrogated privity in relation to the special areas of insurance and maritime contracts of carriage. In Western Australia the *Property Law Act 1969* (WA) section 11(2) provides that where a contract expressly in its terms purports to confer a benefit directly on a person who was not named as a party to the contract, the contract is enforceable by that person in his or her own name. This is subject to the proviso in subsection (3) that, unless the contract provides, the contract may be cancelled or modified by the mutual consent of the persons named as parties at any time before the beneficiary has adopted it, either expressly or by conduct.

280. The Property Law Act 1974 (Qld) section 55(1) and the *Law of Property Act 2000* (NT) section 56 both provide that a promisor who, for a valuable consideration moving from the promisee, promises to do or refrain from doing an act or acts for the benefit of a beneficiary shall, upon acceptance by the beneficiary, be subject to a duty enforceable by the beneficiary to perform that promise.

But note that in all instances where the statutory provisions cannot be applied, such as where the requirement of acceptance has not been complied with, the common law is still applicable.

281. In Australia today insurance cases are the subject of legislation enacted to overcome the privity rule. This is in line with *Vandepitte v. Preferred Accident Insurance Corporation* of New York where the Privy Council applied the privity rule to an insurance policy that was expressed to be for the benefit of persons who were not parties to the contract. As a consequence, persons who were named as beneficiaries under the insurance policy, but who were not actually parties to the policy, were unable to claim coverage under the policy.[262]

262. [1933] AC 70.

Chapter 5. The Termination of the Contract

§1. Performance and Breach

282. Performance of the contract according to its terms is the aim of the parties in all contracts – that is to say that the mutual obligations of the parties should be discharged through their proper performance in strict accordance with the contract terms, leaving nothing outstanding. In *In re Moore & Co Ltd and Landauer & Co*[263] it was held that this may be accomplished in either of two ways (as specified according to the terms of the contract), with actual performance corresponding as nearly as practicable to the terms of the contract. A contract may be terminated by the giving of 'reasonable notice' by one of the parties. However, such a term will not be implied into the contract if, on a construction of the contract, it was not intended by the parties, with the courts determining the rights and obligations of the parties on an objective basis. This often involves an assessment of what a 'reasonable person' would believe they intended, based on their words and behaviour.[264] Generally evidence of surrounding circumstances is inadmissible for the purpose of interpreting a contract unless the contract is on its face ambiguous.[265]

283. The first method of performance is by payment of money. This is limited to the amount of money or legal tender that a creditor is bound to accept in payment of a debt and may be in any recognized and convertible currency. This may be absolute payment, in which full payment in legal tender ensures the debt is discharged, or conditional payment, in which the payment is made by other means, such as by cheque or money order. In *Godfrey v. Sevenoaks* [266] the court held that payment for a car that was made by cheque (that was subsequently dishonoured) was payment made on a conditional basis. As the purchaser had immediately on-sold the car, claiming that they had received good title, the issue of whether the payment had been made in full became of paramount importance. The court held that payment by cheque was conditional and the receipt given could not be regarded as an unequivocal representation that title had passed to the purchaser. The contract was declared void *ab initio*.

284. The second acceptable method is when payment is made by means other than money. This occurs when the parties to the contract fulfil their obligations to each other in some way that does not involve the transfer of money. Examples of this may be found in the bartering of goods and services.

263. *In re Moore & Co Ltd and Landauer & Co* [1921] 2 KB 519.
264. *State Bank of NSW v. Commonwealth Savings Bank Ltd* (1985) 60 ALR 73 at p. 100.
265. See Collins, The Basis of Contract (1933) Harvard Law Review 553,557; *Velvet Glove Holdings Pty Ltd v. Mt Isa Mines Ltd* 2011] QCA 312.
266. *Godfrey v. Sevenoaks* (1957) WN(NSW) 487.

285. Notwithstanding the presence of an apparent right to terminate, this cannot be adjudged to be an absolute right, and there are certain restrictions on its application. For example, the party wishing to exercise their right to terminate the contract must themselves be ready and willing to perform their obligations, and they may even lose their right to termination through their own conduct. Should termination be adjudged to have been unconscionable in all of the circumstances, then equitable principles will be applied.[267] In addition, there may be statutory relief available under the Australian Consumer Law if the contract involves trade or commerce.[268] It is important that the performance of the contract be exactly as specified, and made within the stipulated time. Where there is no express time for performance, the contract must be performed within a reasonable time. A party can perform their contractual obligations through the actions of another party, provided that this is not expressly prohibited in the contract. In circumstances of partial performance of the contract, the degree of non-performance will determine what legal consequences will ensue. If the non-performance is minimal, the law will treat the contract as having been validly discharged.[269] Where the shortfall is significant, there is a prima facie repudiation of the contract, giving rise to liability in damages.[270] The liability of a party under an action in non-performance is subject to the equitable doctrine of substantial performance, under which the courts have recognized that if a party is denied recovery where there has been only partial performance of the contract, this will result in the unjust enrichment of the other party. Where a supplier has supplied most of what he or she contracted to supply, he or she is entitled to recover the contract price minus a sum reflecting the shortfall in performance.

286. Whether a breach has occurred depends on whether there has been compliance with the terms of the contract, not whether the party in breach was blameworthy, careless nor affected by events outside their control, although this is subject to application of the doctrine of frustration.[271] A contract may fail through illegality, that is to say that the contract itself, is by its nature illegal per se either before or during the performance of the contract. Generally, if illegality is present, the contract is prima facie considered to be void at common law and/or on grounds of public policy. It may also include rescission under discharge by operation of law, such as when there is breach of statute (e.g., the *Bankruptcy Act*). This prohibition may be either express (such as through the *Competition and Consumer Act 2010* (Cth))

267. *Foran v. Wight* (1989) 88 CLR 413.
268. Section 20 of the ACL states that a person (which includes a corporation) must not, in trade or commerce, engage in conduct that is unconscionable within the meaning of the unwritten law from time to time. The purpose of this section is principally to widen the range of remedies available to the victim of unconscionable dealing. It also enables the ACCC to investigate unconscionable conduct and, if necessary, bring legal action on behalf of the person who has been treated unconscionably. The section appears to refer to the doctrine of unconscionable dealing as it has been interpreted in case law. However, the words are perfectly general and the courts have not yet settled on what constitutes unconscionable conduct under 'the unwritten law' and it may go beyond the doctrine of unconscionable dealing to include other equitable doctrines.
269. This is under the principle of *de minimis non curat lex.*
270. *Corio Guarantee Corp v. Macallum* [1956] VLR 755 at 760.
271. See *Codelfa Contruction Pty v. State Rail Authority of NSW* (1982) 149 CLR 337.

or may be implied (such as where a licence is required by Parliament and one is not held, thereby rendering the activity illegal per se).

There are contracts that fall into either of two categories established through the operation of the common law:

- illegal contracts; and
- contracts void at law.

287. First, there are illegal contracts at common law, an example of which could be contracts involving the commission of a crime, or involving sexual immorality to an objectionable degree, perhaps collectively described as contracts tending to promote corruption in some way or other.[272] In *Pearce v. Brooks* [273] it was held that contracts involving the letting of premises or the hire of vehicles for an immoral purpose were illegal, and therefore void. This was however not an established rule, and in *Barac (t/as Exotic Studios) v. Farnell*,[274] the court held that the employment of a receptionist at a brothel (when the brothel itself was illegal) was not void for illegality, because the employment as a receptionist was itself legal, and that therefore she could claim compensation for a broken arm sustained on the way to work. Second, there are void contracts, such as a contract intended to oust the jurisdiction of the courts, or one that involves unreasonable restraint of trade. In *Equuscorp* the High Court held that where a contract for the loan of funds was deemed illegal, those funds were not recoverable.[275]

288. In addition, there are contracts in restraint of trade, which fall under the provisions of the *Australian Consumer Law 2010 (Cth)*. An example of this is to be found in the case of *Drake Personnel Ltd v. Beddison* [1979] VR 13.[276] The plaintiff sought an injunction to restrain the defendant carrying on the business of an employment agency in breach of his covenant with the plaintiff. It was held that it represented unreasonable restraint of trade and was therefore illegal.

289. A court possessing equitable jurisdiction may order a party which has only partly executed a contractual obligation to complete this obligation. This is a discretionary remedy that is usually applied by the courts in circumstances where damages would be inadequate compensation for the innocent party's loss. Damages may be awarded in lieu of an order of specific performance. The courts are less likely to order specific performance of a contract for personal services:

- where the court's supervision of the contract's performance would be difficult;[277]
- where the performance of the contract would offend public policy or;
- where ordering performance would have futile consequences.

272. *Public Service Credit Union Co-Operative Ltd v. Campion* (1984) 56 ACTR 39.
273. *Pearce v. Brooks* (1866) LR 1 Ex 213.
274. (1994) 125 ALR 241.
275. *Equuscorp Pty Ltd v. Haxton* [2012] HCA 7.
276. *Drake Personnel Ltd v. Beddison* [1979] VR 13.
277. *Skywest Airlines Pty Ltd v. Northern Territory* (1987) 45 NTR 29 at p. 50.

I. Breach

290. In recognition that not all of what are generally described as terms of a contract are of fundamental importance to the performance of that contract, different rules apply according to this distinction when a party fails to live up to its contractual obligations, which may result in the breaching of the contract. The different classifications of terms were dealt with in detail in Chapter 3 above. A breach of contract occurs when a party to a contract is unable for whatever reason to carry out their obligations under the terms of the contract, and may be by operation of the contract itself[278] or by the exercise of a right conferred by law, and whether the breach is of a condition or a warranty. This latter distinction is important, because in essence only if it is a condition that is breached, it confers on the innocent party the option of continuing with, or seeking discharge of, the contract. It is important to note, however, that only serious breaches fall into this category, and in *Shevill v. Builders Licencing Board*[279] the High Court of Australia set down three categories of breach justifying termination:

(i) breach of an essential term (breach of a condition);
(ii) breach going to the root of the contract (a fundamental breach); and
(iii) repudiation of the contract.

291. As discussed above, whether a breach is of a condition or warranty is more than an academic distinction, as an actual breach of the former (this generally being clear on the facts) represents grounds for termination, whereas the latter does not. The second category is more complex, with the possibility that a term that is breached, although not in itself qualifying as a condition, may nonetheless be fundamental to the performance of the contract, and therefore its absence justifies termination. Repudiation represents the unwillingness or inability of one party to perform an essential term of the contract, and may occur in two situations: in the first, one party repudiates the whole contract whether by act or by deed (i.e., to say, unilaterally). This does not of itself automatically terminate the contract, and instead gives the other party(ies) the option of either ignoring the breach and insisting upon performance when due, or accepting the repudiation and deeming themselves as discharged from any further obligation under the contract. For this to occur, the contract must be entirely renounced.[280] The second situation is where there is an anticipatory breach, where one party renounces it before the contract is due for performance. In *Foran v. Wight*,[281] time was specified in a contract as being of the essence – that is to say, it was clearly a condition – and two days before settlement was due the vendor's solicitors advised that a delay was necessary. In this case, although the purchasers failed to lodge a claim for anticipatory breach when it thus became available to them, they were themselves not ready to proceed. The High

278. In *Commonwealth v. Amman Aviation Pty Ltd* (1991) 174 CLR 64 the inclusion of such a right in the contract itself was held to be operable over any right to termination on other grounds.
279. (1982) 149 CLR 620 at 625–626 per Gibbs CJ.
280. *Hochster v. De La Tour* (1853) 2 E&B 678, 118 ER 922.
281. *Foran v. Wight* (1989) 88 CLR 413.

Court held that as the vendors were not ready, they were at fault, and freed the purchasers from their obligations and allowed them to recover their deposit.

292. A party found by a court to have breached a contract where no quantifiable loss can be found, will nonetheless be held liable for nominal damages.

293. Breach of a particular and *essential* term (as opposed to a condition) of a contract by one party may entitle another party to the contract to regard themselves as being discharged from performance, and they may refuse to carry out their own obligations that are otherwise due under the contract. Whether this option is available to the innocent party largely turns on whether the term alleged to have been breached is an essential term and not a warranty. In *Bettini v. Gye*,[282] the court held that it may be expressly provided that a particular term is essential to a contract, for example by a stipulation that it is the basis for, or the essence of, the contract, and that therefore a breach of that term by one party entitles the innocent party to act in this way.

294. In *Tramways Advertising Pty Ltd v. Luna Park (NSW) Ltd*,[283] the NSW Supreme Court held that 'the test of essentiality is whether it appears from the general nature of the contract considered as a whole, or from some particular term or terms, that the promise is of such importance to the promisee that he would not have entered into the contract unless he had been assured of a strict or a substantial performance of the promise ... and that this ought to have been apparent to the promisor'. This position was reinforced by the High Court of Australia in *Shevill v. Builders Licensing Board*,[284] where it was held that consistently late payment of rent alone does not constitute repudiation of a lease, and it would be premature for the other party to consider the contract at an end and would render that party potentially liable for breaching the contract themselves.

295. Any decision to declare that a party has committed a sufficiently serious breach of what is undeniably a term of a contract, sufficient to enable the innocent party themselves to breach the contract with impunity, turns therefore on this categorization of the terms, and on this there is some judicial uncertainty. The High Court of Australia held in 1987 that 'a term in a contract may stand somewhere between a condition and a warranty'.[285] The court gave some useful guidelines when it went on to hold that the status of a term ought to be determined 'according to the gravity of the breach', noting that 'nothing less than a serious breach of an innominate (or intermediate) term entitles the innocent party to treat the contract as at an end'. Termination is not however required for a right to damages to arise,[286] but when a party does elect to terminate the contract, the terminating party is

282. *Bettini v. Gye* (1846) 1 QB 183.
283. *Tramways Advertising Pty Ltd v. Luna Park (NSW) Ltd* (1938) 38 SR (NSW) 632.
284. *Shevill v. Builders Licensing Board* (1982) 149 CLR 620.
285. *Ankar Pty Ltd v. National Westminster Finance (Australia) Ltd* (1987) 162 CLR 549 at 561–562.
286. *Luna Park (NSW) Ltd v. Tramways Advertising Pty Ltd* (1938) 61 CLR 286.

entitled to recover damages for all losses resulting from the breach, but not for expectation loss.

A person may be liable in tort for inducing or procuring conduct that they know will be in breach of a contract, and this includes whether a party was 'recklessly indifferent' as to whether the conduct would give rise to a breach of contract.[287]

296. The law imposes a duty upon the party claiming damages to mitigate or to take all reasonable steps to reduce or minimize their loss, failing which the amount or quantum of damages to be awarded will be reduced. If the plaintiff is able to avoid a loss (whether they do so or not), damages will not be recoverable for the potential loss that the plaintiff may have suffered.

§2. Impossibility, Frustration and Hardship: 'the Unforeseen'

297. Under impossibility, an unforeseen event can result in such a fundamentally different situation that a party to the contract is unable to perform its obligations under the contract, and the law regards it as being discharged from any further obligation under the contract. In *Davis Contractors Ltd v. Fareham Urban District Council*,[288] the court held that 'mere hardship, inconvenience or material loss will not in themselves justify the application of principle … there must be as well, such a change in the significance of the obligation that the thing undertaken would, if performed, be a different thing from that contracted for'.

298. It may be that although all parties to the contract are ready and willing to perform their obligations under the contract, due to circumstances beyond the control of any of the parties performance is not possible, and this is recognized by the rules relating to impossibility, frustration and hardship. Impossibility may be created by one party before the contract is due for performance, although this is not a situation that can be induced by the party seeking to benefit from this rule, and in *Synge v. Synge*,[289] the court held that a party cannot by his or her own act rid themselves of obligations under a contract and escape liability, although impossibility may be created by one party during the performance of the contract.[290]

I. Frustration

299. Termination by frustration represents the doctrine by which events that occur after the contract has been concluded and without fault of any of the parties make its performance pointless, impossible or more difficult or costly than anticipated, enabling courts to make appropriate orders terminating the contract and compensating the parties accordingly. The effect of frustration is that it discharges a contract immediately from the time of the frustrating event, but only as to the future

287. *LED Technologies Pty Ltd v. Road Vision Pty Ltd* [2012] FCAC 3.
288. *Davis Contractors Ltd v. Fareham Urban District Council* [1956] AC 696.
289. *Synge v. Synge* [1894] 1 QB 466.
290. *Ogden's Ltd v. Nelson* [1905] AC 109.

and not *ab initio*. The lead case for this doctrine is *Codelfa Constructions Pty Ltd v. State Rail Authority of NSW*.[291] In this case, mentioned above, Codelfa Constructions contracted to dig tunnels and do other work for an underground railway in the eastern suburbs of Sydney pursuant to a strict timetable, with time cited as the essence of the contract. The work generated considerable noise and vibrations, to which local residents objected, and a court injunction was obtained restricting the hours available to work, with the result that the company could not complete its obligations under the contract. It was held by a majority of the High Court that the granting of the injunction had made the thing (the contract) radically or fundamentally different from that specified in the contract documentation, resulting in frustration of the contract. It is reasonable to assume, however, that performance of contractual obligations will not readily be excused by a court simply because it might appear that frustration can be applied, where there was opportunity for the parties to cater for foreseeable eventualities within the terms of the contract, and that a clear case will need to be made out.[292] The frustrating event must not have been induced by the parties to the contract, and must not have been foreseen or reasonably foreseeable. For example, a contract would be frustrated in circumstances where the subject matter of the contract suddenly ceases to exist, where there is an outbreak of war rendering the performance of the contract impossible, or where there is a change in the law that renders the performance of the contract illegal. Parties wishing to maintain a contract on foot after a frustrating event may include a term in the contract to that effect. Alternatively, a term can be included stating what consequences shall ensue upon the occurrence of a frustrating event. In the absence of a contractual term specifying the consequences of frustration of the contract, the result at common law is an automatic discharge of contractual obligations. Where the contract has been partly performed, rights accruing under the contract prior to the date of frustration remain on foot. Legislation in New South Wales and Victoria[293] supplements this common law principle in those jurisdictions. Although that legislation does not define the concept of a frustrating event, it adjusts the rights and liabilities of parties to a frustrated contract, and deals with compensation for partial performance of the contract.

300. In particular, in New South Wales, the *Frustrated Contracts Act 1978* (NSW) adjusts the rights of the parties in the case of frustration (but not for impossibility of performance), by allowing for:

- repayment of moneys paid before frustration;
- payment for any benefit that a party has obtained from the actions of another party under the contract and;
- payment of half of the reasonable costs incurred by a party for the purpose of performing the contract.

291. *Codelfa Construction Pty Ltd v. State Rail Authority of NSW* (1981) 149 CLR 337.
292. *Scanlan's New Neon Ltd v. Tooheys Ltd* (1943) 67 CLR 169, cited with approval in *Codelfa Constructions*.
293. Frustrated Contracts Act 1978 (NSW); Frustrated Contracts Act 1959 (Vic).

However, it is important to note that under this legislation provision has been made to allow the courts to apply the common law and award compensation as they deem appropriate, if, mindful of the particular circumstances before them in a case involving frustration, they feel that these statutory remedies are manifestly inadequate.[294]

301. There are, however, limits to the doctrine of frustration. Each case is taken by the courts on its merits, and where, given the nature of the contract, after removal of the obstruction, any delay has not been so long as to make it unreasonable to resume performance, frustration will not be granted.[295] Self-induced frustration will not generally be regarded as sufficient grounds, with the onus on the party seeking to invoke frustration[296] to show that they are not responsible for the event relied upon, and this has been described as being 'both logical and satisfactory'.[297]

302. Frustration is generally agreed to represent a failure of a contract that is not the fault of any of the parties, but is in fact a confluence of circumstances preventing its performance to fruition. In such a case, it would be inappropriate to apportion blame or financial penalty to any of the parties; rather, it is appropriate to determine their entitlements under the contract up to the point of frustration. In such a case, and in addition to recovery of monies paid,[298] the equitable principle of quantum meruit is applied, and payment (generally under the terms and processes stipulated in the contract) is made to the parties according to their participation under the contract to that point, at least where tangible benefits have been conferred on a party who would be unjustly enriched in the absence of compensation.[299]

§3. Discharge by Agreement

303. Discharge by agreement may be as agreed between the parties at any time, and involves the entering into a further agreement that terminates the original one. This further agreement may be made:

- by cancellation of the original contract, such as through mutual discharge, prior to full performance of their contractual obligations, in which case both parties agree to cancel the original contract, but that requires that the contract is still wholly or partly executory on both sides. An example is novation, where a new contract is substituted for the old one. A written contract can be discharged or varied either in writing or orally (in which case provided the intention to rescind the

294. In Victoria, the *Frustrated Contracts Act* 1959 similarly applies, being based substantially on the *Law Reform (Frustrated Contracts) Act* 1943 (UK), and in South Australia the *Frustrated Contracts Act* 1988 applies.
295. *Ringstad v. Gollin & Co Pty Ltd* (1924) 35 CLR 303 at 316/317.
296. *Scanlan's New Neon Ltd v. Tooheys Ltd* (1943) 67 CLR 169.
297. Carter & Harland *Contract Law in Australia* 734 (3d ed., Butterworths 1996).
298. Obiter comment made in *Baltic Shipping Co v. Dillon* (1993) 176 CLR 344 by Chief Justice Mason.
299. *Restitution Law in Australia* 1995 paras 305–309 and 1228–12231 Mason and Carter cited in *Cheshire & Fifoot's Law of Contract*, 7th Australian Edition 1997 at 721.

contract is clear). The agreement may provide that termination of the contract is to ensue upon the occurrence of a stipulated event. The agreement to terminate is in itself a binding contract, with consideration in the form of a promise to release the other party from its contractual obligations. Otherwise, a contract may be terminated under an agreement known as 'accord and satisfaction'. A party under a contractual obligation to another may purchase a release from this obligation by offering something of value as consideration. The agreement to release is known as the 'accord' and the consideration is known as 'satisfaction'. A contract embodied in a deed can only be terminated by deed at common law (this does not apply where there is a substituted agreement);[300]

- by release, in a situation in which only one party has completed its obligations, in which case the contract may be completed under seal or by providing additional consideration;[301] or by varying the terms of the original contract, such as by substituted agreement, where a new agreement is made providing for an alteration in the terms of the original contract. Fresh and valuable consideration is required. A party may unilaterally release another from his or her contractual obligations by means of a waiver of the party's rights of enforcement in relation to those obligations. The waiver may pertain to the other's contractual obligations in general terms, or may pertain to specific obligations under the contract. The waiver is unsupported by consideration, but in cases where problems of enforcement do arise, the doctrine of promissory estoppel is available to enforce the waiver; or
- by express or implied agreement, where an executed or partly performed contract is terminated. For example, the contract may be deemed to have been abandoned in circumstances where there has been a long period of inactivity by both parties in relation to the contract.[302] The implication of abandonment is defeated where there is clear evidence of an intention to keep the contract in existence.

304. In *Noble v. Ward*,[303] the court ruled that discharge may in general be accomplished orally, but it is important to note the effect of the statute of frauds on alteration of certain written contracts. It is sufficient to show that the obligation under the deed has been varied or discharged by a subsequent simple contract for valuable consideration.[304]

---

300. The strictness of the common law principle is mitigated in equity.
301. Consideration must be valuable, but need not be adequate, that is to say, it must have some value which may be independent of the value of the thing offered in return.
302. *Fitzgerald v. Masters* (1956) 95 CLR 420; *Summers v. Commonwealth* (1918) 25 CLR 144; *cf. Rian Financial Services Pty Ltd v. Alfred Investment Projects Pty Ltd* (1988) 90 FLR 215.
303. *Noble v. Ward* (1867) LR2 Ex 135.
304. *Berry v. Berry* [1929] 2 KB 316.

Chapter 6. Remedies

§1. General Provisions

305. If a breach of the conditions of the contract is established, the aggrieved party will have a right to seek damages to compensate for identified losses flowing from that breach. Remedies are the redress available to the innocent party where there has been a breach of contract, and the usual remedy is an award of damages, which is a common law as opposed to equitable remedy. They can broadly be divided according to whether:

- the contract is treated as discharged for the breach, such as when a condition or essential term of the contract is breached, at the option of the innocent party, who can then sue for damages;
- the contract is not discharged for the breach, such as where a warranty is breached, and it is therefore of a less serious nature, or where the innocent party has not elected to terminate the contract notwithstanding the existence of sufficient grounds for doing so; or
- an innocent party is faced with a breach of a condition or an anticipatory breach by the other party to the contract. Such conduct vests in the innocent party the right to elect, within a reasonable time, either to affirm or to terminate the contract. The innocent party must nevertheless have been prepared and able to perform the contract before the right of election may vest. Otherwise, he or she is not an 'innocent' party. Where the party intends the contract to remain in effect, there must be an unequivocal act of affirmation, either by words or conduct. Mere inactivity will not amount to a valid affirmation. However, undue delay in electing to terminate may mean that the party loses the right to terminate in circumstances where the position of the other party is unfairly prejudiced by the delay.[305] The innocent party may also be estopped from relying on termination where he or she has evinced an intention to keep the contract in effect. Such conduct may amount to a waiver of the right to terminate. Where the party intends the contract to end and the parties to be discharged from further obligations under the contract, there must be an unequivocal act of termination, either by words or conduct. Whether the termination needs to be communicated to the party in breach is the subject of conflicting authority.[306]

306. In addition, a remedy may be available based on estoppel, whereby under the equitable principle of estoppel, a contract is held to exist when at common law it did not. In such a case, remedies are limited to those necessary to cure the unconscionability involved, as was the case in *Waltons Stores (Interstate) v. Maher* [1988] 164 CLR 387. In that case the High Court found that when the legal representatives of the defendant prevaricated over their client's signature on contract documents and encouraged the plaintiff to commence building work, on the assumption that this had in fact taken place, their existed a binding contract and Waltons was

305. *Sargant v. ASL Developments Ltd* (1974) 131 CLR 634.
306. *Wood Factory Pty Ltd v. Kiritos Pty Ltd* (1985) 2 NSWLR 105.

estopped from denying its existence. A failure to perform a contractual obligation without lawful excuse amounts to actual breach of contract. A breach may be compared with the concept of anticipatory breach, or repudiation, which arises when a party expressly or impliedly evinces an intention not to be bound by the contract prior to the time of performance of the contract. While an actual breach does not necessarily give rise to a right by the other party to terminate, conduct amounting to an anticipatory breach implicitly gives rise to a right to terminate. Conduct amounting to repudiation must be motivated by an unwillingness or an inability to perform the contractual obligations. A party that does not intend to abandon the performance of the contract cannot be viewed as having repudiated it.[307] The test of intention is objective.

307. Remedies may range from self help (where the parties sort out the problem between themselves by direct or even assisted negotiation and without recourse to the legal system), through mediation to court decisions issuing injunctions, making orders for damages or compelling performance.

I. Tortious and Equitable Relief

308. Where the strict application of the law of contract (known as the 'black letter' approach to law) would produce an unjust or unreasonable result, the innocent party may seek as an alternate remedy relief under either tort or equity, but damages as a general rule are not recoverable for disappointment, distress, injured feelings or mere inconvenience. In *Dillon v. Baltic Shipping Co 'Mikhail Lermontov'* [308] the court held that as the plaintiff had enjoyed eight days out of a nine-day cruise, there had not been a total failure of consideration, and to award full restitution of the fare in addition to damages would represent excessive compensation.

309. There exists a range of equitable remedies, and it has been said that the list of available equitable actions is not closed and is therefore always open to addition. The list of available remedies includes:

- specific performance (i.e., an order compelling the responsible party to complete their obligations under the contract, rather than pay damages), which is dealt with below;
- injunctions;
- rescission; and
- unconscionability (see *Waltons Stores (Interstate) v. Maher*,[309] dealt with above.

II. Injunctions

310. An Injunction is an order of the court restraining a person from doing a wrongful act. In contract law, this means prohibiting a party from breaching

---

307. *Nina's Bar v. MBE Corporation (Sydney)* (1984) 3 NSWLR 613 at p. 615.
308. *Dillon v. Baltic Shipping Co 'Mikhail Lermontov'* (1993) 176 CLR 344.
309. *Waltons Stores (Interstate) v. Maher* [1988] 164 CLR 387.

contractual obligations by order. It is important to note that there are restrictions on when and for how long injunctions will be ordered, and the court will not grant an injunction where:

(i) an order for specific performance would accomplish the desired result;
(ii) the contract is for personal services; or
(iii) the effect would be to require specific performance.

Specific performance (on which see *below*) is an order of the court requiring a party to perform their obligations under a contract, in effect enforcing the original agreement as between the parties. The rules for its application are cited under §2. Specific performance and injunctions *astreinte* below. In *Page One Records Ltd v. Britton*,[310] a music group, The Troggs, dismissed their manager and, despite having signed an agreement not to hire any other manager for five years, proceeded to hire a new one. Briton sought an injunction preventing them from doing so, but this was denied, as the court felt that to have done so would have had the effect of enforcing a contract for personal services, as any rock group must have a manager to operate, and to do this would be against public policy and could not guarantee the desired result. An injunction will however be granted to enforce negative covenants (i.e., promises not to do something), and in *Beyond Productions Pty Ltd v. Curro*,[311] an injunction was granted to prevent the host of television station Channel Seven's show 'Beyond 2000' from switching to rival Channel Nine's 60 minutes show in direct breach of a contractual undertaking not to act as a presenter for anyone else's show. The courts may enforce a prohibitory injunction to stop or prevent a continuing or threatened breach of contract

311. Rescission may be available where there is a vitiating factor in existence at the time of the formation of the contract (e.g., where there is actionable misrepresentation), and the contract is rendered void or voidable (at the option of the innocent party). Where the contract is voided, it is terminated retrospectively as well as prospectively *ab initio*, and the law treats the contract as if it had never existed.

III. Injunctive Relief as an Aid to Damages

312. There are some specialist injunctions available not as remedies in contract but as the tools for obtaining this, the most prominent of which is the 'Mareva' injunction, which is a legal procedure initially devised by the English courts, and the 'Anton Piller' order. The first of these gained its name from one of the initial cases in which such an injunction was granted, *Mareva Campania Naviera SA v. International Bulk Carriers SA*.[312] In *Jackson v. Sterling Industries Ltd*[313] the High

310. *Page One Records Ltd v. Britton* [1968] 1 WLR 157.
311. *Beyond Productions Pty Ltd v. Curro* (1993) 30 NSWLR 337.
312. *Mareva Campania Naviera SA v. International Bulk Carriers SA* [1980] 1 All ER 213 [1975] 2 Lloyd's Rep 509.
313. *Jackson v. Sterling industries Ltd* (1987) 162 CLR 612; 71 ALR 457.

Court expressly recognized it and held that, as a general proposition, it should now be accepted in Australia that a Mareva injunction can be granted if the circumstances are such that there is danger of the defendant absconding, or a danger of his or her assets being removed from the jurisdiction or disposed of within the jurisdiction, or otherwise dealt with so that there is a real danger that a successful plaintiff will not be able to have his or her judgment satisfied. The High Court further expressed the view that the Mareva jurisdiction is based on the court's power to prevent an abuse of its process. Any attempt by a defendant to frustrate the enforcement of judgment, for example by moving or concealing assets, is an abuse of its process.

A Mareva injunction may be granted either before or after judgment has been obtained, and even in support of a costs order prior to taxation of costs. To this end, it represents a limited exception to the general rule that a plaintiff must obtain their court judgment and then enforce it.[314]

Another injunction available in contract dispute that is not itself a remedy but, as with a Mareva injunction, is a means for obtaining a remedy, is an *Anton Piller order*. In *Anton Piller K.G. v. Manufacturing Processes Ltd* [315] the plaintiff filed an affidavit ex parte (without notice to the defendant, its UK agent) that the agent was selling confidential design information to other companies. The court granted an order, again ex parte, allowing the plaintiff to search the defendant's premises and remove documents belonging to the plaintiff. Strictly speaking, this was not a 'civil search warrant' because it did not allow the plaintiff to enter at will. It had the same effect, however, because it directed the defendant, on pain of being held in contempt of court, to the entry and the seizure of the documents. As with an interim freezing injunction, the plaintiff must demonstrate that it has an extremely strong prima facie case, the actual or potential damage to the plaintiff must be very serious, there must be clear evidence that the defendant has incriminating documents or other evidence, there must be a real possibility that the defendant might destroy them and that the harm likely to be caused to the defendant and his business by the order is not excessive or out of proportion to the legitimate object of the order. Like freezing injunctions, an Anton Piller order may also require the defendant to disclose where certain assets, information or evidence are located (e.g., bank accounts). However, the courts have generally been more reluctant to order a defendant to produce documents that are held abroad, on the theory that this may intrude on a foreign state's sovereignty.

§2. Specific Performance and Injunctions Astreinte

313. As noted above, specific performance is an order of the court requiring a party to perform their obligations under a contract, in effect enforcing the original agreement as agreed between the parties. The awarding of this type of injunction is generally restricted to particular circumstances, and will not be granted in the following circumstances:

314. Legal Database of the Australian Taxation Office.
315. *Anton Piller K.G. v. Manufacturing Processes Ltd*, 1976 1 All ER 779 [1976] Ch. 55 (CA).

- where damages are considered by the court to provide an adequate remedy for breach of contract;
- where the contract is for personal services;
- where performance of the contract would require constant supervision by the court; or
- where the order is not mutually available.

Injunctions for specific performance will however be granted in the following instances:

- contracts for the sale of land and buildings;
- contracts for the sale of personal property; and
- other circumstances as determined by the court.

In *Turner v. Bladin* [316] the court found that a threatened refusal to perform a contract was sufficient to entitle the other party to apply for an order directing specific performance. In *Ryan v. Tontine Westminster Chambers Assoc* [317] the court held that specific performance will not be granted where the court cannot supervise its enforcement, such as in the case before it, in building contracts.

314. *Astreinte*, or the German *Geldstrafen*, is a civil law concept referring to a pecuniary court order supplementing a main order if the latter is not executed within the time-limit prescribed by the court. Fixed at a certain sum payable for each day of non-execution, it is intended to coerce the obligor into executing the main order under the threat of the mounting debt that it would otherwise incur. In France, for instance, it can be used as a means of enforcement against an employer who has been ordered to supply a certificate of employment to an employee or to a public authority such as the Employment Service (for the purposes of awarding and calculating unemployment benefits, etc.).[318] It is not available under Australian law.[319]

§3. Termination

315. This is covered in detail in Chapter 5 above.

316. *Turner v. Bladin* (1951) 82 CLR 463.
317. *Ryan v. Tontine Westminster Chambers Assoc* [1893] 1 Ch. 116.
318. Bulletin sur la terminologie juridique anglais-français Dictionnaire du droit privé français, Serge Braudo at www.dictionnaire-juridique.com/dictionnaire-juridique.php.
319. Some guidance for common law acceptance may be found in the Supreme Court of South Africa case of *Stassen v. Stoffberg* (1973) (3) SA 725 (C).

§4. *Exceptio Non Adimpleti Contractus* (The Defence of Non-Performance by the Other Party)

316. Non-performance is not the same as a breach of contract, since it may be excused.[320] *Exceptio non adimpleti contractus* is a principle available under civil law and, under some circumstances, under common law. The grounds for its application in the former could be generally described as force majeure and, under the common law, as impossibility of performance and frustration. It represents an exception to the normal laws of contract regarding adherence by both parties to the terms of their contract.

317. Although in general terms the common law of Australia follows the principle that performance of an obligation may be withheld if the other party has itself failed to perform the same or a related obligation, the principle of *exceptio non adimpleti contractus* has not been directly absorbed into its common law.[321] There are different types of loss recoverable at law where one party has not performed their obligations under the contract, and in order to be liable, the defaulting party must contemplate the kind of loss suffered, but not necessarily the exact amount of loss suffered. The categories of loss for which the party may be liable are financial loss (which includes the loss of a real chance of economic gain), and non-financial loss.[322] Subject to what the parties have specifically provided in the contract, unliquidated damages at common law may be available, with reliance damages being prima facie recoverable to compensate the innocent party for expenses incurred in entering the contract and performing his or her obligations under the contract.[323] In addition, expectation damages may be awarded for lost profits, in which case the date of assessment for such damages is the date of breach, and inflation must be taken into account where applicable.

§5. Faulty Behaviour of the Debtor

318. As the a contract in Australia is regarded as a bargain between parties that acquire rights and incur responsibilities, the parties are required to completely and without qualification complete their obligations under the contract in order to be able to regard themselves as discharged from further obligations and to be eligible to claim the benefits due to them. It follows, that if one party defaults on its obligations, then they incur a liability to all other parties to the contract. The extent of this liability is determined using the processes detailed in *Breach* at Chapter 5 above.

---

320. *Breach of Contract* M.P. Furmston (1992) *40 American Journal of Comparative Law* 671.
321. There is weak common law authority in the Scottish case of *Luigi Macari v. Celtic Football and Athletic Co Ltd* 8 Jun. 1999 Scot SC.
322. *David Securities Pty Ltd v. Commonwealth Bank of Australia* (1990) 93 ALR 271 at 293.
323. *Amann Aviation Pty Ltd v. Commonwealth of Australia* (1990) 92 ALR 601 at.610.

§6. Limitation of Actions

319. Under the limitation of actions legislation in all states and in the Australian Capital Territory (ACT), as a general rule an action for breach of contract must be commenced within six years of the breach occurring.[324] Where a contract is under seal or falls within the 'specialty' classification, the statutory periods are twelve years in the ACT,[325] New South Wales,[326] the Northern Territory,[327] Queensland[328] and Tasmania.[329] In South Australia and Victoria the period is fifteen years, and in Western Australia it is twenty years. Unusually in the common law of Australia, however, with respect to contractual agreements, such legislation is subject to any agreement made by the parties, and in, for example, *Port Jackson Stevedoring Pty Ltd v. Salmond & Spraggon (Aust) Pty Ltd*,[330] the High Court upheld a one-year limit specified in the contract. In addition, one of the parties may waive the limitation period and thereby be estopped from seeking its application as in the *Commonwealth v. Verwayen*.[331] In that case, the Commonwealth of Australia, in its defence in an action brought by a sailor who was injured when his ship was run down and sunk by an Australian aircraft carrier, sought the protection of the statutory limitation period, but was held to have itself previously assured potential claimants that it would not argue the statute of limitations in defence of the claim.

320. In all cases, the time runs from the time that the breach occurs, and this in turn depends on the terms and construction of the contract itself. The fact that the damage might not actually be suffered until sometime after that date does not automatically extend the limitation period, although this may be done through the mutual agreement of the parties. Generally, part payment or acknowledgment by the party liable for the debt may extend the period by restarting the period of limitation, although these provisions are not uniform throughout Australia.

321. If there is fraud or mistake involved, in most States and Territories the period does not begin to run until the plaintiff has discovered the fraud or mistake, or should reasonably have done so, with the courts generally having the discretion to extend the time appropriately.

322. Generally, although equitable actions are not affected by the statute of limitations (except where this can be achieved through analogy) and where the suit in equity corresponds with an action at common law, the same limits will be applied. It is possible, however, for a court sitting in equity to refuse relief where there has

324. In the Northern Territory, and in the Commonwealth under the *Australian Consumer Law* 2010, the period is three years.
325. *Limitation Act 1985* s. 13.
326. *Limitation Act 1969* s. 16.
327. *Limitation Act 1981* s. 14.
328. *Limitation of Actions Act 1974* s. 10(3).
329. *Limitation Act 1974* s. 4(3).
330. *Port Jackson Stevedoring Pty Ltd v. Salmond & Spraggon (Aust) Pty Ltd* (1978) 132 CLR 231.
331. *Commonwealth v. Verwayen* (1990) 170 CLR 394; 95 ALR 321.

been unacceptable delay in bringing an action (*laches*), on the grounds that to do so would be unjust,[332] with the onus on the party arguing *laches*.

§7. Damages and Exemption Clauses

323. As discussed above, damages generally form the basic common law remedy for a breach of contract and form compensation for the innocent party, payable by the party responsible for the breach. The common law provides for the calculation of damages in such circumstances. In *Hungerfords v. Walker*,[333] the High Court ruled that under this rule, non-compensatory damages, such as punitive or exemplary damages, will not be awarded. Termination is not required for a right to damages to arise.[334]

Damages are divided into:

- ordinary damages (the most important kind, and that flow from the loss);
- nominal damages (where there has been an infringement of a legal right, but the plaintiff is unable to establish that they have actually suffered a loss; such damages are usually a token sum, e.g., one dollar). As noted above, a party found by a court to have breached a contract, where no quantifiable loss can be found, will nonetheless be held liable for nominal damages;[335] and
- exemplary damages (that are awarded not only to compensate the injured party but also to punish the party in default as appropriate in the circumstances).

The contractual remedies for breach and anticipatory breach are distinct from the remedy of rescission, which may be pursued in respect of a vitiating factor affecting the formation of the contract. The most common remedy sought for the unlawful termination of an unperformed or partly performed contract is that of damages.

324. The general principle in damages is that the innocent party should be placed to the extent possible in the position they would have been but for the breach. In *Robinson v. Harman*,[336] it was held that 'where a party sustains a loss by reason of a breach of contract, he is, so far as money can do it, to be placed in the same situation, with respect to damages, as if the contract had been performed'. More recently, in *Commonwealth v. Amman Aviation Pty Ltd*, the High Court adopted the finding in *Robinson v. Harman*. Whereas unliquidated damages pertain to those that are not certain and that are assessable in accordance with the above principles, liquidated damages refer to those that take the form of a certain sum stipulated under a contractual term to be payable for a breach of contract.

325. A decision to award damages for breach of contract will require that:

---

332. R.P. Meagher, W.M.C Gummow, & J.L.R Lehane, *Equity: Doctrines and Remedies* 800 (3d ed., Butterworths 1992).
333. *Hungerfords v. Walker* (1989) 63 ALJR 210 perv Mason, C.J. and Wilson, J.
334. *Luna Park (NSW) Ltd v. Tramways Advertising Pty Ltd* (1938) 61 CLR 286.
335. *Ibid.*
336. *Robinson v. Harman* (1848) 1 Ex 850 at 855; 154 ER 363 at 365.

- a loss was incurred by the plaintiff;
- the loss was the result of that breach;
- the loss was of a foreseeable kind; and
- it could not have been prevented by a reasonable attempt to mitigate the loss.

In these circumstances, a loss is considered to have occurred where the benefit actually gained under the contract is less than the actual outcome achieved, and it is this amount that is generally awarded in damages. The onus of proving failure to mitigate[337] or take reasonable actions to offset the impending loss is on the defaulting party.[338] A claim for damages is subject to the principle of causation, which provides that monetary compensation can only be sought in relation to those losses 'caused' by the breach of the defaulting party.[339] The claim for damages is limited to those losses that can 'fairly and reasonably be considered (as) either arising naturally according to the usual course of things from such a breach of contract, or such as may reasonably be supposed to have been in the reasonable contemplation of the parties at the time they made the contract, as a probable breach of it.'[340] A probable breach has been interpreted as a breach that causes a real, serious or significant risk of loss in order to be deemed not too remote. The causal nexus between the breach of the defaulting party and the loss of the innocent party is determined by a *sine qua non* (but for) test. A prima facie nexus will be broken by the interruption of a wholly unpredictable supervening event that becomes the dominant causal factor. The act of the defaulting party need not however be the sole cause of the loss.[341] Where there are other causal events operating to bring about the loss, the defaulting party's act must amount to a significant, rather than peripheral, contribution to the loss.

326. The calculation of any award of damages is a two-stage process. The first of these involves establishing whether damages should be awarded on the basis that a contract exists, and then if they should, the second stage involves calculation of the quantum (the amount) of the damages. The court will look to the following issues:

- whether the loss has been incurred will be a matter of evidence;
- whether the loss was the result of the breach is a matter of causation, with the English case of *Hadley v. Baxendale* [342] establishing the principle that the party who is in breach of the contract is liable for damages to the other party for losses

337. The duty to mitigate requires a party claiming loss due to a breach to endeavour to find a viable alternative, serving to reduce the loss claimed, and serves to deny recovery of any part of damages that could have been reasonably avoided. 'Reasonably avoided' has no specific definition, but generally means what a reasonable person would do under similar circumstances. An innocent party is not required to take extraordinary efforts or sacrifice any substantial right to avoid losses from a breach of contract.
338. *TCN Channel Nine Pty Ltd v. Hayden Enterprises Pty Ltd* (1989) 16 NSWLR 130 at 158; *Goldburg v. Shell Oil Co of Australia Ltd* (1990) 95 ALR 711 at 713.
339. *Hadley v. Baxendale* (1854) 9 Ex 341; 156 ER 145.
340. *Ibid.*, at.354 *per* Alderson B.
341. *Alexander v. Credit Cambridge Corp Ltd* (1987) 9 NSWLR 310 at 314–315.
342. *Hadley v. Baxendale* (1854) 156 ER 145.

arising naturally from the breach, i.e., losses occurring in the usual or normal course of things (flowing naturally) from the breach; or losses that are actually contemplated by the parties as a probable result of the breach, i.e., losses occurring as the result of exceptional circumstances where such circumstances were made known to the party in breach, so that they could have reasonably foreseen and considered them if the contract were to be broken;

- an attempt must be made by the party seeking damages to mitigate their loss. That is to say they must do whatever is reasonable to offset their loss. This may be by any means, for example, by sourcing goods from an alternate supplier even if to do so would result in additional expenditure (that would be recoverable under the head of damages). In *Brace v. Caulder* [343] it was held that a person discharged from employment would be obliged to accept a reasonable offer of new employment in a similar type of job or else be limited to nominal damages only. However, this requirement is not stringently applied, with the burden of proof on the defendant to prove it has not been attempted;[344] and
- where there is no strict entitlement to damages based on the existence of a contract under the usual tests, the court may apply quasi-contractual remedies (see Chapter 13 for further details). These compel the payment of money by one party to another in circumstances where it would be unjust for that party to retain money or some other benefit at the expense of the other. The recovery of money by means of a quasi-contractual remedy need not be grounded in an agreement between the parties (see quantum meruit *above*) – for example, an action to recover a reasonable price for goods or services supplied in circumstances where the defaulting party has breached his or her obligation to pay for them as stipulated under the contract. Alternatively, an action can be sought where the contract is unenforceable because it did not comply with a particular formality, or where the contract is void, thereby excluding the pursuit of contractual remedies. A party may sue to recover money paid under a contract where there has been total failure of consideration under the contract, or where the money was paid as a result of a mistake of fact or under compulsion or duress.[345] Money cannot be recovered where the payment can be construed as a gift. In addition to common-law and equitable remedies, specific legislation such as the *Australian Consumer Law 2010 (Cth)* and fair trading act of each State and Territory will authorize remedies in addition to, and often subject to fewer restrictions, than those available at common law. An example of this is the remedy of corrective advertising that is available for a breach of the *Australian Consumer Law*.[346]

I. Defences

327. Contributory negligence is a defence to actions for breach of contract and acts to negate the claims of the other party, either in full or in part, depending on

343. *Brace v. Caulder* [1895] 2 QB 253.
344. *Payzu v. Saunders* [1919] 2 KB 581.
345. *David Securities v. Commonwealth Bank of Australia* (1992) 175 CLR 353 at 356.
346. See s246(s)(d) of the Australian Consumer Law (Schedule 2, *Competition and Consumer Act 2010*).

the circumstances. The court apportions damages recoverable in tort actions according to what it judges to be the 'fault' of the party.

II. Establishing the Quantum

328. Once the conditions for an award of damages have been satisfied, then the quantum of those damages must be calculated, and the courts again have given guidance as to how this is to be achieved. Broadly, the rule established in *Commonwealth v. Amman Aviation Pty Ltd* (see *below*) is applied, but only after the court is satisfied that there has been no provision for such calculation made in the terms of the contract itself. Where such a provision has been made, these are termed 'liquidated damages', applying only where the plaintiff is able to sue for a precise, fixed sum in compensation for their claimed loss, usually included as a express (and clear and unambiguous) term of the contract. *Wallis v. Smith* [347] established the rule that 'liquidated damages means that it shall be taken as the sum that the parties have by the contract assessed as the damages to be paid, whatever may be the actual damage', although the court retains the right to limit these under the rule against enforcing unconscionable penalties. A liquidated damages clause that was adjudged to be 'out of all proportion' or 'extravagant, exorbitant or unconscionable' in all the circumstances[348] will be declared void.

329. Unliquidated damages apply where it is not possible to assess the quantum of damages in this way, and instead an estimate is made of the loss, based on all of the facts tendered in court.[349]

330. There is a traditional and important distinction between contract damages and tort damages. Whereas contract damages seek to put the claimant in the position that they would have been in had the contract been performed, tort damages aim to put them in the position they would have been had the tort not been committed.[350] In *Commonwealth v. Amman Aviation Pty Ltd* [351] the court held that damages can generally be assessed as (a) expectation damages and (b) reliance damages, a distinction that is perhaps somewhat illusory, as there exists a considerable degree of overlap. Expectation damages are generally regarded as being those damages applicable where the claimant is awarded the full value of the expectancy created by the contract, and reliance damages are those applicable where the damages are intended to 'undo' the harm that their reliance on the promise of defendant has caused.[352]

---

347. *Wallis v. Smith* (1882) 21 ChD 243 at 267.
348. *AMEV-UDC Finance Ltd v. Austin* (1986) 162 CLR 170 at 190.
349. *Dunlop Pneumatic Tyre Co v. New Garage and Motor Co Ltd* [1915] AC 79.
350. *Gates v. City Mutual Life Assurance Society Ltd* (1986) 160 CLR 1 at 11–12.
351. *Commonwealth v. Amman Aviation Pty Ltd* (1991) 174 CLR 64.
352. G.C. Cheshire, N.C. Seddon & M.P. Ellinghaus, *Cheshire & Fifoot's Law of Contract* 778–780 (Butterworths 1997).

III. Exemption Clauses

331. Exemption clauses are more commonly known in Australia as limitation of liability or exclusion clauses, and are inserted into a contract to allocate risk to a party or parties to a contract in ordinary commercial transactions. This often dictates which party should take out insurance against that risk. Although there is sometimes an attempt to use these in consumer transactions, they risk offending against the *Australian Consumer Law 2010* (Cth) that takes precedence over any purported contractual agreement. Australian courts have adopted the *contra proferentem* rule, which means that an exclusion clause will be construed by the court against the person seeking the benefit of such a clause, and in doing so have limited its attractiveness. In *Darlington Futures Ltd v. Delco Aust Pty Ltd*,[353] the High Court found that in a commercial setting such clauses are allowed on the basis that businesses can be expected to have a greater knowledge of the law and its application, and, correspondingly, less need for protection against poor judgment. By contrast, in the consumer case of *Bright v. Sampson and Duncan Enterprises Pty Ltd*,[354] the NSW Court of Appeal appears to have gone to great lengths to find fault with such a clause. In such cases, damages will be applied according to the principles laid down above.

§8. Restitution

332. Restitution is available if the court feels that compelling the payment of money by A to B would be equitable because it would be unjust to allow A to retain the benefit of money, goods or services that A has received from B. It exists outside of contract law, and is always available to the court, but only to the innocent party, and therefore may not be awarded to a party in breach of contract. This amount may be an amount equal to money paid or the value of goods or service supplied, in which case, the court will assess them on a quantum meruit basis. In *Pavey & Mathews Pty Ltd v. Paul*[355] the High Court held that quantum meruit is available in restitution or to prevent unjust enrichment because of the client's acceptance of benefits from the builder's performance of an unenforceable oral contract (legislation required it to be in writing). Goff and Jones[356] identify three essential elements that underlie the principle of unjust enrichment:

(1) the defendant must have been *enriched* by the receipt of a benefit;
(2) the benefit must have been *gained at the claimant's expense;* and
(3) it would be *unjust* to allow the defendant to retain the benefit.

353. *Darlington Futures Ltd v. Delco Aust Pty Ltd* [1986] HCA 82; (1986) 161 CLR 500 FC 86/083.
354. *Bright v. Sampson and Duncan Enterprises Pty Ltd* (1985) 1 NSWLR 346.
355. *Pavey & Mathews Pty Ltd v. Paul* (1987) 162 CLR 221.
356. Jones, Goff and Jones Law of Restitution (7th ed., 2007) 1-106, and see also *Lumbers v. W Cook Builders Pty Ltd (in liquidation)* (2008) 232 CLR 635 per Gummow, Crennan and Keifel JJ.

Part II. Specific Contracts

Chapter 1. Agency

§1. Introduction

333. Agency law is about the relationship between a principal, an agent and a third party.[357] The parties involved as follows:

(i) the agent – this person is authorized to act on behalf of a principal;
(ii) the principal – the person represented by the agent; and
(iii) the third party – the person who the agent brings into a legal relationship with the principal.

334. Strictly speaking, any contract formed will be between the principal and the third party. The agent only acts as an intermediary. The legal meaning of agent is narrower than the conversational meaning. Agents can take many forms, these can include the following:

(i) a universal agent with unrestricted authority to act on behalf of the principal (e.g., by way of power of attorney);
(ii) a general agent – that is, a person authorized to act for a particular matter usually within the normal business of the principal (e.g., a person authorized to purchase cars for a car yard);
(iii) a special agent – a person authorized to act in relation to a specific matter that is outside the normal course of events (i.e., an agent with particular expertise in antiques authorized to sell a house);
(iv) a *del credere* agent – this is a person authorized by the principal to sell goods on behalf of the principal and who guarantees that if the goods are not paid for, that the agent will pay. The agent will normally receive a higher commission for taking on this risk;
(v) a mercantile agent – a person authorized to sell goods, or assign goods, with this type of agent established under factors legislation;[358]
(vi) an insurance agent;

357. *International Harvester Co of Australia Pty Ltd v. Carrigan's Hazeldene Pastoral Co* (1958) 100 CLR 644.
358. *Mercantile Law Act* 1962 (ACT); *Factors (Mercantile Agents) Act* 1923 (NSW); *Factors Act* 1892 (Qld); *Mercantile Law Act* 1936 (SA); *Factors Act* 1891 (Tas); *Goods Act* 1958 (Vic).

(vii) an auctioneer; and
(viii) an estate agent (though it will be an unusual situation where an estate agent can sign the contract on behalf of the principal).[359]

335. An agency relationship can be created by express (in writing or orally)[360] or implied agreements (e.g., by relationship such as partnership), or by apparent authority (i.e., a holding out or representation leading to an estoppel), by operation of law (i.e., necessity);[361] or by the principal ratifying the contract made by the agent.[362] Generally, if the principal has the authority to contract in respect of a matter, then the principal can appoint an agent to act as an intermediary.[363] There are two exceptions to this. The first is where the statute prescribes that something must be executed by the principal.[364] A second exception is where the competency to undertake the act arises from the person (e.g., a statutory duty that cannot be delegated).[365] Outside of this, the only exceptions that would apply to a principal appointing an agent arise out of the normal contractual restrictions such as infancy, insanity, enemy alien, or intoxication. As the agent only acts as an intermediary, the lack of capacity of an agent to contract is not relevant. However, lack of capacity in the agent may be relevant to enforcement of the agency relationship by the principal. In certain professions, such as law, real estate and finance, pre-conditions must be met before one can act as an agent.[366] In a dispute between a third party and a principal, the third party has the onus of proof in establishing that an agency relationship existed.[367]

§2. Obligations of the Agent

336. An agent is required to:

(i) follow the directions given to her or him by the principal;
(ii) act to further the interests of the principal;
(iii) act with reasonable care;
(iv) not misuse their position;[368]
(v) not delegate;[369] and

359. *Peterson v. Moloney* (1951) 84 CLR 91.
360. In certain instances, writing will be required. For example in Tasmania where the contact of agency is to exceed one year: *Mercantile Law Act* (Tas) s. 6; and in South Australia, where the agency relationship is formed concerning the sale of a business: *Land and Business (Sale and Conveyancing) Act* s. 21.
361. An example of which can be seen in *Burns Philp & Co Ltd v. Gillepsie Bros Pty Ltd* (1947) 74 CLR 148.
362. *Bolton Partners v. Lambert* (1889) 41 ChD 295.
363. *Deputy Commissioner of Taxation (Vic) v. Boxshall* (1988) 19 FCR 435; 83 ALR 175.
364. *Christie v. Permewan, Wright & Co Ltd* (1904) 1 CLR 693.
365. *Corsellis v. London County Council* [1908] 1 Ch. 13.
366. These professions all have specific educational qualifications that must be met.
367. *Hoare v. McCarthy* (196) 22 CLR 296.
368. *Consul Developments Pty Ltd v. DPC Estates Pty Ltd* (1975) 132 CLR 373. This is part of the agent's fiduciary obligations to the principal.
369. See *John McCann & Co v. Pow* [1975] 1 All ER 129.

(vi) keep separate the proceeds of the principal's money from the agent's personal monies.[370]

An example of a failing to follow the directions given by the principal can be seen in *Bertram, Armstrong & Co v. Godfrey*.[371] The stockbroker was instructed to sell shares at a certain price. He failed to do so, and was subsequently forced to sell at a lower price. The plaintiff was able to recover the difference. The agent can also be liable where he fails to clarify the principal's instructions.[372] Another illustration can be seen in *Mitor Investments Pty Ltd v. General Accident Fire and Life Assurance Co Ltd*.[373] In this case, an insurance broker was instructed to obtain cover for flooding (with the direction given that the cover was to provide protection for flooding by any means). In doing so, he failed to obtain cover where the flooding was caused by the sea; however, he advised the insured that the cover sought had been obtained. When the area was flooded by the sea, the agent was held liable to the principal. Two reasons were advanced. First, the agent had failed to follow instructions. Second, the agent had been negligent in advising the plaintiff that the appropriate cover had been obtained. As noted, an agent must act in the interests of the principal. This will be breached where there is a conflict of interest. An example of this can be seen in *Lintrose Nominees Pty Ltd v. King*.[374] The buyer commissioned an agent to find an investment property for him. The agent sold a property that was owned by the agent's father and brother. The lack of disclosure entitled the buyer to rescind the contract.

337. Two further points should also be noted. A professional agent with particular expertise is likely to have a higher standard of care.[375] An agent who receives a bribe is in breach of duty, and is liable to civil and criminal consequences.[376]

§3. The Principal's Obligations

338. The principal is required to:

(i) remunerate the agent as per the agreement between the two;[377] and
(ii) reimburse the agent for any liabilities or payments made in dealing on behalf of the principal (with this giving the agent a lien over the property of the principal until the agent is paid).

---

370. *Re Todd (No. 2)* (1910) SR (NSW) 490.
371. (1830) 12 ER 364.
372. *Veljkovic v. Vrbogen* [1985] VR 419.
373. [1984] WAR 365.
374. [1995] 1 VR 575.
375. *Yates Property Corp Pty Ltd (in liq) v. Boland* (1988) 85 FCR 84 – matter was reversed on appeal, though this point was not questioned: *Boland v. Yates Property Corp Pty Ltd* (1999) 167 ALR 575.
376. *Boston Deep Sea Fishing and Ice Co v. Ansell* (1888) 39 Ch. D 339. The criminal offence breached is Conspiracy to Defraud.
377. *Luxor (Eastbourne) Ltd v. Cooper* [1941] AC 108.

339. For the agent to be remunerated, the transaction must result from the agency.[378] A remote connection between the agent and the transaction is insufficient.[379] The indemnity the agent enjoys extends to the full amount of the losses incurred by the agent[380] and, to claim the lien, the goods must be held pursuant to the agency under which he or she claims the lien.[381]

§4. EFFECTS OF DIRECT REPRESENTATION

340. Actual authority is given to an agent by express agreement with the principal. Actual authority can also be implied where the intention of the parties is to give the agent the authority, or where it is necessary to give business efficacy to the contract.[382] Words or conduct can extend the ambit of a written authority.[383] Where there is a lack of express direction, the agent is entitled to use her or his discretion to act in the best manner possible.[384]

§5. APPARENT AUTHORITY

341. Express authority provides less concern to the Court than apparent (or, as it is sometimes known, ostensible) authority. In this scenario, the principal can be liable to a third party on the basis that, by the words or conduct of the principal, there has been a representation that the principal has conferred authority on the agent. The question of the extent of this apparent authority was considered in the decision of *Panorama Developments (Guildford) Ltd v. Fidelis Furnishing Fabrics Ltd.*[385] The secretary of a company hired cars purportedly for the company's use, but in reality for his own use. The company was held liable to the third party on the basis that a contemporary company secretary has the apparent authority to be able to enter such contracts. This case reversed previous authority that held that a company secretary was limited in what they could do.[386]

342. The third party cannot rely on apparent authority where they have knowledge that the authority of the agent is restricted.[387] In addition, apparent authority cannot be relied upon where the person holding out that an individual has authority has only apparent authority himself or herself.[388]

378. *LJ Hooker Ltd v. WJ Adams Estates Pty Ltd* (1977) 138 CLR 52.
379. *Moran v. Hull* [1967] 1 NSWR 723.
380. *Jones v. Canavan* [1972] 2 NSWLR 236.
381. *Barratt v. Gough-Thomas* [1951] Ch. 242.
382. *Australia and New Zealand Bank Ltd v. Ateliers de Constructions Electriques de Charleroi* (1966) 39 ALJR 414.
383. *Pole v. Leask* (1860) 28 Beav 562; 54 ER 481.
384. *Donaldson v. Noble* (1888) 14 VLR 1021.
385. [1971] 2 QB 711. See also *Freeman & Lockyer v. Buckhurst Park Properties (Mangal) Ltd* [1964] 1 QB 480.
386. See generally *Osborne v. Boral Resources (NSW) Pty Ltd* [2012] NSWCA 155.
387. *Overbrooke Estates Ltd v. Glencombe Properties Ltd* [1974] 3 All ER 511.
388. *Crabtree Vickers Pty Ltd v. Australian Direct Mail Advertising & Addressing Co Pty Ltd* [1975] 133 CLR 72.

§6. Relationship between Agent and Third Party

343. The agent will not normally be liable to the third party. The contract has been made on behalf of the principal and it is this person that is responsible.[389] However, the agent will be liable where he or she has failed to make it clear that they have acted on behalf of another. Similarly, the agent will be liable where the circumstances indicate that the intent was to contract personally.[390] The agent can also be liable where they contract on behalf of a non-existent principal.[391] Other times when the agent will be liable include the agent executing a deed in her or his own name,[392] the agent signing a bill of exchange in her or his own name,[393] the agent contracting as principal,[394] trade usage renders the agent liable,[395] or where liability is imposed pursuant to the contract as agreed.[396]

344. The agent will not be liable where the existence of a principal is known, but the name of this person is not disclosed.[397] If neither the fact of agency is disclosed, nor the name of the principal is disclosed (i.e., the doctrine of undisclosed principal), the third party has the option of either proceeding against the agent or the principal, though either of the agent or the principal can also sue the third party.[398] The third party must elect who they are to proceed against. An example of the doctrine of undisclosed principal can be seen in the High Court decision of *Construction Engineering (Aust) Pty Ltd v. Hexyl Pty Ltd.*[399] The appellants contracted with an owner of land for the construction of a building development. The owner and Hexyl had previously entered into a relationship concerning the building. This relationship provided that the owner should contract as principal. When a dispute arose between Construction Engineering and the owner, and with Construction Engineering becoming aware of the agreement with Hexyl, Construction sought to join Hexyl as a party to the litigation. This was denied by the High Court – the owner had not purported to contract for Hexyl, and Construction neither knew or believed Hexyl to be a party to the agreement.

345. The undisclosed principal doctrine will not operate unless the principal is in existence and identifiable at the time of making the contract.[400]

---

389. *Wakefield v. Duckworth* [1915] 1 KB 218.
390. *Cooper v. Fisken* (1912) 18 ALR 155.
391. Such as may happen in the steps leading to the formation of a company, though the circumstances may show that no personal liability was intended: *Black v. Smallwood* (1966) 117 CLR 52.
392. *Chapman v. Smith* [1907] 2 Ch. 97.
393. *Bills of Exchange Act* 1909 (Cth) s. 31.
394. *Whinfield v. Lovell* [1926] VLR 185.
395. *Cooper v. Gardiner* (1902) 19 WN (NSW) 54.
396. Such as in circumstances where the agent is the real principal: *Salim v. Ingham Enterprises Pty Ltd* (1998) 55 NSWLR 7.
397. *Southwell v. Bowditch* (1876) 1 CPD 374.
398. *Cooke v. Eshelby* (1887) 12 App Cas 271.
399. (1985) 155 CLR 541.
400. *Keighley Maxsted & Co v. Durant* [1901] AC 240.

§7. Relationship between Agent and Principal

346. The principal can be liable for the torts committed by the agent. The basis on which this is established is vicarious liability.[401] For example, in *Colonial Mutual Life Assurance Society Ltd v. Producers and Citizens Co-operative Assurance Co of Australia Ltd*[402] an insurance company was held liable for defamatory statements made by an agent during the course of the agent's employment.

347. An agent will be liable to a third party for breach of warrant of authority where the third party suggests that he or she has the authority to act on behalf of a principal, but in fact does not have such authority.[403] An action for breach of warrant of authority can only be brought by the third party, but the agent, will not liable if the third party knew of the agent's lack of authority.[404] The measure of damages in an action for breach of warrant of authority is the loss incurred.[405]

§8. Termination of Agency Agreement

348. The agency agreement can be ended in either of two ways:

(i) by the conduct of the parties; and/or
(ii) by operation of law.

349. The principal and agent can decide to terminate the relationship by agreement, by the performance of the agreement, by the agent renouncing his agency[406] or by the revocation of authority by the principal.[407] Operation of law will deem the agency relationship to be revoked where either party dies,[408] where either the agent or principal begins to suffer from a mental incapacity[409] or becomes insolvent,[410] where the subject matter of the agreement is illegal,[411] the contract is frustrated, rendered impossible or the principal becomes an enemy alien.[412] An interesting illustration of the effect of legal incapacity can be seen in *Drew v. Nunn.*[413] The principal had given authority to his wife to act as his agent and had held her out as being his agent. He later became afflicted with a mental disorder, and during this time, the wife ordered clothing apparel from a third party. The principal was held liable for

401. *Lloyd v. Grace, Smith & Co* [1912] AC 716.
402. (1931) 46 CLR 41.
403. *Black v. Smallwood* (1966) 117 CLR 52.
404. *Halbot v. Lens* [1901] 1 Ch. 344.
405. *Firbank's Executors v. Humphreys* (1886) 18 QBD 54.
406. *Balfe v. West* (1853) 13 CB 466.
407. *Tynan v. A'Beckett* [1923] VLR 412.
408. *Re Overweg* [1900] 1 Ch. 209.
409. *Wright v. Gibbons* (1954) 91 CLR 423.
410. *Salton v. New Beeston Cycle Co* [1900] 1 Ch. 43; *Markwick v. Hardingham* (1880) 15 Ch. D 339.
411. R.B. Vermeesch & K.E. Lindgren, *Business Law of Australia* 465 (LexisNexis Butterworths 2005).
412. *Ibid.*
413. (1879) 4 QBD 661.

payment (having recovered from this mental illness) as whilst his insanity had revoked his actual authority, there had been no revocation of the apparent authority.

§9. Indirect Representations

350. As noted above, indirect representations can bind the principal where that person has by their words or conduct given rise to an indication or expectation that authority has been conferred upon an agent. Thus, it will be acceptable to bind the principal to the third party, even though subsequent events reveal that this was not actually the case. In this scenario, an agency by estoppel arises. For example in *Soanes v. London & SW Rly Co*[414] a rail passenger gave his luggage to a man wearing a porter's uniform. The luggage was stolen, and the railway company denied liability on the basis that the porter was off-duty. The court held that by the indirect representation given by the railway company through the appearance of the porter, the company had authorized the person to receive the luggage, and it was therefore liable to the passenger.

§10. Broking

351. A broker can be considered a type of mercantile agent. That is, a person authorized to buy and sell on behalf of another, rather than in the broker's name. Common examples can be seen with stockbrokers, finance brokers and insurance brokers.[415] Insurance brokers are generally considered to be agents of the insured, even though their remuneration may well be by way of commission from the insurer.[416]

§11. Distributors

352. Routinely, distributors will not cause contractual relationships to be brought about between a third party and a consumer. For example, a distributor of Mercedes Benz motor cars will generally contract as principal in selling that car to the consumer. There will be no direct contractual relationship between the manufacturer and the consumer brought about by the actions of the distributor.[417]

414. (1919) 88 LJ KB 524.
415. Chapter 7 of the Corporations Act 2001 (Cth) regulates persons acting in the financial services industry.
416. See *further Insurance (Agents and Brokers) Act* 1984 (Cth). As an illustration see *Derham v. Amev Life Assurance Co Ltd* (1982) 2 ANZ Ins Cases 60-459.
417. Consumer protection legislation such as the *Competition and Consumer Act 2010* (Cth) will assist a consumer in bringing an action against a manufacturer.

Chapter 2. Bailment

§1. Introduction

353. Bailment is that situation where the bailee comes into possession of goods that belong to the bailor. As described in *Compania Portorafti Commerciale SA v. Ultramar Panama Inc (The Captain Gregos (No. 2)*[418] a bailment will result where the bailor delivers possession of goods to a bailee and the bailor has the right to receive the goods back when the bailment ends. The key components of bailment are as follows:

(i) the passing of exclusive possession by the bailor;[419]
(ii) the bailee taking possession;[420]
(iii) the bailee undertaking the responsibility to keep the goods safe;[421] and
(iv) an obligation on the bailee to return.[422]

354. Many situations illustrate the practical relevance of bailment:

(i) the loaning of goods to a person without receiving any reward (e.g., loaning of a lawn mower to a neighbour);
(ii) the deposit of goods with someone for work to be undertaken – such work without reward (e.g., leaving a lawn mower with a neighbour to fix);
(iii) the leaving of goods with another for safe custody (e.g., leaving valuables with a neighbour when going on holidays);
(iv) the hiring of chattels;
(v) the pawn or pledge of a good;
(vi) the deposit of goods for safe custody, with a charge imposed (e.g., leaving a certificate of title with a bank, with the bank charging for this service); and
(vii) the leaving of goods with another for repair (e.g., leaving a car at a motor mechanic's garage).

355. The first three categories were traditionally classified as gratuitous bailments, with the latter categories described as bailments for reward.[423] Despite the width of the concept of bailment, there must be a change in possession. This aspect was not established in *Greenwood v. Council of the Municipality of Waverley*.[424] The plaintiff hired a locker at a beach in which he put his clothes before going for a swim. The key to the locker was left with the attendant. The clothes were stolen in his absence, and the plaintiff sued the Council as bailee. He was unsuccessful.

418. [1990] 2 Lloyd's Rep 395 at 405.
419. *Midland Silicones Ltd v. Scuttons Ltd* [1949] 2 QB 171 at 189.
420. *Compania Portorafti Commerciale SA v. Ultramar Panama Inc (The Captain Gregos) (No. 2)* [1990] 2 Lloyd's Rep 395.
421. *Gilchrist Watt and Sanderson Pty Ltd v. York Products Pty Ltd* [1970] 2 NSWR 156.
422. *South Australian Insurance Co v. Randell* (1869) LR 3 PC 101.
423. The classification was taken from *Coggs v. Bernard* (1703) 92 ER 107 at 109; [1558–1774] All ER Rep 1.
424. (1928) 28 SR (NSW) 219.

The deposit of clothes in a hired space was insufficient to provide evidence of a change in possession.

§2. DUTIES OF THE BAILEE

356. The bailee has a number of duties. Most notably, they are to:

(i) take care of the goods;[425]
(ii) to not misuse the goods;[426] and
(iii) to return the goods.[427]

357. When the goods are not returned, or are returned damaged, the bailor can sue the bailee. However, and contrary to the normal position with litigation where the party bringing the action will have the burden of proof, the onus is on the bailee to show that the loss or damage was not due to any negligence on her or his part.[428] An example of bailee liability can be seen in the case of *Pitt Son & Badgery Ltd v. Proulefco SA*.[429] Bales of wool purchased from the defendant were stored at the defendant's wool store. The store was destroyed following a fire lit by an intruder. The store had inadequate security and no water sprinkler system. It was held by the High Court that the defendant was liable in negligence for failing to keep the wool secure. Another illustration of due care can be seen in *Nightingdale v. Tildsley*,[430] (a case involving the bailment of a car). Did the bailee's duty in respect of a motor vehicle extend to turning over the engine to keep it in good condition? In arguing this the bailor relied on the decision of *Scarfe v. Morgan*[431] in which a court held that a bailee of a horse was required to feed it. The Court distinguished this decision in *Nightingdale* as the bailee did not turn over the engine of his own vehicles.

358. A bailee can use exclusion clauses to limit, restrict or modify liability. However any exclusion or limitation must be in clear and unambiguous terms[432] and

---

425. *Son & Badgery Ltd v. Proulefco SA* (1984) 153 CLR 644; 52 ALR 389.
426. *Cowper v. JG Goldner Pty Ltd* (1986) 40 SASR 457; *Mulgrave v. Ogden* (1591) Cro Eliz 219; 78 ER 475.
427. *Council of the City of Sydney v. West* (1965) 114 CLR 481.
428. *Tottenham Investments Pty Ltd v. Carburettor Services Pty Ltd* (1994) Aust Torts Report 81-292, *Wicks Farming Pty Ltd v. Waraluck Mining Pty Ltd* [1996] 1 Qd R 99; *Port Swettenham Authority v. TW Wu & Co* [1979] AC 580. It should be noted that common carriers (i.e., a person who undertakes to transport goods) and common innkeepers (a person offering lodging to guests) are both under absolute liability for loss or damage of goods entrusted to them. Legislation exists to limit liability in both situations: see *Common Carriers Act* 1902 (NSW); *Carriers Act* 1891 (SA); *Carriers Act* 1920 (WA); *Common Carriers Act* 1874 (Tas); *Common Carriers Act* 1902 (ACT); *Carriers Act* 1891 (NT); *Transport Operations (Road Use Management) Act* 1995 (Qld). *Innkeepers Act* 1968 (NSW); *Carriers and Innkeepers Act* 1958 (Vic); *Liquor and Licensing Act* 1988 (WA); *Liquor and Accommodation Act* 1990 (Tas); *Civil Law (Wrongs) Act* 2002 (ACT); *Accommodation Providers Act* 1981 (NT); *Traveller Accommodation Providers (Liability) Act* 2001.
429. (1984) 153 CLR 644.
430. [1980] 7 CL 134.
431. (1838) 4 M&W 270.
432. *Paterson v. Miller* [1923] VLR 36.

must be read in light of statutory developments such as the consumer protection legislation within the *Competition and Consumer Act 2010* (Cth).[433]

359. The extent of the bailee's duty will also depend on whether the receipt is based on necessity,[434] mistake,[435] an accident[436] or simply involuntary.[437] Whilst traditionally it was thought that the greater the benefit received by the bailee, the higher the standard of care, today, the standard is to take reasonable care according to the circumstances of the case, rather than to look at the particular category in which the matter sits.[438]

360. A finder of a chattel has no obligation to take custody of it.[439] However, if the person does take it into her or his possession, then they are in the same position as a gratuitous bailee.[440]

§3. The Bailor's Duties

361. A bailor is required to notify the bailee if the goods are of a dangerous nature. In *Pivovaroff v. Chernabaeff*[441] a market gardener lent his onion sorting machine to another. The guard had been removed, but the bailor instructed the bailee not to allow children near the machine. The bailee operated the machine with the help of a 13-year old boy who was injured when his hand became caught in the machine. The bailor was not liable as the danger had been communicated to the bailee.

§4. Rights against Third Parties

362. If the bailment is determinable at will, the bailor is the individual entitled to pursue a third party who damages or interferes with the goods.[442] This will most likely be the case with gratuitous bailments. By contrast if the bailor has no immediate right to possession, such as would commonly be the case with a bailment for reward, then it is the bailee that should take action against the third party.[443] The bailor can however take action where the interference with the goods is such that it

433. The *Competition and Consumer Act 2010* does provide that any services must be provided with due care and skill. However, services as defined exclude the business transportation or storage of goods.
434. Such as some form of natural disaster, see *Mulgrave v. Ogden* (1591) Cro Eliz 219; 78 ER 475.
435. Such as where goods are given to the wrong person.
436. E.g., fruit from a branch pruned off an overhanging tree, see *Mills v. Brooker* [1919] 1 KB 555.
437. Where goods are sent unsolicited. This is now regulated by consumer protection legislation such as the *Australian Competition and Consumer Act 2010*.
438. *Houghland v. RR Low (Luxury Coaches) Ltd* [1962] 1 QB 694; [1964] 2 All ER 159.
439. *Hollins v. Fowler* (1875) LR 7 HL 757.
440. *Parker v. British Airways Board* [1982] QB 1004 at 1017.
441. (1978) 21 SASR 1.
442. R.B. Vermeesch & K.E. Lindgren, *Business Law of Australia* 731 (11th ed., LexisNexis Butterworths 2005).
443. Vermeesch & K.E. Lindgren, *Business Law of Australia* 731 (LexisNexis Butterworths 2005).

will not make it possible for the goods to be returned in an appropriate form at the end of the bailment.[444]

363. The *Personal Property Securities Act 2009* (Cth) (PPSA) which became effective in January 2012, expands the range of interests in goods which can be secured through registration. One of the most significant of these is bailment. Under bailment facilities, goods such as cars, boats or equipment is typically bailed or put in the possession of a dealer by a financier. The financier owns the goods, and when there is a pending a sale to a customer the financier sells the goods to a dealer just before hand with the financier retaining title and the seller retaining possession prior to the sale to the eventual buyer. The PPSA applies to commercial consignment of goods contexts as well to bailments. Prior to the new legislation such bailments were not typically registered but are now covered by the new act. This marks a fundamental exception to the *nemo dat* rule in that purchasers may take title to the goods where the security interests have not been registered. To protect themselves, financiers will have to be sure to register their interests so that third parties have notice.

§5. Termination of the Bailment

364. A bailment will be terminated in the following instances:[445]

(i) when the agreed purpose of the bailment ends;
(ii) when the parties agree to end the bailment;
(iii) by unilateral action (in the context of gratuitous bailments);
(iv) where the goods are destroyed; and
(v) where the bailee commits some wrongful act.

444. *Penfold Wines Pty Ltd v. Elliott* (1946) 74 CLR 204.
445. P. Latimer, *Australian Business Law* 1017 (25th ed., CCH 2005).

Chapter 3. Gaming and Wagering

§1. What is a Gaming and Wagering Contract

365. Gambling is very popular in Australia and the vast majority of Australians engage in one or more forms of gambling. Overall, gambling is a multi-billion dollar industry. Most gambling in its various forms is regulated by laws in Australia's states and territories. Online gambling is subject to Commonwealth legislation as discussed below.

The underlying feature of a gaming and wagering contract is that one party is to lose, and another party is to win, based upon a future event, the result of which is uncertain.[446] An obvious example is betting on the result of a future sporting event. By contrast to gaming and wagering contracts, betting with a totalisator agency is not a contract for gaming or wagering as the agency does not run the risk of winning or losing.[447] Gaming and wagering contracts are not supported by consideration in the formal sense of that phrase, as an individual's only stake in the matter is the amount that he or she could potentially win or lose.[448] To be considered a gaming or wagering contract, a common intention to wager must be established.[449] The substance of the transaction is to be determined, not merely its form.[450]

§2. The Enforceability of Gaming and Wagering Contracts

366. Whilst at common law gaming and wagering contracts were enforceable,[451] this position no longer applies in any Australian jurisdiction. Legislation provides that contracts for gaming and wagering are void, rather than illegal.[452] This prevents any action being brought in a court for the recovery of any sum of money.[453] Exceptions apply throughout Australia for contributions to prizes for the winner of some pursuit, for bets made with licensed bookmakers, or for gaming that is otherwise lawful (e.g., with a casino, public lotteries).

---

446. *Morley v. Richardson* (1942) 65 CLR 512 at 517 per Rich J. *Jackson Securities Ltd v. Cheesman* (1986) 4 NSWLR 484; *Carragreen Currencies Corp Pty Ltd v. Corporate Affairs Commission of New South Wales* (1986) 7 NSWLR 705; *Australian Capital Territory Gaming and Liquor Authority v. Andonaros* (1991) 103 FLR 450.
447. *Petranker v. Brown* [1084] 2 NSWLR 177.
448. *Morley v. Richardson* (1942) 65 CLR 512.
449. See *v. Cohen* (1923) 33 CLR 174, 182.
450. *Whittle v. Jennings* [1922] SASR 394; *Jackson Securities Ltd v. Cheeseman* (1986) 4 NSWLR 484.
451. *Middleton v. Cavenett* [1923] SASR 255.
452. *Games Wagers and Betting Houses* 1901 (ACT); *Unlawful Betting Act* 1989 (NT), *Racing and Betting Act* 1983 (NT); *Unlawful Gambling Act* 1998 (NSW); *Racing Act* 2002 (Qld); *Lottery and Gaming Act* 1936 (SA); *Racing Regulation Act* 1952 (Tas); *Lotteries Gaming and Betting Act* 1966 (Vic); *Gaming and Betting (Contracts and Securities) Act* 1985 (WA).
453. *Games Wagers and Betting Houses* 1901 (ACT) s. 13; *Unlawful Betting Act* 1989 (NT) s. 4, *Racing and Betting Act* 1983 (NT) s. 135; *Unlawful Gambling Act* 1998 (NSW) s. 56; *Racing Act* 2002 (Qld) s. 341; *Lottery and Gaming Act* 1936 (SA) s. 50; *Racing Regulation Act* 1952 (Tas) s. 114; *Lotteries Gaming and Betting Act* 1966 (Vic) s. 15; *Gaming and Betting (Contracts and Securities) Act* 1985 (WA) s. 4.

I. Online Gambling

367. Australia passed the *Interactive Gambling Act* (2001)(Cth) on 28 June 2001 and it received royal assent on 11 July 2001. The legislation makes it an offence for to offer 'real-money' online interactive gambling to residents of Australia. It also makes it illegal for online gambling operators to advertise 'real-money' interactive gambling services (such as online poker and casino, other than wagering and lotteries services, save to a limited extent)) to Australian citizens. At the same time, it is not illegal for Australians citizens to access interactive online gambling services. Also, Australian companies are permitted to offer gambling services to gamblers who are located outside of Australia with the exception of certain designated countries. As this publication goes to press, Australia's online gambling legislative regime is presently under review by the Department of Broadband, Communications and Digital Economy especially in relation to pressure to loosen restrictions especially in relation to online sports gambling.

Chapter 4. Sale of Goods

§1. Background

368. Sale of goods contracts are governed by general common law principles. The law relating to the sale of goods may be traced to its origins in 1888 when Sir Mackenzie Chalmers drafted a Bill to codify the law relating to the sale of goods in the United Kingdom (UK). The Bill was enacted as the *Sale of Goods Act* 1893 (UK). Since then the 1893 Act has been replaced by the *Sale of Goods Act* 1979 (UK) that consolidates the law relating to the sale of goods.

369. In Australia, all states and territories enacted similar legislation with little modification. Most jurisdictions in other British Commonwealth countries followed suit and as a result there is a high degree of uniformity between the laws. Until the 1950s in the US, most states enacted the *Uniform Sales Act* which was substantially based on the 1893 Act. The *Sales Act* has since been replaced by the US *Uniform Commercial Code*.

370. Halsbury (4th edition) states that the purpose of codifying the law is in order to 'present an orderly and authoritative statement of the leading rules of law on a given subject whether these rules are to be found in statute law or common law'.

The original 1893 Act codified the rights and obligations of sellers and buyers. Many of the cases on which that Act was based concerned manufacturers and suppliers; albeit the Act applied to every sale of goods transaction. This is because from the time of manufacture till the time a good reaches a consumer there may be many different sale of goods transactions and each of these would fall within the ambit of the Act. The 1893 Act is set against the background of the general law of contract and personal property law.

Since the enactment of the Sale of Goods Act in the various common law jurisdictions there is a considerable mass of case law interpreting the Acts of 1893. However, over time the old case law has been declining in importance despite the Act of 1893 having played a codifying role. It is to be noted however that the Sale of Goods Act makes no attempt to codify the general principles of contract law and indeed expressly leaves them untouched where the rules of common law apply to contracts for the sale of goods. Over time there has also been a change in the type of sale of goods. During the 19th C sales were largely between businessmen and organizations – manufacturers and suppliers. However, sales of goods have been by retailers to the consuming public within a very different social and economic nature of the transaction – both these observations are, in law, sale of goods. Indeed in the 21st C one of the principle trends of legislative change is to distinguish between consumer and non-consumer transactions.

371. In Australia, the various states and territories have passed Sale of Goods legislation. These Acts represent a codification and at times a qualification of common law principles pertaining to sale of goods contracts. The common law still plays a role in such contracts, but where there is a conflict between common law and statute, the statutory rules will prevail. Where however the statute merely reflects the common law, the latter principles may be referred to. The respective state and territory Sale of Goods legislation include: ACT *Sale of Goods Act* 1954; NSW *Sale of Goods Act* 1923; NT *Sale of Goods Act* 1972; Qld *Sale of Goods Act* 1896; SA *Sale of Goods Act* 1895; Tas *Sale of Goods Act* 1896; Vic *Goods Act* 1958 and WA *Sale of Goods Act* 1895.

For present purposes, the NSW *Sale of Goods Act* 1923 and its provisions will be referred to as the basis of all discussion and where relevant, reference is made to sections in other state and territory legislation.

Sale of Goods Act 1923 (NSW).

§2. Part I – Preliminary

372. Definitions are given in section 5 of this Act.

§3. Part II – Formation of the Contract: Sale and Agreement to Sell

373. Contracts for the sale of goods under the Sale of Goods Act refer to contracts for the sale of chattels (including emblements), and things attached to or forming part of the land which are agreed to be severed before the sale or under the contract, and which have not been intended to pass with the land.

374. Contracts for the sale of goods may involve an element of 'services' as an incidental component. Where the work element is a dominant factor in the contract, the contract is classified as one for services rather than the sale of goods.

375. Contract. Section 6(1): 'A contract of sale of goods is a contract whereby the seller transfers or agrees to transfer the property in goods to the buyer for a money consideration called the price.'

376. Goods which form the subject matter of the contract of a sale may be existing goods (goods in existence at the time of contractual formation) or future goods (goods which come into existence after formation, or which are to be acquired by the seller after this point). The contract may provide for specific or ascertained goods, and unascertained goods (goods which at the time of the contract have not been identified or agreed upon as specific goods of which title is to pass). This distinction is important in relation to the passing of legal title in the goods under the contract.

377. Sale or agreement to sell. Section 6(3) defines a sale or agreement to sell. Under this provision where the contract operates to transfer the property in goods then the transaction is a sale, whereas if the property is to pass at some time in the future then the transaction is an agreement to sell. Whether a sale of goods transaction is a sale or agreement to sell will have consequences as to which party bears the risk of loss or damage to the goods. This also will have implications in terms of a breach of contract in which the seller may sue for the price and the buyer may assert rights of ownership against the seller and third parties. Where the transaction is an agreement to sell the remedy is an action for damages.

378. 'Property' (section 5) is defined as general property in goods and not merely a special property such as some limited interest or right in the goods. 'Goods' include all chattels personals other than things in action and money. So, debts, shares, negotiable instruments, patents and copyrights are specifically excluded as is currency. The term 'goods' also includes emblements and things attached to or forming part of the land which are agreed to be severed before sale or under the contract of sale. 'Emblements' are the natural products of the soil, such as crops, and these become 'goods' when they are severed from the land before sale or under the contract of sale. While 'fixtures' are things that have become so attached to the land so as to become part of the land, however, when fixtures are severed from the land, they become again goods to which the Act applies.

379. Without *consideration*, a contract is unenforceable. Section 6(1) requires the consideration to be 'money consideration'. Such a requirement therefore excludes barter or exchange transactions. However, a 'trade-in' of a motor vehicle satisfies the section.[454]

380. Other types of transactions. The sale of goods is thus distinguished from other transactions such as direct exchange without money and hence is not a sale. A gift is the transfer of property without consideration. Where a 'free gift' accompanies a sale, a collateral contract may bind the seller to make the gift.[455] In this case a motorist was entitled to a free medallion on the purchase of four gallons of petrol.

381. The receipt of goods 'on approval', 'sale or return', or 'on consignment' is in the hands of the merchant for the purpose of a sale. Where the merchant holds the goods as agent the contract is one of bailment. In these cases no property in the goods passes and the same goods must be returned when unsold.[456] These distinctions are important from the point of view of the privity of contract reasons as well as in defining the respective rights and duties of the parties.

I. Capacity

382. Section 7 deals with the capacity of parties. At common law, contracts are generally not enforceable against an infant but could be enforced by an infant. There

454. See *Davey v. Paine Bros (Motors) Ltd* [1954] 73 NZLR 1122.
455. See *Esso Petroleum Co Ltd v. Customs & Excise Commissioners* [1976] 1 All ER 117.
456. See *Chapman Bros v. Verco Bros & Co Ltd* (1933) 49 CLR 306; and *Farnsworth v. FCT* (1949) 78 CLR 504.

are, however, a number of exceptions to this general principle such as infants are liable to pay a reasonable price for necessaries, such as education and training.[457]

In relation to goods, legislation in all jurisdictions (except New South Wales) provides that where necessaries are sold and delivered to a minor, the minor must pay a reasonable price.[458]

The statutory definition of necessaries accords with the common law: they are goods suitable to the condition in life of such minor, and necessary to his or her actual requirements at the time of sale and delivery.[459]

383. In New South Wales, the provision concerning necessaries is found in section 7 of the Sale of Goods Act 1923; however, that section only applies to those who are suffering from mental incapacity or drunkenness. In respect of contracts made with minors, the position in NSW is regulated by the *Minors (Property and Contracts) Act 1970.*

As was the case for minors, where necessaries are sold and delivered to a mentally disabled person, there is a statutory requirement that the person pay a reasonable price for them. The definition of necessaries is the same as for minors – goods suitable to the condition in life of such person, and to her or his actual requirements at the time of the sale and delivery.[460]

384. Section 7 deals only with necessaries sold and delivered to the infant. The age of majority has been lowered from 21 years to 18 years and different legislation in each state has altered the common law position. Some states Tasmania and Victoria have followed the *Infants Relief Act 1874* (UK). Other states Queensland, South Australia and Western Australia have inherited English legislation that amends the general law. New South Wales has the *Minors (Property and Contracts) Act 1970* (NSW) which provides a comprehensive scheme for infants' contracts.

385. Insanity and drunkenness will not preclude liability for a reasonable price to be paid for necessaries;[461] whereas contracts by mentally disabled persons are voidable.[462]

At common law a company only has capacity to enter into contracts to the extent it was given such capacity by its constitution. Section 124 of the *Corporations Act*

---

457. *Nash v. Inman* (1908) 2 KB 1.
458. If the goods have not been delivered, any dispute arising under the contract would be determined according to the common law.
459. See Sale of Goods Act 1954 (ACT), s. 7; Sale of Goods Act (NT), s. 7; Sale of Goods Act 1896 (Qld), s. 5; Sale of Goods Act 1895 (SA), s. 2; Sale of Goods Act 1896 (Tas), s. 7; Sale of Goods Act 1895 (WA), s. 2; Goods Act 1958 (Vic), s. 7.
460. Section 7 of the Sale of Goods Act 1954 (ACT) is an example of the relevant provision: 'Where necessaries are sold to an infant or to a person who, by reason of mental incapacity or drunkenness, is incompetent the contract, he must pay a reasonable price for the goods.' See equivalent provisions in the other jurisdictions: Sale of Goods Act 1896 (Qld), s. 5; Sale of Goods Act 1923 (NSW), s. 7; Goods Act 1958 (Vic), s. 7; Sale of Goods Act 1895 (WA), s. 2; Sale of Goods Act 1895 (SA), s. 2; Sale of Goods Act 1896 (Tas), s. 7; Sale of Goods Act 1992 (NT), s. 7; Sale of Goods Act 1908 NZ s. 4(1).
461. *Blomey v. Ryan* (1956) 99 CLR 362.
462. *Gibbons v. Wright* (1954) 91 CLR 423.

2001 (Cth) gives a company the same legal capacity as 'an individual' including the power to make an agreement and section 125 provides that the performance of an act – including entry into an agreement – by a company will not be invalid merely because it is beyond the power of the company's constitution. There are rules regarding companies that are in the process of being 'formed' and the capacity of the promoters to be bound once the company is formed section 13(1). However, an unincorporated association has no legal personality and therefore cannot enter into contracts. A contract that is entered into with the unincorporated association will be void.

II. Formalities

386. Section 8 provides that a contract of sale may be made in writing, orally, partly in writing and partly orally or it may be implied from the conduct of the parties. This reflects the common law position.

387. Section 9, now abolished, introduced formal requirements before contracts will be enforceable where the value of goods is AUD 20 or more. This section was repealed in NSW in 1988, Queensland (1972), ACT (1975), SA (1982) and Victoria (1987). In WA, Tasmania and NT the value of goods must be AUD 50 or more.

III. Subject Matter

388. The subject matter of a contract of sale may be existing goods owned and possessed by the seller or future goods – section 10(1). 'Future goods' include goods to be manufactured or acquired by the seller after the making of the contract of sale. This includes goods already in existence but which need to be acquired by the seller.

However, an agreement to agree in the future offends against the general principle of completeness. Although the parties in such a case have turned their minds to the issue of price, this will not necessarily mean that the contract will be upheld. Unfortunately, the case authorities are not entirely consistent. It is suggested that the outcome is likely to differ depending on the nature of the contract. If the contract is for a sale of goods, there is authority to suggest that a court may imply a term that the goods will be sold at a reasonable price, and the contract will be upheld.[463]

463. *Foley v. Classique Coaches Ltd* [1934] 2KB 1. *Contrast May and Butcher v. The King* [1934] 2 KB 17. The Sale of Goods legislation in the various jurisdictions will be relevant here. Where the parties agree to agree on price in the future, they may not be regarded as having fixed the price in accordance with the relevant provision of various state and territory Sale of Goods legislation (noted above and cited here in abbreviated form): Qld s. 11(1); NSW s. 13(1); Vic s. 13(1); SA s. 8(1); WA s. 8(1); Tas s. 13(1); NT s. 13(1); ACT s. 13(1). Therefore, the buyer may be required to pay a reasonable price for the goods: Qld s. 11(2); NSW s. 13(2); Vic s. 13(2); SA s. 8(2) WA s. 8(2); Tas s. 13(2); NT s. 13(2); ACT, s. 13(2).

However, an agreement by the parties to agree later on a price in a contract to sell land, or on rental in an option to renew a lease, is unlikely to be upheld.[464] Given this, it is submitted that contracts dealing with land where parties agree to agree in the future about price or rental are likely to be treated in the same way as contracts that are silent on those matters.

389. Where specific goods have perished without the knowledge of the seller when the contract is made, the contract is void – section 11. Such 'specific goods' include goods identified and agreed upon at the time a contract of sale is made.

390. Under the common law, where the subject matter of a contract is not in existence, two things can take place. First, if both seller and buyer assume the existence of the good, and the assumption proves to be wrong, there is a common mistake and both parties are released from all liability.[465] Second, there may be a good contract about non-existence and on the construction of the contract the risk of non-existence is assumed by one party. If the seller warrants the existence of the goods then the seller is liable for non-delivery and the buyer will not be liable for the price. However, if the buyer has taken the risk that the goods do not exist then the buyer will have to pay the price and the seller is not liable for non-delivery. The question is essentially one of construction of the contract.[466]

391. Section 11 is focused on the existence of goods that may then have perished but does not apply when the goods have never existed.

392. The doctrine of frustration is dealt with in section 12. This doctrine discharges parties to a contract where without fault, performance becomes impossible due to some external circumstance.[467] In *Allied Mills v. Gwydir Valley Oilseeds Pty Ltd* [1978] 2 NSWLR 26 goods sold but not delivered in accordance with the contract were destroyed by fire. It was held that section 12 did not apply. However, section 25 applied as the risk lay on the seller and the buyer cannot be compelled to pay the price but the seller may be liable in damages for non-delivery. Where the risk has passed to the buyer he/she may be liable for the price of damages for non-acceptance.

393. Legislation has been introduced to relieve the inadequacies of the application of the doctrine of frustration.[468]

---

464. *Stocks & Holdings (Constructors) Pty Ltd v. Arrowsmith* (1964) 112 CLR 646; 650 per Barwick CJ; *Randazzo v. Goulding* [1968] QdR 433, 441.
465. *Couturier v. Hastie* (1856) 5 HLC 673; 10 ER 1065.
466. *McRae v. Commonwealth Disposals Commission* (1951) 84 CLR 377.
467. *Taylor v. Caldwell* (1863) 3 B&S 826.
468. See *Frustrated Contracts Act* 1959 (Vic); *Frustrated Contracts Act* 1978 (NSW) and *Frustrated Contracts Act* 1988 (SA).

IV. Price, Valuation and Stipulation as to Time

394. In section 13(1) the price in a contract of sale may be fixed by the contract or left to be fixed in any agreed manner or may be determined by the course of dealing between the parties. Further section 13(2) states that where the price is not determined in the provisions, the buyer must pay a reasonable price. What is a reasonable price is a question of fact that is dependent on the circumstances of each particular case. In any contract for sale the price must be money consideration.

395. The presumption in section 13 is the existence of a contract. Where the agreement between the parties is too uncertain so that no contract exists, then section 13 has no application. With the enactment of the sale of goods legislation throughout Australia, the position is now clear for contracts for the sale of goods. If the contract is silent as to price, the buyer is required to pay a reasonable price.[469]

If no price is fixed the agreement may be so uncertain that the court may treat the agreement as void. It has been suggested by the High Court that the section should not apply to executory contracts.[470]

396. Section 14 states that where there is an agreement to sell goods on terms and the price is to be fixed by valuation, the agreement is void if the valuation is not or cannot be made. It is noted that different principles apply where the contract is for the sale of goods and the price is to be fixed by the valuation of a third party.[471]

Where the third party cannot or does not make such valuation, the agreement is void.[472] However, if the third party is prevented from so doing by the fault of one party, the other may maintain an action in damages against the former.[473] Further, notwithstanding the above, if any of the goods have been delivered to and appropriated by the buyer, he or she must pay a reasonable price for them.[474]

Also if goods have been delivered to, and appropriated by the buyer, then a reasonable price must be paid. If a party prevents a valuation then damages may lie against the party at fault.[475]

397. In section 15(1) stipulations as to time of payment are not of the essence of the contract unless there is a specific term in the contract to that effect.

---

469. Sale of Goods legislation: Qld s. 11(2); Vic s. 13(2); NSW s. 13(2): WA s. 8(2); SA s. 8(2); Tas s. 13(2): ACT s. 13(2); NT s. 13(2). These provisions will only be of assistance where the parties have attached agreement on all other essential terms of the agreement: *Australia and New Zealand Banking Group Ltd v. Frost Holdings Pty Ltd* [1989] VR 695, 703.

470. See *Hall v. Busst* (1960) 104 CLR 206.

471. *Sale of Goods Act 1896* (Qld), s. 12; *Sale of Goods Act 1923* (NSW), s. 14; Goods Act (Vic), s. 14; *Sale of Goods Act 1895* (WA), s. 9; *Sale of Goods Act 1895* (SA), s. 9; *Sale of Goods Act 1896* (Tas) s. 14; *Sale of Goods Act 1972* (NT), s. 14; *Sale of Goods Act 1954* (ACT), s. 14.

472. Qld s. 12(1); NSW s. 14(1); Vic s. 14(1); WA s. 9(1); SA s. 9(1); Tas s. 14(l); NT s. 14(1); ACT s. 14(1).

473. Qld s. l2(2); NSW s. l4(2); Vic s. 14(2); WA s. 9(2); SA s. 9(2); Tas s. 14(2); NT s. 14(3); ACT s. 14(2).

474. Qld s. 12(1A); NSW s. 14(1); Vic s. 14(1); WA s. 9(1); SA s. 9(1); Tas 14(1); NT s. 14(2); ACT s. 14(1).

475. See *Wenning v. Robinson* (1964) 64 SR (NSW) 157.

V. Terms of the Contract: Condition and Warranty

398. The original 1893 Sale of Good Act was basically a statement of the common law in regards to matters to be implied in contracts by sellers and buyers and the consequences of non-performance. Benjamin's *Sale of Goods* [476] gives a typology of express statements made about goods in a contract of sale. Such express statements include those involving no legal liability, for example, 'mere puffs' and those involving legal liability, including misrepresentation inducing the contract (fraudulent, negligent or innocent), contractual promises separate from the main contract, and contractual promises which are terms of the main contract. The test used in all cases is objective.

399. The various State and Territory Sale of Goods Acts have preserved the common law distinction between conditions, warranties and intermediate terms, as well as the legal consequences of their breach. Whether a particular term in the contract is a condition or warranty depends upon the intentions of the parties, as can be construed from the document.

400. Section 16(2) distinguishes between a *condition* and a *warranty*. A *condition* is a term so vital that if it was breached then the other party could treat the contract as discharged; whereas a *warranty* is to be applied to less important terms of the contract, the breach of which may give rise to a claim for damages but not to a right to reject the goods and treat the contract as repudiated. However, *innominate* terms are promises that cannot be designated as conditions or warranties because the consequences of their breach varies in importance. Whether a term is a condition or warranty is left to the courts to decide.[477]

The main implications of the contract of sale of various conditions and warranties may be listed below:

- Implied condition that the seller has title to the goods being sold, or will have title at the time property in the goods is to pass.[478]
- Implied warranty that the buyer will have quiet possession of the goods.[479]
- Implied warranty that the goods are free from any charge or encumbrance.[480]
- In a contract for the sale of goods by description, an implied condition that the goods correspond with the description (and if the sale is by sample as well as by

476. 7th edition AG Guest (ed.), London: Sweet & Maxwell, para. 10-001.
477. See *Blakney v. Savage & Sons Pty Ltd* (1970) 119 CLR 435.
478. Sale of Goods Act 1896 (Qld), s. 15(a); Sale of Goods Act 1923 (NSW), s. 17(1); Goods Act 1958 (Vic). s. 17(a); Sale of Goods Act 1895 (WA), s. 12(a); Sale of Goods Act 1895 (SA), s. 12(a); Sale of Goods Act 1896 (Tas), s. 17(a); Sale of Goods Act 1972 (NT), s. 17(a); Sale of Goods Act 1954 (ACT), s. 17(a).
479. Sale of Goods legislation: Qld, s. 15(b); NSW, s. 17(2); Vic, s. 17(b): WA, s. 12(b); SA, s. 12(b); Tas, s. 17(b); NT, s. 17(b); ACT, s. 17(b).
480. Sale of Goods legislation: Qld, s. 15(c); NSW, s. 17(3); Vic, s. 17(c); WA, s. 12(c); SA, s. 12(c); Tas, s. 17(c); NT, s. l7(c); ACT, s. l7(c).

description, it is not sufficient that the bulk of the goods corresponds with the sample if the goods do not also correspond with the description).[481]

401. Where the buyer (expressly or by implication) makes known to the seller the particular purpose for which the goods are required, so as to show that the buyer relies on the seller's skill or judgment, and the goods are of a description that it is in the course of the seller's business to supply, an implied condition that the goods are reasonably fit for that purpose.[482]

When goods are bought by description from a seller who deals in goods of that description, an implied condition that the goods are of merchantable quality.[483]

In a contract for sale by sample, implied conditions that the bulk corresponds with the sample in quality, that the buyer will have a reasonable opportunity of comparing the bulk with the sample, and that the goods are free from any defect, rendering them unmerchantable, which would not be apparent on reasonable examination of the sample.[484]

In some cases, the parties may contract out of the statutory conditions and warranties that are implied in the contract of sale.[485]

In the case of a sale of goods only, although strictly speaking the term 'condition' is not defined in the sale of goods legislation, it is clear that the legislation contemplates that a condition is a term the breach of which gives rise to a right to 'repudiate' (terminate) the contract.[486]

However, in most jurisdictions, where the contract is for specific goods and the contract has been executed, any breach of condition must be treated as a breach of warranty ex post facto.[487]

The effect of these provisions is that where a contract for specific goods has been executed, there will only be a right to claim damages. Any claim to terminate for a breach of condition will have been lost.

---

481. Sale of Goods legislation: Qld, s. 16; NSW, s. 18,Vic, s. 18; WA, s13; SA, s13; Tas, s. 18; NT, s. 18; ACT, s. 18.
482. Sale of Goods legislation: Qld, s. 17(a); NSW, s. 19(1); Vic, s. 19(a); WA, s. 14(2); SA, s. 14(a); Tas, s. 19(a); NT, s. 19(a); ACT s. 19(2).
483. Sale of Goods legislation: Qld, s. 17(c); NSW, s. 19(2); Vic, s. 19(b); WA, s. 14(3); SA, s. 14(b); Tas, s. 19(b); NT, s. 19{b); ACT, s. 19(3). Also Fair Trading Act 1987 (WA), s. 38(1).
484. Sale of Goods legislation: Qld, s. 18; NSW, s. 20; Vic, s20; WA, s. 15; SA, s. 15; Tas, s. 20; NT, s. 20; ACT, s. 20.
485. Sale of Goods legislation: Qld, s. 56; NSW, s. 57; Vic, s. 61; WA, s. 54; SA, s. 54; Tas, s. 59; NT, s57. Some jurisdictions prohibit parties to a 'consumer' transaction from excluding these terms: Sale of Goods Act 1923 (NSW), s. 64; Australian Consumer Law and Fair Trading Act 2012 (Vic), s. 31; Fair Trading Act 1987 (WA), part III.
486. Sale of Goods Act 1954 (ACT), s. 16(2); Sale of Goods Act 1923 (NSW), s. 16(2); Sale of Goods Act (NT), s. l6(2); Sale of Goods Act 1896 (Qld), s14(2); Sale of Goods Act 1895 (SA), s. 11(2); Sale of Goods Act 1896 (Tas), s. 16(2); Goods Act 1958 (Vic), s. 16(2); Sale of Goods Act 1895 (WA), s. 11(2).
487. Sale of Goods Act 1923 (NSW), s. 16(3); Sale of Goods Act (NT), s. 16(4); Sale of Goods Act 1896 (Qld), s. 14(3); Sale of Goods Act 1895 (SA), s. 11(3); Sale of Goods Act 1896 (Tas), s. 16(3); Goods Act 1958 (Vic), s. 16(3); Sale of Goods Act 1895 (WA), s. 11(3). No equivalent provision appears in the ACT.

402. In section 19(3) – custom or trade usage may attach a condition or warranty to a contract. The existence of the custom is a question of fact and must be well-known so that anybody entering a contract in the circumstance would be presumed to know the custom or usage as a term of the contract.[488]

403. Section 19(4) states that an express warranty or condition will not negative a warranty or condition implied by the Act unless inconsistent with it.[489]

404. Federal and state legislation also provide for terms to be implied in certain circumstances. Schedule 2 Pt 3-2 Div 1 Competition and Consumer Act 2010 (Cth) implies a series of conditions and warranties. However, conditions and warranties implied by the Competition and Consumer Act 2010 (Cth) cannot be contracted out of by the parties – Schedule 2 section 64. The right to rescind a contract for breach of a condition is provided in Schedule 2 sections 82, 83.

405. The *Consumer Transactions Act* 1972 (SA) prohibits contracting out of conditions and warranties where there is a consumer sale. The position is similar in WA[490] and in the NT.[491]

VI. Implied Conditions as to Title

406. Section 17 provides for the fact that unless the contract shows a different intention it is an implied condition that the seller has a right to sell; a warranty that the buyer shall have quiet possession; and, a warranty that the goods are free from charges or encumbrances.

407. Unless the parties expressly provide otherwise, a contract for the sale of goods contains the following implied terms as to title. There is an implied condition that the seller has the right to sell the goods (good title) or at least, will have such a right when title is to pass under the contract. There is an implied warranty that the buyer shall have and enjoy quiet possession of the goods.[492] Furthermore, there is an implied warranty that goods will be free from any charge or encumbrance in favour of a third party which has not been declared to the buyer when the contract is made – see *Rowland v. Divall*.[493]

408. If a seller has no title and attempts to sell goods and later acquires a title the seller can hold the buyer to the bargain provided that the title is acquired before the buyer rejects the goods. In *Pattern v. Thomas Motors Pty Ltd*[494] a hirer under a hire purchase agreement sold a car to a dealer who then resold it to a third party.

488. *Con-Stan Industries of Australia Pty Ltd v. Norwich Winterthur Insurance (Aust) Ltd* (1986) 60 CLR 226.
489. *Gemmel Power Farming Co Ltd v. Nies* (1935) 35 SR (NSW) 469.
490. *Fair Trading Act* 1987.
491. *Consumer Affairs and Fair Trading Act* 1990.
492. See *Healing (Sales) Pty Ltd v. Inglis Electrix Pty Ltd* (1968) 121 CLR 584; (1968) 42 ALJR 280.
493. (1923) 2 KB 500; (1923) All ER Rep 270.
494. [1965] NSWLR 1457.

The car changed hands a number of times over the next two years when it was seized by a finance company who claimed to hold a bill of sale over the vehicle. The hirer had used the borrowed money to pay out the hire purchase agreement. The court held by paying out the hire purchase agreement, the hirer had acquired title to the car.

409. In *Steinke v. Edwards*[495] it was held that the right to levy a tax on a vehicle with a right to seize the chattels to enforce collection was a 'charge or encumbrance' within the meaning of section 17(3). In *Stego Securities Pty Ltd v. Csaszar*[496] a hire purchase interest registered under the *Chattels Security Act* 1987 (Vic) was held to be an encumbrance under section 17(3) of the *Sale of Goods Act* 1979 (NSW).

410. Schedule 2 section 51 Competition and Consumer Act 2010 (Cth) contains a more elaborate version of the condition and warranties found in section 17 of the *Sale of Goods Act* 1979 (NSW). Subsection (1)(a) states that where goods are supplied by a corporation to a consumer there is an implied condition that the seller has a right to sell at the time when property is to pass. Subsection (1)(b) quiet enjoyment warranty recognizes lawful disturbance whereas the freedom from encumbrances warranty spells out that the goods are free and will remain free from encumbrances until the time when property passes.

411. Schedule 2 section 51 Competition and Consumer Act 2010 (Cth) recognizes the existence of a floating charge over the assets of a corporation and is not a breach of the freedom from encumbrances warranty. Further recognition is also given to the transfer of a limited title by the vendor.

A. Sale by Description

412. Where there is a contract for the sale of goods by description, for example a contract to sell goods through a catalogue, advertisement or even through the description on the packaging of the goods, there is an implied condition that the goods shall correspond to the description in terms of identity or character (rather than quality).[497]

413. If the sale of the goods is by sample as well as description, there is an implied condition that the goods correspond to the sample as well as the description.

414. Section 18 of the *Sale of Goods Act* 1979 (NSW) states that there is an implied condition that the goods shall correspond with the description; and if it is

495. (1935) SA.
496. (1992) Vic.
497. See *Grant v. Australian Knitting Mills Ltd* [1936] AC 85; and *Ashington Piggeries Ltd v. Christopher Hill Ltd* [1972] AC 441.

a sale by sample as well as by description, it is not sufficient that the bulk of the goods corresponds with the sample if the goods do not also correspond with the description. However, 'sale by description' is not defined even though it is also used in section 23, rule 5.

415. In practical terms there are two areas which the section has been held to cover. In the first instance, there is the failure to conform exactly to the full description of the goods – *Re Moore & Co v. Landauer & Co*,[498] where 3,000 tins of Australian fruit were to be packed 30 tins to the case. Although the total number of tins consigned was correct, most cases contained 24 tins. In the second instance, there is a total failure to perform contract when there is a discrepancy between the goods ordered and the goods supplied.[499]

416. While the Competition and Consumer Act 2010 (Cth) Schedule 2 section 56 is similar to section 18 of the *Sale of Goods Act* 1979 (NSW) there is a limitation to sales 'in the course of business'. Section 56(2) provides that 'a supply of goods is not prevented from being a supply by description only because, having been exposed for sale or hire, they are selected by the consumer'. Thus, a purchase from a self-serve store may still be a sale by description.

B. Fitness for Purpose

417. There is no general implied term as to fitness of purpose or merchantable quality, except for in certain cases under the Act. This reflects the common law principle of *caveat emptor* [let the buyer beware], under which the buyer must satisfy him/herself as to the quality of the goods to be purchased.

418. Section 19(1) of the Sale of Goods Act 1979 (NSW) relates to the implied condition as to quality or fitness. There are three elements in this section. The first refers to the 'particular purpose' which should be made known. In *Frost v. Aylesbury Dairy Co Ltd*,[500] 'supply of milk, pure and unadulterated and free from germs or disease' was held to spell out the particular purpose. The second element refers to a reliance on the seller's skill or judgment. Disclosure of purpose may be insufficient as the purpose must be communicated in a way 'as to show' that the buyer has relied on the seller's skill.[501] In this instance there was a reliance on the skill of animal feed compounders to use ingredients fit for feeding to animals.

419. The final element is that the seller deals in goods of that kind. This is similar to the provision in section 19(2) where the seller must 'deal with goods of that description'. Thus, the ambit of section 19 is limited to business sales rather than private sales.

498. [1921] 2 KB 519.
499. See *Christopher Hill Ltd v. Ashington Piggeries Ltd* [1969] AC 441.
500. [1905] 1 KB 608.
501. *Christopher Hill Ltd v. Ashington Piggeries Ltd* [1969] AC 441.

420. The Competition and Consumer Act 2010 (Cth) Schedule 2 section 54 guarantee as to acceptable quality provides for a condition as to fitness to be implied similar to those under the *Sale of Goods Act* 1979 (NSW). However, Schedule 2 section 54 is different in four respects. The section applies only to consumer transactions; where goods are supplied in the course of a business rather than the sale of goods by a dealer; there is no requirement that the consumer must rely on the supplier's skill or judgment as a presumption exists that the consumer is relying on such skills; and finally, the supplier cannot contract out of the section. However, this last issue is resolved if the seller can show that the consumer did not rely on the skill or judgment or that it was unreasonable to rely on it.

421. The Competition and Consumer Act 2010 (Cth) provisions while limited to corporations extends to the supply of goods and not simply the sale of goods.

C. Merchantable Quality

422. Where goods are purchased by description and the seller deals with goods of that description in his/her ordinary course of business, there is an implied condition that the goods are of 'merchantable quality'. The term 'merchantable quality' is taken to mean fit for normal use to which goods of that description are put –*Anthony v. Esanda Ltd.*[502]

423. If the buyer has examined the goods prior to sale, the implied condition does not cover defects which might have been revealed by a reasonable examination.

424. Section 19(2) Sale of Goods Act 1979 (NSW) 'where goods are bought by description from a seller who deals in goods of that description (whether he be the manufacturer or not), there is an implied condition that the goods shall be of merchantable quality'.

'Merchantable' here implies 'commercially saleable' which means that the goods were suitable for the actual purpose for which the buyer bought them under that description. Alternatively, goods would be merchantable if they could be sold for any purpose. Both of these meanings impact differently on sellers and buyers respectively.

Hence, it is important to classify the subject matter of the sale. In *George Wills & Co Ltd v. Davids Pty Ltd*[503] what may be merchantable quality as 'beetroot canned in vinegar' may not be merchantable as 'canned beetroot' or 'beetroot canned in brine'.

425. The extant cases suggest that goods will be merchantable if:

– they are bought by description;

---

502. (1980) 32 ALR 627 at 635.
503. (1957) 98 CLR 77.

- they are bought from a seller who deals in goods of that description;[504] and
- the buyer has not examined the goods, or if he/she has, the defects would not be discoverable on such examination made before the contract. This proviso will not apply if no examination is made. Section 19(2) provides that 'if the buyer has examined the goods there shall be no implied condition as regards defects which such examination ought to have revealed'.

426. Schedule 2 sections 54, 55, 56 Competition and Consumer Act 2010 (Cth) applies definitions of 'acceptable quality' to consumer transactions and uses the same definition in the *Sale of Goods Act* 1979 (NSW) applying to consumer sales.

427. Schedule 2 section 54 Competition and Consumer Act 2010 (Cth) implies a condition or acceptable quality where goods are supplied to a consumer in the course of a business. Where defects are drawn to the attention of the consumer before the contract is made, or where the consumer examines the goods and ought to have discovered the defect, then merchantability is not implied.[505]

D. Sale by Sample

428. Under a sale by sample, a sample of goods is presented prior to the formation of the contract. The Act will imply that there is a condition that the bulk of the goods shall correspond to the sample in terms of quality. There is also an implied condition that the buyer shall have reasonable opportunity to compare the bulk with the sample and that the goods shall be free from any condition rendering them unmerchantable which would not be apparent on a reasonable examination of the sample.

429. Under the *Sale of Goods Act* 1979 (NSW) a 'sale by sample' as defined in section 20(1) is where there is a 'term in the contract express or implied to that effect'. The parties must intend it to be a sale by sample otherwise the production of samples by the seller will be a sale by description from the samples. Further section 20(2) provides three conditions for a sale by sample:

- that the bulk shall correspond with the sample in quality;
- that the buyer shall have reasonable opportunity to compare the bulk with the sample; and
- that the goods shall be free from any defect rendering them unmerchantable which is not apparent on reasonable examination of the sample. This reasonable examination test is stated in *Godley v. Perry Burton & Sons (Bermondsey).*[506]

430. Schedule 2 section 57 Competition and Consumer Act 2010 (Cth) implies conditions in the contract identical to those set out in the previous discussions on goods that are supplied 'by reference to a sample'.

---

504. *Christopher Hill Ltd v. Ashington Piggeries* [1969] AC 441.
505. See *Lockhart v. Osman* [1982] VR 57.
506. [1960] 1 WLR; [1960] 1 All ER 36.

§4. PART III – EFFECTS OF THE CONTRACT

I. Transfer of Property

431. Where the contract is for the sale of specified or ascertained goods, title will pass when the parties intend it to pass, as determined by the terms of the contract, the conduct of the parties and the circumstances of the case. Where the contract is for the sale of unascertained goods, title will pass once they have been ascertained.

432. Section 21 of the *Sale of Goods Act* 1979 (NSW) provides that in a sale 'goods must be ascertained'. Sale of unascertained goods means that no property in the goods is transferred unless and until the goods are ascertained. There is no definition of 'unascertained goods' in the Act but the term generally covers generic goods; goods to be manufactured or grown by the seller; and, an unidentified part of a specific whole. The key is that the goods cannot be identified but only referred to by description.

433. Subsection 1 provides for property to pass on sale of ascertained goods at a time intended by the parties. 'Property' is defined in section 5 as general property in goods and not merely a special property.

434. The intention of the parties is to be obtained from all the circumstances set out in sections 22(3) and 23 and the five rules for ascertaining intention, subject to any contrary intention appearing in the contract.

II. Passing of Risk

435. Property in goods is different from possession of goods. The transfer of title determines which of the parties to the contract assumes liability for the loss of the goods. Prima facie risk of loss passes with the title in the goods. Where there is destruction of or damage to the goods after the contract is formed, the seller must bear the risk of loss in circumstances where title has not passed upon the making of the contract, and must be prepared to insure the goods accordingly. However, the *Sale of Goods Act* 1979 (NSW) provides that where delivery has been delayed through the fault of either the buyer or seller, the party at fault is liable for any loss which occurred as a result of the fault, except in the case where either the buyer or seller is a bailee of the goods for another party.

436. Section 25 of the *Sale of Goods Act* 1979 (NSW) states that risk prima facie passes with property. The issue of risk arises if the goods have been lost or damaged. If the risk is with the seller, the buyer cannot be compelled to pay the price but the seller may be liable in damages for non-delivery. Where the buyer has taken on the risk, he/she may be liable for the price of damages for non-acceptance.[507]

---

507. *Healey v. Howlett & Sons* (1917) 116 LT 591.

437. Two provisos attach to section 25. The first relates to where delivery has been delayed through the fault of either buyer or seller; the goods are at the risk of the party at fault in regards to any loss which might not have occurred but for such fault. In *Sharp v. Batt*[508] a delivery of apples was delayed at the request of the buyer. The fruit deteriorated and the seller could rely on the proviso.

In *Allied Mills v. Gwydir Valley Oil Seeds Pty Ltd* [1978] 2 NSWLR 26 the court considered both provisos in section 25. The first proviso relates to a delayed delivery. A part of the goods which had not been delivered was destroyed in a fire. The buyer had to replace those goods on a rising market as it had already been sold. The goods were held to be at the seller's risk.

438. The second proviso states that nothing in section 25 shall affect the duties or liabilities of either seller or buyer as a bailee of the goods of the other party. See also section 36 which relates to risk where goods are delivered at a distant place: 'The seller of the goods agrees to deliver them at his own risk at a place other than that where they are when sold, the buyer must nevertheless unless other agreed, take any risk of deterioration in the goods necessarily incident to the course of transit'.

III. Transfer of Title

439. In general, a seller of goods cannot pass to another any better title than that which is possessed by the seller. However, the Sale of Goods Act 1979 (NSW) creates a number of important exceptions to this general rule.

440. Section 26(1) partially sets out the *nemo dat* rule that says that nobody can give a better title to goods than that which the person possesses. This rule is made subject to the other provisions of the Act which recognize exceptions to the rule. The first exception is found within section 26(1) which states that 'unless the owner of the goods is by his conduct precluded from denying the seller's authority to sell' invokes the common law doctrine of estoppel. Where estoppel exists the buyer acquires a title which is good against all the world.[509]

IV. Registration of Interests

441. The *Personal Property Securities Act 2009* (Cth) now provides a national legislative scheme that allows and encourages people with an interest in goods to register that interest.

508. (1930) Tas LR 33.
509. See *Thomas Australia Wholesale Vehicle Trading Co Pty Ltd v. Marac Finance Australia Ltd* (1985) 3 NSWLR 452.

V. Sale by Factor or Mercantile Agent

442. A second exception found in section 26(2) provides that 'nothing in this Act shall affect – (a) the provisions of the *Factors (Mercantile Agents) Act* 1923 (NSW)'. Where an owner entrusted goods to a dealer for sale, the common law protected a third party who purchased those goods in the ordinary course of business.

443. The *Factors Act* was originally passed in the UK which was directed at commercial agents of English merchants who pledged imported goods to raise funds pending the landing and resale of the goods. Today the Act is commonly applied to motor dealers entrusted with vehicles for sale. The provisions in the *Factors Act* are an amplification of the common law. Apart from Western Australia, all other states and territories have enacted a *Factors Act.*

VI. Sale under Common Law or Statutory Power

444. Section 26(2) further states that '(b) the validity of any contract of sale under any special common law or statutory power of sale, or under the order of a court of competent jurisdiction' is not affected by the Act. Powers of sale are given in various legislation such as *Disposal of Uncollected Goods Act* 1966 (NSW), the *Bankruptcy Act* 1966 (Cth); and section 50 of the *Sale of Goods Act* 1979 (NSW). A sheriff may seize and sell goods of a defendant at common law.

VII. Sale under Voidable Title

445. Section 27 provides that 'where the seller of goods has a voidable title thereto but his title has not been avoided at the time of the sale, the buyer acquires a good title to the goods, provided he buys them in good faith and without notice of the seller's defect of title'. In *Car & Universal Finance Co Ltd v. Caldwell*[510] a fraudulent seller disappeared and so made it impossible to communicate the rescission. The court held that a clear intention to rescind the contract and taking all necessary steps to do so would be sufficient.

VIII. Sale by Seller in Possession

446. Section 28(1) of the *Sale of Goods Act* 1979 (NSW) relates to where a person having sold goods continues or is in possession of the documents of title to the goods will protect an innocent buyer as if the person making the delivery or transfer were expressly authorized by the owner of the goods. This is illustrated by *Pacific Motor Auctions Pty Ltd v. Motor Credits (Hire Finance) Ltd.*[511]

510. (1965) 1 QB 525.
511. [1965] AC 867.

The Privy Council here reversed on appeal a decision of the High Court of Australia and applied section 28(1). A motor dealer sold a number of vehicles to a finance company under an agreement where he was allowed to keep possession and sell the cars as agent for the company. The authority to sell was revoked when the dealer got into financial difficulties. A bona fide purchaser, who had had previous dealings with the dealer, bought a number of vehicles. The purchaser knew of the display plan agreement but did not know that the authority had been revoked. As the financial difficulties were not resolved the finance company demanded the return of the cars. The High Court held that this was a case of ostensible agency rather than ownership; the purchaser would only have been protected if the sale had been in the ordinary course of business – the sale took place outside business hours. The Privy Council reversed this decision and held that the purchaser was entitled to the protection of section 28(1).

IX. Sale by Buyer in Possession

447. Section 28(2) states that the buyer must be bound to buy the goods. However, this section will not apply if the buyer has an option to buy, such as in a hire-purchase agreement. The possession of the goods by the buyer must be with the consent of the seller.

§5. Part IV – Performance of the Contract

448. The seller is under a statutory duty to deliver the goods and the buyer is under a duty to pay for them in accordance with the terms of the contract. The performance of these duties is concurrent, unless the parties intend otherwise.

449. Section 30 provides that 'it is the duty of the seller to deliver the goods and of the buyer to accept and pay for them in accordance with the terms of the contract for sale'. 'Delivery' defined in section 5(1) is the voluntary transfer of possession from one to another. The contract determines each party's obligations to the other.

450. Payment and delivery are concurrent conditions: section 31. The five rules about delivery are set out in section 32.

I. Quantity

451. The right quantity available is paramount: section 33(1). A delivery of less than the required quantity with a statement that the balance will be delivered in due course may not assist the seller because section 34(1) provides that unless otherwise agreed, the buyer of goods is not bound to accept delivery by instalments.

452. Section 33(2) applies where more than the contracted quantity is delivered. The buyer may reject the whole, retain the correct quantity and reject the rest or accept the whole and pay at the contract price.

453. Section 33(3) applies where the contract goods are delivered in full mixed with additional goods and also where the correct contract amount is delivered but is made up by goods of different descriptions. Subsection 4 states that the whole of section 33 is subject to any usage of trade, course of dealing between the parties or special agreement.

II. Instalment Deliveries

454. Unless agreed, the buyer is not bound to accept delivery of the goods by instalment. But, where it is agreed that delivery is to be by stated instalments to be paid for separately and a breach occurs, it is a question of construction of the contract and the circumstances of the case as to whether the whole contract is repudiated or there is a severable breach giving rise to damages: section 34.

455. A divisible contract for delivery of goods by instalment is different from a series of separate contracts for separate deliveries. The former is a single contract and the provisions for instalment delivery are usually treated as subsidiary clauses bearing upon performance.

III. Delivery to a Carrier

456. Prima facie, delivery to a carrier is delivery to the buyer: section 35(1), but this subsection will not apply to carriers who are servants or agents of the seller.[512]

457. Unless agreed, there is no duty to insure the goods but section 35(3) may require the seller, where the goods are to be sent by sea, to give notice to the buyer so that he/she can effect insurance.[513]

IV. Buyer's Right of Examining the Goods

458. In section 37(1) of the *Sale of Goods Act* 1979 (NSW) a buyer is deemed not to have accepted the goods unless he has had a reasonable opportunity of examining them to ensure the goods conform to the contract. The buyer is deemed to have accepted the goods in one of three circumstances:

– intimates to the seller that he has accepted them; or

512. See also s. 23, r 5 and *Nissho (WA) Australia Ltd v. Malaysian International Shipping Corp Berhad* (1989) 167 CLR 219.
513. *Wimble Sons & Co Ltd v. Rosenberg & Sons* [1913] 3 KB 743.

- when the goods have been delivered to him and he does an act in relation to them which is inconsistent with the ownership of the seller; or
- when after the lapse of a reasonable time he retains the goods without intimating to the seller that he has rejected them.

459. With specific goods the right is lost when property passes to the buyer. This becomes problematic when there is no chance to examine the goods before delivery and acceptance especially when section 23, rule 1 operates to pass property on completion of the contract. In South Australia, the Australian Capital Territory, NZ and UK, this difficulty has been overcome by legislation.

460. Under the Competition and Consumer Act 2010 (Cth) Schedule 2 sections 82, 83 a right of rescission is provided where there has been a breach of a condition or warranty in a consumer transaction implied by Schedule 2 Pt 3-2 Div 1. Notice must be given to the seller specifying the breach or the goods returned with a notice specifying the breach. This right is in addition to any other right available by law.

461. Section 39 states that buyers are not bound to return rejected goods. Further section 40 states that a buyer is liable for reasonable charges for the care and custody of the goods.[514]

§6. Part V – Rights of Unpaid Seller against the Goods

462. Where the seller has received only part of the contract price or a negotiable instrument which is subsequently dishonoured, the seller may pursue a number of legal remedies, irrespective of the fact that title may have passed to the buyer under the contract.

463. The rights of the seller against the goods are summarized by sections 42(1) and (2). 1 states that the unpaid seller of goods has a lien on the goods for the price while the seller is in possession of them; in the case of insolvency of the buyer a right of stopping the goods *in transitu* after the seller has parted with the possession of them; a right of resale as limited by this Act. In subsection 2 – where property in goods has not passed to the buyer, the unpaid seller has in addition to the seller's other remedies a right of withholding delivery similar to and co-extensive with the seller's rights of lien and stoppage *in transitu* where the property has passed to the buyer.

464. A seller is 'unpaid' when the whole of the price has not been paid or tendered; or when a negotiable instrument has been received as conditional payment and the condition has not been met – section 41(1).

514. See *Francis v. Lyon* (1907) 4 CLR 1023.

I. Unpaid Seller's Lien

465. The seller's lien is a qualification on his duty (section 30) to deliver the goods. Under section 43, for the lien to arise the seller must be unpaid, the goods not sold on credit and the seller still be in possession. There are two exceptions to a lien arising where goods are sold on credit: sections 43(1)(b) and (c) – where the goods have been sold on credit but the term of credit has expired and where the buyer becomes insolvent, respectively.

466. Under section 43(2) the right of lien remains even if the seller is in possession as agent or bailee for the buyer.

II. Termination of Lien

467. The lien is lost if the price is paid or tendered: section 45(1). There are three ways this may happen. First, when the goods are delivered to a carrier or other bailee for transmission to the buyer, without reserving a right of disposal. Second, when the buyer lawfully obtains possession of the goods and third, by waiver. However, compare this to section 49 which refers to a situation where a seller assents to a sub-sale or other disposition of the goods; or where documents of title to goods are lawfully transferred to the buyer who then transfers the documents to another for valuable consideration.

In *Hewett v. Court*[515] the High Court outlined how an equitable lien might arise. *Electrical Enterprises Retail Pty Ltd v. Rodgers*[516] held that an equitable lien would only be available if the contract could be specifically performed.

III. Right of Stoppage *in Transitu*

468. Section 46 of the *Sale of Goods Act* 1979 (NSW) states that 'when the buyer of goods becomes insolvent, the unpaid seller who has parted with the possession of the goods has the right of stopping them *in transitu*, that is to say, he may resume possession of the goods as long as they are in course of transit and may retain them until payment or tender of the price'.

469. Goods are 'deemed to be in course of transit from the time when they are delivered to a carrier by land or water or other bailee for the purpose of transmission to the buyer until the buyer or his agent in that behalf takes delivery of them from the carrier or other bailee' – section 47(1).

470. At common law there is no particular formality to exercise a right to effect stoppage *in transitu*: section 48(1). This right is 'not affected by any sale or other disposition of the goods which the buyer may have made unless the seller has

515. (1983) 149 CLR 639.
516. (1989) 15 NSWLR 473.

assented thereto': section 49. A sale is not generally rescinded by lien or stoppage *in transitu*: section 50. The right to recover damages for any loss occasioned by breach of contract arises when goods are perishable or where a notice is given to the buyer of an intention to resell and the buyer does not pay. This right allows the seller to rescind the contract: section 50(3).

§7. Part VI – Actions for Breach of Contract

471. As well as the seller's rights against the goods, a seller has personal rights to sue the buyer for breach of contract. This is an action for the price of the goods sold or there may be an action for damages for non-acceptance.

I. Action for the Price

472. The seller may sue in debt for the price of the goods after title in the goods has passed to the buyer where the buyer wrongfully neglects or refuses to pay for the goods according to the terms of the contract; or where title has not passed the buyer does the same.

473. Section 51(1) provides for a seller maintaining an action against the buyer for the price of the goods. The property must have passed and there must be a neglect or a refusal to pay for the goods. The claim by the seller is for the specific sum of money fixed by the contract; no loss need be shown by the seller. There may also be no duty on the seller to mitigate loss by attempting to resell the goods.

474. Further section 51(2) states that 'where under a contract of sale the price is payable on a day certain irrespective of delivery, the buyer wrongfully neglects or refuses to pay such price, the seller may maintain an action for the price, although the property in the goods has not passed and the goods have not been appropriated to the contract'.

II. Damages for Non-acceptance

475. The seller can seek damages when the buyer wrongfully neglects or refuses to pay for the goods. The measure of damages is the loss estimated to arise naturally and directly from the breach. Further, where there is an available market for the goods, the damages are estimated to be the difference between the contract price and the market price.

476. Section 52(1) provides: 'Where the buyer wrongfully neglects or refuses to accept and pay for the goods, the seller may maintain an action against the buyer for damages for non-acceptance.'

This is a wide section in that it covers non-acceptance when the property has passed so that a choice is presented in an action for the price or an action for damages for non-acceptance.

477. In section 52(2) 'the measure of damages is estimated loss directly and naturally resulting in the ordinary course of events from the buyer's breach of contract'. This subsection uses language of the first rule in *Hadley v. Baxendale*[517] (see *below* at section 54(2)).

478. Section 52(3) concerns the available market for the goods in question. 'The measure of damages is prima facie to be determined by the difference the contract price and the market or current price at the time or times when the goods ought to have been accepted, or if no time was fixed for acceptance, then at the time of the refusal to accept.' The doctrine of mitigation is one basis for this provision. An innocent party is required to act immediately on the breach to minimize loss by reselling in the market.

III. Remedies of the Buyer

479. As against the goods a buyer has a statutory right to reject goods when a condition of the contract is breached so that sections 16(3), 37 or 38 will operate. The right may be lost if under section 16(3) the buyer elects to treat the breach as one of warranty rather than condition or if property has passed or if under section 38 the goods have been accepted.

480. As against the seller, damages for non-delivery are provided by section 53(1). A buyer may maintain an action against the seller for damages for non-delivery. The measure for damages provided under section 53(3) prima facie is 'ascertained by the difference between the contract price and the market or current price of the goods at the time or times when they ought to have been delivered, or if no time was fixed, then at the time of the refusal to deliver'.

As in section 52(3) the doctrine of mitigation applies as given in section 53(3). The assumption is that the buyer goes into the market for substitute goods immediately following the seller's breach. The damages so awarded would put the buyer in the same financial position as if the seller had performed the contract.

481. The rules for an anticipatory breach by the seller are similar to those where there is an anticipatory breach by the buyer. A buyer may accept the anticipatory breach as repudiation of the contract and sue for damages. If the buyer does not accept the anticipatory repudiation, the contract remains on foot and the breach will be committed when the seller fails to deliver. The duty to mitigate commences on the failure to deliver.

517. (1854) 9 Exch 341; 156 ER 145.

482. In section 54 a breach of warranty by the seller:

> or where the buyer elects or is compelled to treat any breach of a condition on the part of the seller as a breach of warranty, the buyer is not by reason only of such breach of warranty entitled to reject the goods, but the buyer may: (a) set up against the seller the breach of warranty in diminution or extinction of the price; or (b) maintain an action against the seller for damages for the breach of warranty.

483. The measure of damages is from the first rule in *Hadley v. Baxendale*[518] which is 'the estimated loss directly and naturally resulting from the ordinary course of events from the breach of warranty': section 54(2). But where there is a defect in quality section 54(3) applies. If the goods are so defective as to have no value the damages will be the full value of the goods.

484. Where the loss is unusual the innocent party must show that the guilty party knew or had the means to know that the loss would arise from the breach.[519]

IV. Remedies for Buyer or Seller

485. Section 55 in relation to interest and special damages preserves the second rule in *Hadley v. Baxendale*.[520] The rule states that if the special circumstances of the contract were communicated by the plaintiffs to the defendants, the damages recoverable are those which the parties could reasonably contemplate flowing from a breach of the contract.

486. Section 56 discusses savings of proceedings in equity and applies to seller and buyer and extends to 'any remedy in equity'.

A general principle for a contract for the sale of specific goods that is either custom-built goods (bespoke) or articles that are one or few of a kind-may be specifically enforced. This rule has been given statutory endorsement in all sale of goods legislation except in New South Wales.[521]

In New South Wales it seems that this section permits specific performance of a sale of goods contract where the remedy of common law would be inadequate: *Aristoc Industries Pty Ltd v. RA Wenham (Builders) Pty Ltd* [1965] NSWR 581, 588. In considering the application of this principle, a court will take into account the nature of the transaction in which the sale is embodied, the nature of the goods involved

518. (1854) 9 Exch 341; 156 ER 145.
519. See *Victoria Laundry (Windsor) Ltd v. Newman Industries Ltd* (1949) 2 KB 528.
520. (1854) 9 Exch 341; 156 ER 145.
521. Goods Act 1958 (Vic), s. 58; Sale of Goods Act 1894 (Qld), s. 53; Sale of Goods Act 1895 (SA), s. 51; Sale of Goods Act 1895 (WA), s. 51; Sale of Goods Act 1954 (ACT), s. 55; Sale of goods Act 1972 (NT). Sections 53 and 56 of the Sale of Goods Act 1923 (NSW) provides that nothing in the Act shall affect any remedy in equity of the buyer or the seller in respect of any breach of a contract of sale or any breach of warranty.

in that transaction and the general question of the inadequacy of damages should specific performance be refused.[522]

Certain other statutory provisions alleviate the position of the buyer in circumstances where the buyer would not otherwise be entitled to terminate the contract for breach of condition, for example, Competition and Consumer Act 2010 (Cth) Schedule 2 sections 82, 83. The Fair Trading Acts in Victoria and New South Wales vest the courts with wide powers to make orders upon the application of an aggrieved party. In South Australia, the buyer has a statutory right to rescind the contract within a defined cooling off period.

The buyer may seek interest or special damages in circumstances where there has been a complete failure of consideration.

487. The courts may exercise their inherent equitable jurisdiction in relation to contracts for the sale of goods. The buyer may therefore seek equitable remedies such as injunctions or specific performance. The issue of whether equity is applicable has been the subject of some contention, but recent authority in relation to equitable rescission of sale of goods contracts indicates that equitable principles are applicable to sale of goods contracts – see *Graham v. Freer*;[523,524] *Leason Pty Ltd v. Princes Farm Ltd.*

V. Exclusion Clauses

488. Section 57 provides the exclusion of implied terms and conditions 'where any right, duty, or liability would arise under a contract of sale by implication of law, it may be negative or varied by express agreement, or by the course of dealing between the parties, or by usage, if the usage be such as to bind both parties to the contract'. Hence, under this section it might be possible to contract out of the implied conditions as to fitness or merchantable quality.

In *Liaweena (NSW) Pty Ltd v. McWilliams Wine Pty Ltd*[525] defective corks were supplied to a winery and a quantity of wine became contaminated. Although there had been a course of dealing between the parties, the notice excluding the implied terms and conditions was misleading as it claimed there was no change from the previous terms on which business was carried out. Accordingly, the seller was unable to rely on the notice.

489. Legislative controls in regard to exclusion clauses feature in the Competition and Consumer Act 2010 (Cth) especially Schedule 2 Pt 2-2 Consumer Protection and the *Contracts Review Act* 1980 (NSW). The latter piece of legislation empowers a court to review a contract where there were 'unjust' circumstances at the time of making the contract. In order to avoid 'an unjust consequence or result' the court may make all or any of the orders set out in section 7 of the Act. The orders

522. *Timmerman v. Nervina Industries (International) Pty Ltd* [1983] 1 QR1.
523. (1980) 35 SASR 424.
524. [1983] 2 NSWLR 381.
525. (1991) ASC 56-038.

may set aside or vary part or the whole of the contract. The scope of this Act was considered by the Court of Appeal in *West v. AGC (Advances) Ltd.*[526] Section 16(2) of the *Market Court Act* 1978 (Vic) is similar to the provisions of the NSW Act.

§8. Part VII – Consumer Sales

490. Section 62 provides the definition of what constitutes a 'consumer sale' – namely, a sale of goods other than a sale by auction by a seller in the course of a business. The goods are to be of a kind commonly bought for private use or consumption, and, are sold to a person who does not buy or hold himself or herself out as buying them in the course of business. In section 63 the onus on proving that a sale is not a consumer sale is on the party so contending. Section 64 provides for conditions and warranties in contracts for consumer sales.

I. Commonwealth and State Consumer Protection

491. A fundamental doctrine in contracts on the sale of goods is 'let the buyer beware' (*caveat emptor*). Parties were assumed to have an equal bargaining power and so could freely enter into contracts. More recently, however the focus is on 'let the seller beware' (*caveat venditor*) because of mass production, technological developments, and sophisticated marketing which have worked to introduce an imbalance in the respective bargaining positions of the parties. The Commonwealth and the states have passed legislation aimed at protecting the consumer against market abuses. Credit sales legislation have also endeavoured to regulate all forms of credit sales.

492. Consumer protection is largely the domain of legislation rather than the common law.

In general, the federal provisions are broader that state legislation in that they apply to 'supply' rather than to 'sale' in the Competition and Consumer Act 2010 (Cth). However, the federal legislation is narrower in scope because Commonwealth powers limit the provisions to a contract between a 'corporation'[527] to a 'consumer'.[528]

II. Commonwealth

493. The Competition and Consumer Act 2010 (Cth) is the pre-eminent piece of legislation dealing with the subject of consumer protection. Schedule 2 Pt 2-2 is entitled 'Unconscionable Conduct'. The validity of the Competition and Consumer

526. (1986) 5 NSWLR 610.
527. Defined in s. 4(1).
528. Defined in s. 4b.

Act 2010 (Cth) rests on a number of vested powers of the Commonwealth, including trade and commerce, postal telegraphic services, power, banking power, corporations power, and the territories power among others. Much of the Act is directed at the behaviour of corporations although there are parts that extend to individuals who deal with the Commonwealth, use Commonwealth facilities or engage in interstate trade or operate in a territory.

494. Section 4B of the Competition and Consumer Act 2010 (Cth) defines a consumer by reference to the price of goods rather than by reference to the class of goods and the purpose of the purchase (see also Schedule 2 section 3).

495. Under section 3(1) of the Australian Consumer Law, a person is taken to have acquired particular goods as a consumer if, and only if:

(a) the amount paid or payable for the goods, as worked out under subsections (4) to (9), did not exceed:
  (i) $40,000; or
  (ii) if a greater amount is prescribed for the purposes of this paragraph – that greater amount; or
(b) the goods were of a kind ordinarily acquired for personal, domestic or household use or consumption; or
(c) the goods consisted of a vehicle or trailer acquired for use principally in the transport of goods on public roads.

496. The prescribed amount is AUD 40,000. If the purchaser acquires the goods for re-supply or for transforming them in production or manufacture he/she is not a consumer.

A. *Division 1 – Unfair Practices*

497. Schedule 2 section 22 Competition and Consumer Act 2010 (Cth) prohibits unconscionable conduct in less substantial business transactions. The section lists a diverse range of factors that a court may consider in determining whether or not a party has contravened this section. One of the factors identified is the extent to which the parties 'acted in good faith'.[529] The case suggests that reference to good faith in contracts either in general law or statute are equivalent standards.

This may be contrasted to the provisions of the Victorian *Fair Trading Act* 1999 Part 2B which classifies bad faith conduct as a subset of unconscionable conduct.

498. Schedule 2 section 18 Competition and Consumer Act 2010 (Cth) is wide and prohibits a corporation in a commercial transaction from engaging in conduct which is 'misleading or deceptive or is likely to mislead or deceive'. Conduct which is regarded as misleading under this section is one where it has a tendency to lead

529. See *Garry Rogers Motors (Aust) Pty Ltd v. Subaru (Aust) Pty Ltd* [1999] ATPR (41-703).

into 'error'. The concept of misleading conduct covers and goes beyond the general law governing misrepresentation.

499. The liability created is civil. The remedies are damages or an injunction. The time limitation for taking action is three years. Offences under Pt VI Competition and Consumer Act 2010 (Cth) are found under section 79, injunctions under section 80, and actions for damages section 82. See also Schedule 2 section 236.

500. Schedule 2 section 18 Competition and Consumer Act 2010 (Cth) provides that this Schedule extends to conduct engaged in outside Australia by companies incorporated in Australia or carrying on business in Australia or by Australian citizens or persons ordinarily resident in Australia. A foreign company will be 'carrying on business' in Australia if it establishes a branch office or subsidiary in Australia or appoints an Australian representative. The Competition and Consumer Act 2010 (Cth) also applies if the 'conduct engaged in' occurs in Australia which will depend upon the nature and quality of the involvement of the trader in the jurisdiction. Conduct is defined in section 4(2) and Schedule 2 section 52 of the Competition and Consumer Act 2010 (Cth) to include refraining (otherwise than inadvertently) from doing an act. It need not constitute an active representation and silence may suffice, for example, should the trader give incomplete information.

501. These provisions have been reproduced in almost identical terms in the fair trading legislation of all states and territories.[530]

1. Puffs

502. In *John Glass Real Estate Pty Ltd v. Karawi*[531] a statement made by a real estate agent about the net lettable area of a building was held not be mere puffery but a statement of fact. Also in *Petty v. Penfold Wines Pty Ltd*[532] the statement that Petty was getting Penfold's 'best discount' was held to be a statement of fact. However, mere puffery has also been found, for example, in the cases of *Dynamic Lifter Pty Ltd v. Incitec*[533] and *Sabre Corp Pty Ltd v. Laboratories PharmaA-Care Pty Ltd.*[534] In Dynamic Lifter the statement was directed at graziers to the effect that the defendant provided fertilizer 'as it had for generations' was held to be a classic puff because it could not be read as meaning 'always' whereas in Sabre Corp the statement 'if you like that hairdressing product you will love this one', was held to be a classic example of puffing.

530. *Fair Trading Act* 1992 (ACT); *Fair Trading Act* 1987 (NSW); *Consumer Affairs and Fair Trading Act* 1990 (NT); *Fair Trading Act* 1989 (Qld); *Fair Trading Act* 1987 (SA); With the introduction of the Australian Consumer Law, Tasmania deleted its Fair Trading legislation. *Fair Trading Act* 1999 (Vic); and *Fair Trading Act* 1987 (WA).
531. (1993) ATPR 41-249.
532. (1994) 42-247.
533. (1994) 30 IPR 198.
534. (1995) ATPR 41-396.

2. Statements of Law

503. A misstatement of law may constitute misleading conduct. In *Qanstruct Pty Ltd v. Bongiorno Ltd*[535] representation that the payment of life insurance policies would be tax deductible was held to be misleading. In *SWF Hoists and Industrial Equipment Pty Ltd v. State Government Insurance Commission*[536] advice by the Commission that its workers compensation insurance cover would extend to employees injured during work interstate was held to be misleading within section 52.

3. Promises

504. Contractual promises are enforceable and may relate to facts or to some future event. How a misrepresentation may be resolved in the light of the provision about a 'representation as to any future matter' now Schedule 2 section 54 Competition and Consumer Act 2010 (Cth) has occupied judicial minds. In *Holt v. Biroka Pty Ltd*[537] the defendant argued that the making of a representation and its subsequent non-fulfilment did not itself constitute misleading or deceptive conduct. This argument was rejected by the court as it could be too restrictive an approach. In this case Kearney, J. held that the definition of 'engaging in conduct' section 4(2)(a) of the *Trade Practices Act* 1974 (Cth) (now in section 4 Competition and Consumer Act 2010 (Cth)) envisaged acts of a contractual nature as constituting misleading conduct. The distinction has to be drawn between the bare making of a contract and representations or promises as to the carrying out such a contract.

505. A contractual promise may relate to a presently existing state of affairs. This is sometimes called a warranty. A promisor may warrant that the house is free of termites or that the promisor is the sole beneficial owner of copyright in a computer program. If the promised state of affairs does not exist, that person may be deemed to have engaged in conduct that is misleading as provided under section 4(2) of the *Trade Practices Act* 1974 (Cth) (now Competition and Consumer Act 2010 (Cth) section 4) as found in the case of *Accounting Systems 2000 (Developments) Pty Ltd v. CCH Australia Ltd.*[538]

506. Where a breach of a contractual promise constitutes misleading conduct, it will be more significant under the Competition and Consumer Act 2010 (Cth) and Fair Trading Acts than under general law for breach of contract. This is because the remedies available are more attractive under legislative provisions. It will also be significant where the contract itself is unenforceable, void or illegal.[539]

535. (1993) 113 ALR 667.
536. [1990] ATPR 51,599.
537. (1988) 13 NSWLR 629.
538. (1993) 114 ALR 355.
539. See *Futuretronics Pty Ltd v. Gadzhis* [1992] 2 VR 209.

507. Part IVA of the Competition and Consumer Act 2010 (Cth) deals with misleading or deceptive conduct and unconscionable conduct in trade or commerce.

508. Schedule 2 section 29 Competition and Consumer Act 2010 (Cth) prohibits a corporation in a commercial transaction from making false or misleading representations or false or misleading statements in connection with the supply of goods or services. The matters covered include quality, standard or age of the goods, the consumer's need for the goods and statements about conditions, warranties and guarantees. Liability for breach of this section is criminal and fines are imposed.

509. Other sections under this Division deal with land sales, bait advertising, coercion at place of residence, pyramid selling, product information and safety standards and the supply of unsolicited credit cards and goods.

510. Schedule 2 section 29 Competition and Consumer Act 2010 (Cth) provides tests for determining if goods are Australian made.

511. Schedule 2 Pt 3-2 safety of consumer goods and product related services has a comprehensive scheme dealing with product safety – banning goods and product recalls, and the dissemination of product information.

The ACCC recently (2013) lost a High Court case relating to misleading and deceptive conduct. The ACCC alleged Google had engaged in misleading or deceptive conduct in relation to its display of sponsored links. The High Court held that Google was not responsible for misleading or deceptive representations contained in the links themselves. These representations were the responsibility of the advertisers themselves. See *Google Inc v. ACCC*.[540]

B. Schedule 2 Pt 3-2 Div 1 Consumer Guarantees

512. This Division applies where there is a relationship of seller and buyer between the corporation and the consumer. The provisions are designed to give consumer protection against exclusion clauses.

513. Schedule 2 section 64 makes void any contractual term which excludes, restricts or modifies the provisions of Schedule 2 or the terms of Schedule 2 sections 82, 83 (rescission of contracts).

In relation to standard form contracts, legislation has been introduced to protect consumers. Section 68 implies certain conditions as to fitness and quality into consumer contracts for the sale of goods or services and prevents these provisions from being excluded by the supplier.

514. Section 68 and Schedule 2 section 64 guarantees not to be excluded by contract renders void terms which purport to exclude, restrict or modify terms implied and certain rights conferred under the Act or which have that effect. In certain

540. *Google Inc v. ACCC* [2013] HCA 1.

circumstances, the legislation permits the use of clauses to limit liability where 'fair and reasonable': Schedule 2 section 64A limitation of liability for failures to comply with guarantees.

515. Section 68A allows a corporation to include a term in a contract to limit its liability under section 68 for breach of an implied condition or warranty. But such a term may not be used if the goods are 'of a kind ordinarily acquired for personal domestic or household use or consumption'. The term may be used in a business transaction where the goods are not intended for resale or use in a manufacturing process.

The court is given jurisdiction to decide if the term is fair and reasonable. It has to take into account all the circumstances of the case and in particular the bargaining strength of the parties, whether the buyer received an inducement to enter the contract, if the buyer knew of the extent of the term and whether the goods were made to the special order of the buyer.

516. Schedule 2 applies to the supply of services as well as goods. Schedule 2 section 60 guarantee as due care and skill creates two new warranties for services supplied to business and Schedule 2 Pt 5-5 Div 1 linked credit contracts exempts financiers from liability for breach of terms implied by the Division.

Schedule 2 is silent about the consumer's rights to damages for breaches of the implied terms. The penal provisions and section 82 (but see also Schedule 2 section 236) do not apply to a claim for damages for a breach of an implied term imported into a contract by Division 2. Actions for damages under Schedule 2 section 236 are for contraventions of Parts VI Enforcement and Remedies and Schedule 2 Pt 2-2 unconscionable conduct of the Act.[541]

517. A consumer has the right to rescind a contract where there has been a breach of a condition implied in the contract by Schedule 2.

C. Division 2A – Manufacturers

518. Schedule 2 section 138 liability for loss or damages suffered by an injured individual is provided under section 138.

519. Privity rules preclude effective remedies to consumers against manufacturers for defective goods. Similarly, liability in tort is difficult to establish.[542] Schedule 2 now provides significant means for the consumer to redress against a manufacturer.

520. Schedule 2 does not apply where there is a contract between manufacturer and the consumer. However, it applies where the manufacturer supplies goods to a person who acquires them for re-supply to a consumer. The types of goods included

541. See *Arturi v. Zupps Motors Pty Ltd* (1980) 49 FLR 283; 33 ALR 243.
542. See *Grant v. Australian Knitting Mills Ltd* [1936] AC 85.

are of a kind ordinarily acquired for personal, domestic or household use. A manufacturer is given an extended definition to include importers. The obligations of manufacturers are similar to those implied between supplier and consumer and these provisions act to create a code of product liability. The provisions include:

- Schedule 2 sections 54, 259, 260(e), 271(1) and (2) Actions in respect of unsuitable goods – fitness for the purpose;
- Schedule 2 sections 54m 259, 260(e), 271(1) and (2) Action in respect of goods of unmerchantable quality;
- Schedule 2 sections 54, 259, 260(b)(ii) Actions in respect of non-correspondence with samples;
- Schedule 2 section 58 Actions in respect of failure to provide facilities for repairs or parts – liability to compensate a consumer for damages where facilities for the repair of goods or the supply of parts necessary for such repairs are not available;
- Schedule 2 section 59 Guarantees due care and skill – where there is a failure to comply with an express warranty, liability for damages to consumer is present;
- Schedule 2 section 274 Indemnification of suppliers by manufacturers – right of indemnity by a direct seller to a consumer against a manufacturer. This liability is limited to the cost of repair or replacement: Schedule 2 section 276A limitation in certain circumstances of liability of manufacturer to seller;
- Schedule 2 section 143 Time for commencing defective goods action – actions to be brought within three years of the right of action accruing;
- Schedule 2 section 150 Application of all or any provisions of this Part not to be excluded or modified – contractual terms purporting to exclude the provision of this division are void.

§9. Schedule 2 Pts 3-5 – Liability of Manufacturers for goods with safety defects

521. Part 3-5, Division 1 of the Australian Consumer Law imposes strict liability on manufacturers for goods with a safety defect. The only defence available is what is known as the state of the art defence. Manufacturers can escape liability if they can show that the defect in the product could not have been discovered given the current technical and scientific knowledge.

I. State Legislation

522. Each state and territory has passed general legislation on consumer protection. In addition some jurisdictions have legislation directed to particular areas of consumer abuse such as door-to-door sales, misleading advertising, motor vehicle sales and the supply of unsolicited goods.

523. The states of New South Wales, Victoria and South Australia have reformed their Sale of Goods Acts to give special protection to consumers. In general terms, these reforms provide for non-excludable conditions and warranties (of title, merchantability, fitness for use, etc.) which must be part of every consumer contract.

These reforms have now been implemented and can be found in ss 23-28 of the Australian Consumer Law.

524. While Schedule 2 section 64 Competition and Consumer Act 2010 (Cth) is restricted to contracts with corporations, these provisions are supplemented by state legislation that are not so restrictive.[543]

525. The *Sale of Goods Act* 1923 (NSW) was amended in 1974 to insert Part VIII – Consumer Sales. Section 62 of the Sale of Goods Act 1923 (NSW) defined a 'consumer sale' as goods commonly bought for private use or consumption and which are sold to a person who does not buy them for use in the course of a business. Where a transaction is a consumer sale, any contractual term to restrict the operation of sections 18, 19 and 20 of the Act is void.

526. Section 64(3) of the Sale of Goods Act 1923 (NSW) provides a definition for merchantability if the transaction is a consumer sale. The definition is similar to Schedule 2 sections 54, 55, 56 Competition and Consumer Act 2010 (Cth) on interpretation.

Where defects are drawn to the buyer's notice before the contract is entered into, there is no implied condition of merchantability: section 64(4).

527. By section 64(5) of the Sale of Goods Act 1923 (NSW) the Court may join a manufacturer to proceedings and may order the defect to be remedied or the cost of doing so paid.

II. Contracts Review Act 1980 (NSW)

528. This Act was enacted following a report in 1976 on harsh and unconscionable contracts by John Peden.[544,545] This Act is generally seen as beneficial remedial legislation but which has given rise to considerable litigation over twenty years.

III. Unfair Contracts

529. In June 1997 the Government released its *Fair Trading Report: Finding a Balance – Towards Fair Trading in Australia*, which made a list of 31 recommendations calling for legislative remedies for such small business problems as unfair retail tenancy agreements, misuse of power by big businesses and power imbalances in the franchising sector. The Report recommends an amendment to section

543. See *Consumer Affairs and Fair Trading Act* 1990 (NT), ss 68, 69; *Sale of Goods Act* 1923 (NSW), ss 62–64; *Consumer Transactions Act* 1972 (SA), s. 16; *Goods Act* 1958 (Vic), ss 95, 97, 110; *Fair Trading Act* 1987 (WA), ss 34, 35.

544. See Peden, J. (1982) *The Law of Unjust Contracts*.

545. For appraisals see Carlin, *The Contracts Review Act 1980 (NSW) – 20 years on*, 123 Sydney L. Rev. 125 (2001); Zipser, *Unjust Contracts and the Contracts Review Act 1980 (NSW)*, 17 J. Contract L. 76 (2001).

51 of the *Trade Practices Act* 1974 (Cth) now the Competition and Consumer Act 2010 (Cth) to allow for exceptions and a broader definition of unfair and unconscionable conduct and with the Australian Competition and Consumer Commission (ACCC) administering complaints under this section. These reforms have now been implemented and are discussed elsewhere under the Competition and Consumer Act 2010 (Cth) (*supra*).

530. In 2003, Victoria amended its *Fair Trading Act* 1999 (Vic) to insert a new Part 2B prohibiting the use of unfair terms, to the detriment of the consumer, in consumer contracts. The provisions explicitly target issues of substantive fairness, although as noted previously, concerns about procedural and substantive fairness may often be interrelated. This Act is more protective of consumer rights in that it makes void unfair terms in consumer contracts.

531. Onerous terms in the consumer contract are read in favour of the consumer through the application of legislative provisions. It seems that the various legislative initiatives have now expanded the power of courts to deal with unconscionability and unfairness beyond existing powers. The criteria laid down by the federal and state legislation provide guidance to courts in terms of flexibility of interpretation as well as to ensure consistency and certainty in decision-making.

532. Exclusion clauses may also be affected by general legislative provisions such as those prohibiting unconscionable conduct. For example, in Victoria, Part 2B of the *Fair Trade Act 1999* (Vic) prohibits the use of unfair terms, to the detriment of the consumer in consumer contracts. This prohibition is likely to limit the use of broad exclusionary clauses

IV. International Sale of Goods

533. While Sale of Goods legislation in each jurisdiction governs the sale of goods within Australia, every Australian jurisdiction has also passed legislation enacting the United Nations Convention for the International Sale of Goods (Vienna Convention) 1980 to cover contracts which involve a significant non-Australian element. Importantly, however, this Convention does not apply to sales (a) of goods bought for personal, family or household use; (b) by auction; (c) on execution or otherwise by authority of law; (c) of stocks, shares, investment securities, negotiable instruments or money; (e) of ships, vessels, hovercraft or aircraft; or (f) electricity.[546]

546. See *generally* L. D'Archy, C. Murray & B. Cleve, *Schmitthoff's Export Trade: The Law and Practice of International Trade* (10th ed., Sweet & Maxwell 2000); and Islam, MR, *International Trade Law* (LBC Information Services 1999). The full text and commentary of the United Nations Convention on Contracts for the International Sale of Goods, Vienna 1980 (Official Text) Available at http://www.uncitral.org/ last accessed on 18/08/03.

Chapter 5. Hire of Work and Skills

§1. CONTRACT OF SERVICE VERSUS CONTRACT FOR SERVICE

534. In general, a *contract* of *service* is merely a contract under which a person undertakes to serve another. However, a *contract* for *service* is a contract between two independent parties whereby one agrees to perform some service for the other. It differs from contracts *of* service in that it is not an employer-employee relationship, but a principal-independent contractor relationship. The following discussion will address that of a contract of service and a beneficial contract of service and then that of a contract for service and a consideration of performance in a given time and where personal performance is necessary.

§2. CONTRACT OF SERVICE

535. Contracts of service are those contracts under which one party agrees to serve or to work for another – standard employment contracts. Such contracts can and do include restraint of trade clauses to restrict an employee's freedom to divulge or use sensitive information belonging to the employer where it is only disclosed to that employee for use in the course of employment and for the employer's benefit. Three such restraints may be readily identified.

In the first instance such information could be in the form of generally increased knowledge and skills acquired and developed during the course of employment. Any employer will not be able to restrict an employee's freedom to use these new knowledge and skills when he/she leave the employment as an employer may have no proprietary interest in them.

Second, trade secrets may be involved. Trade secrets include secret manufacturing processes which are not commonly known to competitors. When divulged to employees the secrets are meant to be used in order that the employee may perform tasks more effectively. Consequently, an employer may validly restrain unauthorized use of that information both during employment and after the employee leaves the employment.[547]

Third, the employer's trade connections. This refers to the employer's clients and customer base. An employer is entitled to prevent a former employer either using the list or enticing customers away. Such use is dependent on the employee's status and ability to entice customers away.

More generally, the restraint of trade clause can limit an ex-employee's freedom to find alternative employment in the same trade or industry. However, this is only valid where the employee had been in a position in which his/her skills, judgment and expertise were paramount. Hence, where an ex-employee were to set up an enterprise in competition and the customers followed that employee then it may seem justifiable that the restraint of trade clause in the contract of employment will

547. See *Forster & Sons Ltd v. Suggett* (1918) 35 TLR 87.

be valid. A restraint of trade clause was found to be valid if only to protect an employer's legitimate trade connections in *Hamilton v. Lethbridge*.[548] (see *below*).

§3. BENEFICIAL CONTRACT OF SERVICE

536. Contracts of service are contracts under which a person is employed. Applied to minors (those under 18 years of age), the term beneficial contracts of service will apply. These usually include contracts for the employment of minors where either (a) the employment provides a means of self-support; or (b) provide the minors with a means of obtaining instruction or education – the so-called necessaries, to prepare them for a suitable trade or profession. Examples of these include apprenticeships, cadetships, clerkships, internships and the like. There could also be beneficial contracts of service where the employment is designed solely to enable them to earn their living with no element of instruction or education involved.

§4. ENFORCEABILITY

537. No contract of service is specifically enforceable. It means that no one can be forced to remain in a master's employ or to do the work that he/she is employed to do. It also means that in a beneficial contract of service only the minor will be liable for any breach he/she commits. An employer can sue for damages or, in the case of major breach, can dismiss the minor.

538. In *Doyle v. White City Stadium Ltd*[549] the plaintiff was a minor professional boxer. He was contracted to fight for a purse of GBP 3,000 – win, lose or draw subject to the rules of the British Boxing Board of Control. Under those rules, a boxer who was disqualified forfeited the purse. Doyle was disqualified and the defendants refused to pay him. He sued, alleging that he was not contractually bound by the rules and thus could not be deprived of the money. The court held that the contract was analogous to a contract of service; it was beneficial and as a consequence all of its provisions were binding on him. His disqualification, therefore, meant that his prize had been forfeited.

539. In *Roberts v. Gray*[550] the contract under which Gray, a billiard professional, agreed to accompany Roberts was regarded as a contract for necessaries, the necessary being education or instruction. His breach entitled Roberts to recover damages.

In another case at the Court of Appeal in *Chaplin v. Leslie Frewin (Publishers) Ltd*,[551] a contract, under which the appellant Charlie Chaplin's son, then a minor,

548. (1912) 14 CLR 236.
549. [1935] 1 KB 110.
550. [1913] 1 KB 520.
551. [1966] Ch. 71.

agreed to tell his life story in return for royalties in the resulting book, was held to be binding. The contract was said to be one analogous to a service contract and the court held that as the particular contract was, on balance, beneficial to the minor, it was binding on him.

540. Whether a contract is beneficial therefore is to be viewed as a whole and whether it was for the minor's benefit. Consequently, a minor can be bound, even though some of the clauses of the contract are disadvantageous *see Hamilton v. Lethbridge.*[552] While still a minor, Lethbridge entered into articles of clerkship with Hamilton. The articles contained a covenant to the effect that Lethbridge would not, when qualified, practice as a solicitor within 50 miles of Toowoomba, where Hamilton had his practice. In breach of that covenant, Lethbridge started his own practice within a year of qualifying. Hamilton sought an injunction to restrain him. Lethbridge pleaded his infancy at the time of entering into the articles as an absolute defence. His argument was that the restraint of trade clause was onerous and thus the contract could not be considered 'beneficial'. The High Court unanimously held that the covenant was enforceable even though there was a clause that was prejudicial to Lethbridge because on balance the contract as a whole was beneficial.

However where the contract, on balance, is substantially detrimental to the minor and onerous clauses cannot be validly severed, no part of a contract can be enforced against him or her. In *De Francesco v. Barnum*[553] the whole tenor of the contract was offensive, and the contract as a whole was struck down and no part of it could be enforceable against the minor. Where a contract is objectionable because of one or two clauses, its substantive elements may be saved by excising or severing those clauses and allowing the bulk of the provisions to apply.

§5. Contracts for Service

541. A contract *for* service is one between two independent parties where one agrees to perform some service for the other. Sometimes one party might require the exclusive services of the independent contractor and insert a clause where that contractor may not seek other work without the principal's express consent. Such a clause is valid in that the principal wishes to be able to get access to the contractor's skill and expertise as and when required. However, where the restraint of trade clause is in the form of ensuring that no one else can access them, the clause will be invalid.

Lord Pearce in *Esso Petroleum v. Harper's Garage (Stourport) Ltd*[554] drew the distinction between a restraint of trade clause that was directed towards the *absorption* of a party's services and one that was directed towards their *sterilization*. The former is valid, whereas the latter is not.

552. (1912) 12 CLR 236.
553. (1890) 45 Ch. D 430.
554. [1968] AC 269 at 328.

A valid restraint of trade clause in a services contract is *Warner Bros Pictures Inc v. Ingolia*.[555] The defendant, whose stage name was Connie Stevens, signed a singing and screen contract with Warner Bros. The contract specified that Warner Bros had exclusive rights of her services for the duration of the agreement. Differences arose in the renegotiation of that contract and Ingolia failed to appear on set. Warner Bros suspended her. Without notifying them, she flew to Sydney and opened a twice-nightly show at the Chevron-Hilton Hotel. Warner Bros sued for an injunction to prevent her continuing with the show in breach of the exclusive service provision. The court granted the interlocutory injunction. She was prohibited from performing in continued breach of the contract.[556]

But where a clauses' real purpose is to impede, sterilize or stifle the work of one party, such clauses will be invalid.[557] In both these cases the contracts were deemed harsh and oppressive contracts that had been entered into between composers and/or songwriters and their managers or record companies. The cases were determined on the basis of unacceptable restraint of trade and the relative inequality in bargaining powers of the respective parties.

Less common are mandatory injunctions that compel performance of some obligation arising under a contract. In *Burns Philp Trust Co Pty Ltd v. Kwikasair Freightlines Ltd*[558] the plaintiffs were trustees for the holders of unsecured notes issued by the defendants. The trust deed specified that they were to have access to and a right to inspect the defendant company's register of note holders. The defendants refused to let them inspect it. A mandatory injunction was sought and granted that forbade the defendants from preventing the inspection.

I. Information Technology Personnel Contracts

542. Many personnel contracts are concerned with the performance of services on a temporal basis. In the information technology age, where only maintenance of the computer system is concerned, there are few contentious issues that can arise. However, where personnel are hired for program development work then an employer should be more aware of the pitfalls. The contractor may well wish to contract on a temporal basis to avoid being committed to the performance of a particular task. There is also the prospect of a fixed fee and a minimum of risk. However, the customer needs to scrutinize the contract carefully to see exactly what is being promised. Even with the prospect that the customer may terminate the contract, there are other risks such as incomplete software, the lack of documentation, annotation and source codes and the ease that someone else may complete the task. It may be prudent to tie payments to personnel to the different stages of program development where the nature of the task makes this feasible.

555. [1965] NSWR 988.
556. See also *Curro v. Beyond 2000 Productions Pty Ltd* (1993) 30 NSWLR 337 for a similar result.
557. See *Schroeder v. Macaulay* [1974] 1 WLR 1308; and *Clifford Davis Management v. WEA Records* [1975] 1 WLR 61.
558. (1963) 80 WN (NSW) 801.

Other features of personnel contracts includes place of work, number and quality of personnel involved, rates of remuneration, overhead costs and formula for charging. In this respect it should be absolutely clear the extent to which a customer is to be liable to the contractor's employees where contracts are terminated prematurely.[559]

Appraisals by consultants of the computing needs of an organization is another form of a personnel contract. The difficulties here include assessing the competence of a consultant and avoiding situations where consultants are seen to be feathering their own nests with their recommendations.[560]

Also to be noted is that because the computer industry has grown so rapidly there have been no measures of competence and skill except in the benefit of experience. Aggressive firms have been known to raid employees from their competitors. If the raider can show that it is only interested in an employee and not the training experience or contacts and other information acquired by the employee from the former employer, then there can be little legal difficulty.

However, this is rarely the case and there arises two possible avenues of liability. In contract, a former employee may claim a breach by the employer of the terms restricting employment in a similar industry after termination of employment. However, an employer may rely on unfair competition through torts like conspiracy, inducement for breach of contract, interference with contract and 'passing off'.[561]

Remedies in tort may be possible if it can be shown that the employees have misappropriated trade secrets and confidential materials.[562]

Sometimes contracts of employment have very broad clauses inserted so that courts could strike these down as an unreasonable restraint of trade.[563] An agreement not to actively compete should not be stricken down merely because there would be an overly burdensome effect on the employee.[564]

Restraint of trade. Under English common law, contracts restricting a person's right to pursue a trade or occupation is against public policy. Preparing to leave an employer either to join a competitor or to set up in competition oneself does not constitute such cause if there is no active solicitation of other employees to leave or existing customers to transfer their custom.[565]

A contract for Web page design and hosting services is not a personnel services contract that qualifies for an exception to California procedural rule that prohibits

559. See *Telecomputing Services Inc* 1 CLSR 953 (1968).

560. See *Trilog Associates Inc v. Famularo* 314 A. 2d. 287 (Pa. 1974); and *McArdle v. Board of Estimates of the City of Mount Vernon* 347 NYS 2d. 349 (NY 1973).

561. See *Craig Carnahan v. Alexander Proudfoot Co World Headquarters & Alexander Proudfoot Co of Australia* (1991) 3 CCH Comp. Cases.

562. *Compare Sperry Rand Corporation v. Kinder* 360 F. Supp. 1044 (ND Tex. 1973), and *Republic Systems and Programming Inc v. Computer Assistance Inc* 322 F. Supp. 619 (D. Conn. 1970). Also *Electronic Data Systems Corp v. Kinder*, 360 F. Supp 1044 (1973), and *Kelsey-Hayes Company v. Ali Malehi*, 765 F. Supp. 402 (1991).

563. See *Booth v. Electronic Data Systems Corp* (DC Kan. 1992), 4 CCH Computer Cases 46,801.

564. See *Pinch-a-Penny of Pinellas County v. Chango* [1990–1 Trade Cases 68-961] 557 SO. 2d 940 (Fla 2d. DCA 1990). For 'Employment Contracts' see generally CCH (1992) Guide to Computer Law, CCH 21,100.

565. See *Computer Services Corporation v. Ferguson* 74 Cal. Rptr. 86 (Cal. 1968). See also *Craig Carnahan v. Alexander Proudfoot Co World Headquarters and Alexander Proudfoot Co of Australia* (Fla DC App 1991) 3 CCH Computer Cases.

an injunction from enforcing a contract that would not be specifically enforced under California rules of civil procedure. This ruling was made by the California Court of Appeals, Fourth District, Division 3 in an unpublished decision of *Newport Corp v. Warenet Inc*[566] Web design services, the court found, were so widely available that they could be obtained from many sources and thus the defendant's services were not unique such that specific performance would be available.[567]

§6. Performance in Time and Personal Service

543. Some personnel contracts may stipulate a time by which performance is to occur. Where such a clause exists and the performance does not occur by that time, there is a breach and the innocent party may claim damages. Whether the breach also means a termination of the contract depends on whether the time stipulation was a critical element of the contract or whether it was merely a convenient reference point. Where 'time is of the essence' then a failure to complete on time will permit termination.

544. The other issue is one where a personnel contract stipulates personal performance or service. Here the question is whether a party so engaged may still perform the contractual obligations through others. In one instance unless the contract expressly or impliedly forbids such vicarious performance then personal performance is required. However, where such a stipulation does not exist then that party might delegate some or all of the work to others in his/her employ. The particulars of each case will apply. In the case where the work requires the exercise of a particular skill or expertise, then it is assumed that delegation is not contemplated, and if such work is delegated, the delegation will constitute grounds for the innocent party to discharge the contract.

545. Even in cases where delegation was permissible, the party so delegating will be personally liable for any breach of the contract. Such an eventuality has seen the development of exclusion clauses that seek to exempt liability not only for the proferens' own work but also of those that are sub-contracted to do all or part of the work.

546. Specific performance will not be ordered to enforce a contract of personal service. The reasoning here is that there may be an undue interference with personal liberty in requiring one party to serve a particular master. Conversely, a master cannot continue employing someone who does not want to be a 'servant'. Such a rule not only covers master-servant relationships but also partnerships,[568] agency relationships,[569] share-farming agreements[570] apprenticeships[571] and others. These

566. Cal. Ct. App. 4th Dist., Div. 3, No. G028775, 7/25/02.

567. See (2002) *Electronic Commerce and Law Report*, v. 7 No. 32, 821.

568. *Scott v. Rayment* (1868) LR 7 Eq. 112); *Douglas v. Hill* [1909] SALR 28; *Renowden v. Hurley* [1951] VLR 13.

569. *Chinook v. Sainsbury* (1860) 30 LJ (Ch.) 409.

agreements cannot be enforced by specific performance other than in exceptional circumstances.[572]

547. A contract for personal services is not specifically enforceable at the suit of either party.[573] It would be undesirable as well as impossible to compel an unwilling party to perform personal services within the terms of the contract with another. Courts will also refuse to decree specific performance of contracts requiring continual cooperation between the parties and the supervision of such contracts.

While in general, the rule is that some personal service must be involved, it may be further complicated by other requirements. For example, where the contracts involve some work and items to be produced, then the contract may be specifically enforced.[574]

§7. Professional Services and the Competition and Consumer Act 2010 (Cth)

548. Professional activities for reward fall within the phrase 'in trade or commerce'. In some Fair Trading Acts 'trade or commerce' is defined so as to include professional activity, as well as business not carried on for profit.[575]

549. Moreover, the promotional activities of professional persons within a territory are expressly brought within the ambit of trade or commerce by section 6 Competition and Consumer Act 2010 (Cth) extended application of this Act to persons who are not corporations.[576]

§8. Sale of Goods or Contract for Skill and Materials

550. It may be difficult to decide whether a transaction may be described as a sale of goods or a contract for work or skill to which the supply of materials or other goods is incidental. The parties may choose either form but the ultimate result will be the same. Where the form of the contract does not clearly show the intention of the parties then a court may have to decide. The issue is whether a contract for the exercise of skill is important, with the production of a chattel being incidental or whether it is in essence a contract to produce a chattel.

---

570. *Miotti v. Belford* [1962] NSWR 324; *Bishop v. Taylor* [1968] Qd R 281; *Dudgeon v. Chie* (1955) 92 CLR 342.
571. *Webb v. England* (1860) 29 Beav 44; 54 ER 541.
572. *Byrne v. Australian Airlines Ltd* (1995) 185 CLR 410.
573. per Sugerman J in *Atlas Steels (Australia) Pty Ltd v. Atlas Steels Ltd* (1948) 49 SR (NSW) 157 at 161.
574. See *Thomas Borthwick & Sons Ltd v. South Otago Freezing Co Ltd* [1978] 1 NZLR 538.
575. See *Fair Trade Act* 1987 (NSW) s. 4(1); *Consumer Affairs and Fair Trading Act* (1990) (NT) s. 4(1); *Fair Trading Act* 1989 (Qld) s. 5(1); *Fair Trading Act* 1987 (WA) s. 5(1).
576. See *Presia v. Akner* (1996) 40 NSWLR 165 per Santow, J. at 184.

Schedule 2 of the Competition and Consumer Act 2010 (Cth) provide for consumer guarantees in contracts for the supply of services. Section 60 provides for a guarantee that services supplied to a consumer, in trade or commerce, will be rendered with due care and skill. Section 61 provides for guarantees as to fitness for a particular purpose and section 62 provides for a guarantee that services will be supplied within a reasonable time.

The essential character or substance of the contract test is set out in *Robinson v. Graves*[577] where there was a contract to paint a portrait. The court held that it was not a sale of a good.

In *Delta Nominees Pty Ltd v. Viscount Plastic Products Pty Ltd*[578] the court preferred the earlier test in *Lee v. Griffin*.[579] The test was that if a chattel was produced, no matter how high the skill involved, then it was a sale of goods. However, *Lee v. Griffin* and *Robinson v. Graves* cannot be reconciled.

Sale of goods examples include: *Marcel (Furriers) Ltd v. Tapper*[580] – made to measure suit; *Samuels v. Davis*[581] – making a set of dentures; *Toby Construction Products Pty Ltd v. Computer Bar Sales Pty Ltd*[582] – a computer system comprising software and hardware.

Where the contract provides for supply and installation of the goods so that the chattel becomes a fixture then the contract is for work and materials.[583]

In[584] there was a contract for the sale of goods in the form of an oil heater with a subordinate agreement to install the article.

In certain circumstances, a supply of goods is linked to a supply of services. Today it is commonplace for the purchase of a mobile phone to be linked to a contract for the supply of network services as well. Where the consumer validly notifies the supplier of goods that the consumer rejects the goods and the supplier is required to give a refund, section 265 of the Schedule 2 Competition and Consumer Act 2010 (Cth) provides that the consumer may also terminate the contract for the supply of services. Where a linked service contract is validly terminated, the consumer is entitled to a refund of any money or equivalent paid for the services to the extent that the consumer has not already consumed the services at the time the termination takes effect.[585]

Where a consumer guarantee in relation to services is not complied with, the consumer is entitled to a remedy. The remedy will be available against the supplier of the services.[586]

The nature of the remedy depends upon whether the problem with the services is minor or major. Where the problem is minor, the supplier can choose between providing a repair or offering a refund to the consumer. Where the problem is major,

577. [1935] 1 KB 579; [1935] All ER Rep 935.
578. [1979] VR 167.
579. (1861) 1 B&S 272; 121 ER 716.
580. [1953] 1 WLR 49.
581. [1943] 1 KB 526.
582. [1983] 2 NSWLR 48.
583. See *Aristoc Industries Pty Ltd v. RA Wenham (Builders) Pty Ltd* [1965] NSWR 581.
584. *Collins Trading Co Pty Ltd v. Maher* [1969] VR 20.
585. See Sch 2 s. 265(3) of the Competition and Consumer Act 2010 (Cth).
586. See Sch 2 Ch. 5 Pt 5-4 ss 267–270 Competition and Consumer Act 2010.

the consumer may terminate the contract for the supply of services and seek a refund. Relevant sections of Schedule 2 section 268 Competition and Consumer Act 2010 (Cth) specify what are 'major' failure and the remedies and what are 'minor' failures and the associated remedies to each respectively. In addition damages for consequential losses are available to the consumer if it was reasonably foreseeable that the consumer would suffer such loss or damage as a result of such failure to comply with the guarantee.

§9. Implied Conditions and Warranties

551. The common law will imply conditions and warranties for work and materials where these are not provided for by legislation.[587]

552. However, note that the Competition and Consumer Act 2010 (Cth) Schedule 2 section 60 guarantees as to due care and skill refers to warranties in relation to the supply of services. In particular section 60 states that 'If a person supplies, in trade or commerce, services to a consumer, there is a guarantee that the service will be rendered with due care and skill.'

553. This section implies into contracts for services provided to a consumer by a corporation in the course of business, a warranty that the services will be performed with due care and skill. The warranty is not excludable other than in relation to 'recreational services' *see* Schedule 2 sections 64 and 139K terms excluding consumer guarantees from supplies of recreational services.

554. The remedy for breach of Competition and Consumer Act 2010 (Cth) Schedule 2 section 60 is to sue for breach of the implied condition rather than to proceed for damages under section 82 and see also Schedule 2 section 236.[588]

Schedule 2 section 60 has the effect of including a contractually non-excludable warranty, in relation to the supply of services by a corporation in the course of business, that the services will be rendered with due care and skill.

However, the contract is to be read subject to any applicable state law which places a limitation on those contractual rights or excludes them: Schedule 2 sections 60, 61 (section 60 guarantee due care and skill and section 61 guarantee as to fitness for a particular purpose, etc. Before this subsection was enacted the contrary position applied. State law could not exclude or limit these warranties.[589]

555. While a transaction may not be a 'sale of goods' for the purposes of the Sale of Goods Act, the same transaction may attract the *Fair Trade Act* if there is a 'supply' of goods or services or the acquisition of them by a 'consumer'.

---

587. See for example, *Helicopter Sales Pty Ltd v. Rotor-Work Pty Ltd* (1974) 132 CLR 1.
588. See for instance *Aturi v. Zupp Motors Pty Ltd* (1980) 49 FLR 283; 33 ALR 243.
589. See *Wallis v. Downard Pickford (North Qld) Pty Ltd* (1994) 179 CLR 388; 68 ALJR 395; 120 ALR 440; (1994) ATPR 41-300.

Chapter 6. Agricultural Tenancies

§1. General

556. In New South Wales, specialist legislation applies to agricultural tenancies.[590] Queensland also has a specific division within its *Property Law Act* 1974[591] applying to agricultural tenancies. Apart from this, no Australian jurisdiction has explicit legislation directed to agricultural tenancies, though in Tasmania and Victoria, certain sections of their respective *Landlord and Tenant* legislation are, by their content, directed to agricultural tenancies.[592] The legislation in all of these jurisdictions does not codify the law relating to agricultural tenancies; rather it affects certain aspects peculiar to the landlord and tenant relationship in agricultural law, such as improvements to the farming property, cultivation of crops, inspection by the parties, fixtures,[593] termination and dispute resolution.

§2. New South Wales

557. The object of this legislation is to encourage landowners and their tenants to engage in ecologically sustainable development, to provide a dispute resolution mechanism, and to encourage the use of written agreements.[594] Agricultural purposes is widely drafted and includes grazing, dairying, pig-farming, poultry, viticulture, orcharding, bee-keeping, horticulture, vegetable growing, the growing of crops, forestry, or any combination of these things.[595] The legislation applies to land of not less than one hectare.[596] Either the owner or the tenant can have any agreement reduced to writing.[597] Improvements[598] to the land can be carried out by the tenant with the consent of the owner,[599] with the owner liable to compensate the tenant for those improvements.[600] In addition to this right to carry out improvements with the consent of the owner, the tenant can also make improvements without the owner's consent (with the owner still required to compensate the tenant), where the improvements relate to drainage, the making of roads or bridges, the clearing of stumps, the destruction of pests, the removal of noxious weeds, the making of

590. *Agricultural Tenancies Act* 1990 (NSW).
591. *Property Law Act* 1974 Pt 8, Division 6 (Qld).
592. *Landlord and Tenant Act* 1935 (Tas), ss 19, 25–26; *Landlord and Tenant Act* 1958 (Vic) ss 15–28.
593. This legislation modifying the common law rule that a tenant's right of removal did not extent to agricultural fixtures: *Elwes v. Maw* (1802) 3 East 38; 102 ER 510.
594. *Agricultural Tenancies Act* 1990 s. 3.
595. *Ibid.*, s. 4.
596. *Ibid.*
597. *Ibid.*, s. 5.
598. See *McBean v. Grieve* (1979) 2 SCR (NS) (NSW) L 153.
599. See *Wylie v. McDermott* [1933] St R Qd 1; *Re Brown and Morrisson's Arbitration* [1955] St R Qd 223.
600. *Agricultural Tenancies Act* 1990 s. 6, with Division 1 of Part 3 determining how compensation is to be determined should the parties be unable to agree.

fences, the laying down of pastures, the application of fertilizers, repairs to buildings and repairs to bores, dams and like structures.[601] Improvements can also be carried out by the owner with or without consent (though in the latter instance, this is only possible where the improvement is determined by arbitration to be suitable and desirable in the circumstances.[602] Tenants' fixtures can be removed from the land by the tenant before the conclusion of the tenancy or within a reasonable time after the determination of the lease agreement.[603] Any damage caused in removal must be made good by the tenant.[604] An owner has a right to enter the farm at all reasonable times.[605] A fixed term tenancy is terminated at the end of the period, without any need to give notice.[606] A periodic tenancy is only terminated by the giving of notice equivalent to the length of the tenancy period,[607] with a year-to-year tenancy requiring the giving of six months notice before the end of the tenancy period.[608]

558. Any disputes that occur in respect of the agricultural tenancy can be resolved by arbitration.[609] An application for arbitration is to be made to the Director-General of Agriculture who is to arrange a pre-arbitration conference, encourage the parties to seek mediation, request the parties to provide information, fix the date of hearing and arrange a technical assessor.[610] If the matter is referred to mediation, anything said in that mediation is privileged,[611] and there are only limited grounds when the mediator can disclose any information obtained through the mediation process.[612] If the matter is referred to arbitration, the *Commercial Arbitration Act* 1984 (NSW) applies to the conduct of the arbitration.[613]

559. Any attempt to contract out, or abrogate any right created by the legislation is void.[614]

§3. QUEENSLAND

560. Division 6 of Part 8 of the Queensland *Property Law Act* 1974 applies to holdings of agricultural land where the area of land held by the tenant is not less

601. *Ibid.*, s. 7.
602. *Ibid.*, ss 8–9.
603. *Ibid.*, s. 10.
604. *Ibid.*, s. 10(5).
605. *Ibid.*, s. 11.
606. *Ibid.*, s. 14(1).
607. *Ibid.*, s. 14(2).
608. *Ibid.*, s. 14(4). In this instance, a period of notice to terminate will also not take effect unless it is at least one month after the end of the cropping period.
609. *Ibid.*, Part 4.
610. *Ibid.*, 1990 s. 25.
611. *Ibid.*, 1990 s. 26F.
612. *Ibid.*, s. 26G. Disclosure is permitted if it by consent of the person, where the disclosure is within the context of the mediation, where it is necessary to disclose to prevent injury, or where disclosure is required by law.
613. *Ibid.*, s. 26K.
614. *Ibid.*, s. 27.

than five acres.[615] Any provision in the agreement, which seeks to oust the operation of the legislation in respect of a tenant's right to compensation, is unenforceable.[616] A tenant is entitled to remove any fixtures annexed by the tenant prior to the termination of the tenancy or within two months of its conclusion.[617] The tenant must correct any damage caused by the removal.[618] The tenant is entitled to compensation from the owner for certain improvements made to the land.[619] These improvements include drain construction, the making of fences, improvements to irrigation, the making of dams, the clearing and fertilizing of land, the laying down of pasture, the making of plantations of bananas or pineapples, the planting of sugarcane, or the planting of orchards.[620] If the parties cannot agree as to the amount of compensation, the matter is referred to arbitration.[621] The landlord is entitled to enter at all reasonable times.[622]

§4. Tasmania and Victoria

561. Under the Victorian *Landlord and Tenant Act* 1958, with this mirrored in the Tasmanian legislation, restrictions are placed upon officers of the court, such as the sheriff from dealing with produce on the land.[623] This includes a prohibition on a sheriff from selling grasses growing with corn, and the tenant being able to remove straw, turnips and other articles that the tenant may remove from the farm consistently with some contract in writing.[624] Allied to these provisions is section 27, which provides that if growing crops are seized and sold by any sheriff, then such crops, so long as they remain on the farm or lands shall be liable to the rent that may accrue and become due to the landlord after any such seizure and sale.[625] The tenant is also entitled to remove any farm-buildings or building engines that were attached to the land for agricultural purposes during the term of the tenancy.[626]

615. *Property Law Act* 1974 s. 153.
616. *Ibid.*, s. 154.
617. *Ibid.*, s. 155. Notice must be given to the landlord, and all rent must be paid. *Property Law Act* 1974 s. 155(2).
618. *Ibid.*, s. 155(4).
619. *Ibid.*, s. 156.
620. *Ibid.*, Schedule 4.
621. *Ibid.*, s. 159.
622. *Ibid.*, s. 167.
623. *Landlord and Tenant Act* 1958 ss 15–22 (Vic). *Landlord and Tenant Act* 1935 (Tas) ss 14–22.
624. *Landlord and Tenant Act* 1958 ss 21–22 (Vic). *Landlord and Tenant Act* 1935 (Tas) ss 20–21.
625. *Landlord and Tenant Act* 1958 s. 27 (Vic). *Landlord and Tenant Act* 1935 (Tas) s. 25.
626. *Landlord and Tenant Act* 1958 s. 28 (Vic). *Landlord and Tenant Act* 1935 (Tas) s. 26.

Chapter 7. Compromise Settlement

§1. Compromise Settlement and Compositions

562. Under contract law there is a rule which states that a promise to perform an existing contractual duty is not consideration. However, despite this, courts have attempted to give effect to contracts intended to settle contractual problems. Here it is important to appreciate the reasoning behind the attempts. This reasoning suggests that for problems of this kind it may be necessary to imply that there are two contracts. For example, there may be a contract for the sale of some chattels and a second contract intended to settle a dispute in relation to the first contract. The question that arises in such situations is whether there is consideration for the second contract and the effect of that contract on the rights and remedies which arise from the first contract. The general law has developed such that consideration may be found to exist even though the promisor has in fact promised to do no more than perform an existing duty. This has now come to be known as a compromise settlement.

563. One means by which to characterize such settlements is by way of 'compositions' as deemed in certain legislation. The term compositions is used to describe the enforcement of debtors with creditors. As defined by section 187(1) of the *Bankruptcy Act* 1966 (Cth) 'composition' means an 'arrangement (not being an arrangement entered into for the purposes of a proclaimed law) by which creditors of a debtor:

(i) agree to accept payment of the debts due to them by instalments; or
(ii) agree to accept, in full satisfaction of the debts due to them, less than the full amount of those debts, whether in the form of money or other property and whether by instalments or otherwise.'

564. In practice, compositions seem to work in the commercial world. Commercial practice has found compositions a satisfactory device and the courts have supported this path by 'inventing' and deeming that consideration exists. In Australia, the case in point is that of *McDermott v. Black.*[627] This appears to be another means by which to characterize an agreement to relinquish a cause of action against a party may act as a discharge of the original agreement. Such a contract may be called an 'accord and satisfaction' or a 'compromise' per Scrutton LJ in *McDermott v. Black* 'the accord is the agreement by which is discharged. The satisfaction is the consideration which makes the agreement operative'.[628]

565. A composition is thus an arrangement whereby a creditor of a particular debtor agrees to accept a lesser sum in satisfaction of the whole debt owed. The lesser sum is usually stipulated as a set proportion of each debt (say 60 cents on the

627. (1940) 63 CLR 161 (HCA).
628. (1940) 63 CLR 161, 184.

dollar). As noted above, compositions have statutory force under Part X of the *Bankruptcy Act* 1966 (Cth) which provides that compositions are enforceable and, once they are agreed to by the majority of creditors, the agreement binds them all.

§2. Compromise as an Exception to the Existing Legal Duty Rule

566. Under the general topic of consideration there is a rule relating to an existing legal duty. The general rule states that neither a promise to perform an existing legal duty, nor the performance of an existing legal duty, is regarded as sufficient consideration to support a contract. This legal duty rule covers promises to perform existing public duties, for example, such as a promise to give evidence in court when obliged by a subpoena to do so.

567. However, there are five exceptions in which the existing legal duty rule will not apply. These are: (1) where the beneficiary is providing fresh consideration, (2) where the beneficiary's promise to perform confers a practical benefit on the modifying party, (3) where the promise to perform an existing contractual duty is made by the beneficiary to a third party, (4) where the original contract is terminated by agreement and replaced with a new contract, and (5) where a promise is made by way of a bona fide compromise of a legal claim.

The final exception above may be read as constituting a forbearance to sue. This exception was applied by the High Court in *Wigan v. Edwards*.[629] In this case the Edwards entered into a contract to buy a house from Wigan. After the contract was signed, the Edwards were concerned about some defects in the house and gave a list of defects that required attention. The Edwards refused to complete the transaction unless the defects were rectified. Faced with this Wigan signed a document agreeing to rectify the listed defects. Wigan rectified some of the listed defects before the transaction was completed but did nothing after completion of the transaction to rectify the defects that remained outstanding. The Edwards sued Wigan for damages for breach of contract. Wigan argued that the Edwards had provided no consideration for the promise to rectify the defects. The High Court held that a promise made as part of a bona fide compromise constituted an exception to the existing legal duty rule. The pivotal element in the case was that the compromise must be a bona fide one.

§3. A Promise Not to Sue

568. The principle of the promise not to sue arises when a person seeks to stay the prosecution of a legal claim. There may be two groups – those in which the party threatened admits liability, but offers some promise to postpone litigation; and those where liability is denied but prefers to settle rather than to fight. The first class is classed as a 'forbearance to sue' whilst the second is classed as a 'compromise of the suit'.

629. (1973) 1 ALR 497.

569. In its original guise a promise not to pursue a claim which was without legal basis could not be good consideration. If such a case was submitted to the courts, the promisor would have failed, but it could not be a 'detriment' to be saved from a losing hazard. However, in the 19th C this position was abandoned, and the compromise of a doubtful claim was upheld by the courts. The change was justified on grounds of convenience, per Bowen, L.J. in *Miles v. New Zealand Alford Estate Co.*[630]

570. The modern law of consideration in such cases is said to be the surrender, not of a legal right, which may or may not exist and whose existence, at the time of the compromise, remains untested, but of the *claim* to such a right.

571. An implicit promise of forbearance to sue is sufficient. There need not be an express promise either to compromise or to forbear, if such an understanding can be inferred from the circumstances or from the negotiations between the parties. In *McDermott v. Black*[631] *supra* the plaintiff had been induced to contract with the defendant by the latter's fraudulent misrepresentation, but during negotiations agreed to withdraw all allegations of fraud, provided he was given an extension of time to complete the contract. The defendant granted an extension and, when the plaintiff failed to complete on the new date, repudiated the contract. The plaintiff sued for the return of his deposit on the ground that he had been induced to enter into the contract by fraud.

572. The High Court rejected the claim on the basis that the withdrawal of the allegations of fraud had amounted to a promise not to sue in respect of the misrepresentation and as such was good consideration for the defendant's promise to given an extension of time.[632]

§4. Relinquishment of Cause of Action

573. Where a party undertakes to relinquish a cause of action under a contract, that act normally terminates the obligation to which it relates. A contract to relinquish a cause of action may operate by way of 'accord and satisfaction' or 'compromise'. Under *accord and satisfaction* a plaintiff accepts something else in place of the cause of action – it may be a promise or it may be the act or thing promised. The rule is that some tangible value must be conferred in consideration for the discharge of liability. In *Ballantyne v. Phillott*,[633] Phillott sued his ex-mistress Ballantyne for an amount claimed as a debt. Ballantyne relied on a sworn statement by her and Phillott, stating that he 'waives all and any rights or claims whatsoever' against her, and that she 'has no right or claim' against him. The document was relied on as evidence of an accord and satisfaction.

630. (1886) 32 CLD 266 at 291; [1886–90] All ER Rep 1726 at 1735.
631. (1940) 63 CLR 161 (HCA).
632. See also *Wigan v. Edwards* (1973) 1 ALR 497 above.
633. (1961) 105 CLR 379.

The majority held that she had given no consideration, as she had no apparent claim against Phillott and had in any case made no definite promise.

However, the transaction alleged in *Ballantyne* could also be described as one of *compromise*. It seems that the concepts of accord and satisfaction and compromise are overlapping concepts. But above all, the key requirement is that of a tangible consideration being given.

Chapter 8. Suretyship

§1. Suretyship

574. A contract of guarantee has been defined as 'a contract to answer for the debt, default or miscarriage of another who is to be primarily liable to the promissee'.[634] The person who provides the guarantee is referred to as the 'guarantor' or 'surety'.

The idea of suretyship has a long history which spans over 2,500 years before the dawn of Christianity. The person who makes the promise to be answerable for the debt or obligation of another is called the 'surety' or 'guarantor'; the person to whom the promise is made is called the 'creditor'; and the person on whose behalf the promise is made is called the 'principal debtor' or simply 'the principal'. In Australia and most English common law jurisdictions, the terms 'surety' and 'guarantor' are used interchangeably.

575. Suretyship has become accepted as an accessory contract and more latterly as a contract of guarantee that is entered into for the benefit of another. In addition, equitable principles of contribution, subrogation and reimbursement play a significant part in the law of suretyship. Today, the term 'contract of suretyship' has largely been replaced by the term 'contract of guarantee'. Such contracts are further regulated by statutory provisions affecting their form and enforceability, for example, the respective Australian state and territory *Consumer Credit Act.*

576. Lord Diplock has described subrogation as a remedy that embraced more than one concept in English law. In *Orakpo v. Manson Investments Ltd*[635] Lord Diplock opined that subrogation was a convenient way of describing a transfer of rights from one person to another without assignment or assent from the person from whom the rights are transferred, and which takes place by operation of law in a whole host of circumstances. Some such rights are contractual in origin, for example, contracts of insurance, while others are not contractual in origin. In *Craythorne v. Swinburne*[636] the concept of suretyship was said to depend on natural justice.

577. A surety who discharges the debt of a creditor on behalf of a debtor, for whom he or she has agreed to stand guarantor, has a right to be indemnified by the debtor. By agreeing to become a surety to a debtor, the surety will be legally liable to discharge the debt should the debtor default.

578. Equity will allow a surety to recoup a payment made to discharge a debt from the debtor.

---

634. *Yeoman Credit v. Latter* [1961] 1 WLR 828, 831.
635. [1978] AC 95; [1977] 3 WLR 229.
636. (1807) 14 Ves 160; [1807] 34 ER 1133.

579. A surety has the right to stand in the place of the creditor, to enforce all the securities held by the creditor and to have them transferred to him, even though he may not know of their existence or have stipulated for this in the contract of guarantee once the debt has been paid in full.

580. If a surety's obligations under the contract of guarantee are ambiguous, the contract will be construed *contra proferentem* against the creditor.[637]

581. The common law recognizes the right of a surety to contribution as an action for money paid to the use of another surety or co-obligator. However, equity appears to override the common law in so far as contribution between or amongst sureties is concerned. The doctrine of contribution has been described as founded on doctrines of equity and not in reference to general law. In *Deering v. The Earl of Winchelsea*[638] it was held by Eyre CB that a right of contribution in equity existed irrespective of whether the sureties were bound jointly and severally in the one instrument or had guaranteed a debt in separate instruments, provided that they were co-obligators in relation to the same and not different debts.

582. A surety may claim contribution if he or she has paid more than his or her proportion of the principal debt.

583. Payment of an excessive amount of an instalment of a debt, however, does not entitle the payer to claim contribution since there can be no obligation on a co-surety to pay contribution until the total proportionate share of the debt is paid by the payer.[639]

§2. Guarantee Obligations

584. Two obligations arise in a contract of guarantee – one primary and the other secondary. The principal obligation in a contract of guarantee is based upon the existence of a valid principal obligation owed by the principal debtor. If there is no such principal obligation, generally the guarantee fails. Hence, a valid guarantee depends upon the existence of a promise made to a person to whom a debtor is already answerable or is to become answerable.[640] The principal obligation, however, need not be contractual.

585. Further, in the instant contract of guarantee, a secondary obligation is assumed by the surety or guarantor.[641] A guarantee does not represent that the principal debtor is credit-worthy. The main object of the transaction is that the guarantor, or his or her property, will be answerable to the creditor. It is not necessary for

637. See *Eastern Counties Building Society v. Russell* [1947] 1 All ER 500.
638. (1787) 2 Bos & Pul 270; [1787] 126 ER 1276.
639. *Stirling v. Burdett* [1911] 2 Ch. 418.
640. See *Total Oil Products (Aust) Pty Ltd v. Robinson* [1970] 1 NSWR 701.
641. See *Turner Manufacturing Co Pty Ltd v. Senes* [1964] NSWR 692.

a guarantor to assume personal liability for the debt of another since the person who provides a pledge of property without incurring liability beyond the pledge is nevertheless properly classified as a guarantor.[642] Jordan, C.J. has described the general nature of a contract of guarantee in *Jowitt v. Callaghan*.[643]

§3. The Modern Scope of Suretyship

586. The modern scope of suretyship has been appropriately outlined by Lord Selborne. In *Duncan, Fox & Co v. North and South Wales Bank*,[644] Lord Selborne identified three classic situations in which suretyship arises. In the first, there is an agreement to constitute the relationship of principal and surety for a particular purpose, and the creditor thereby secured is a party to this arrangement in the sense that the creditor and the principal debtor agree from the outset that the surety's liability is merely secondary, and that the primary liability rests with the principal debtor.

587. In the second situation, there is an agreement between two co-debtors that one will assume the primary liability as principal debtor and the other will undertake the secondary liability as guarantor. To this contract of suretyship, the creditor is a stranger.[645] In the absence of notice of this arrangement, the creditor is entitled to treat both co-debtors as principal debtors since there is no contract of suretyship between the creditor and the guarantor. But as between the co-debtors, one is guarantor for the other and, under this contract of suretyship, the guarantor acquires certain rights and incurs certain liabilities vis-à-vis the principal debtor.

588. The third situation is not dependent upon a contract of suretyship. It arises when there is a primary and secondary liability of two persons, say A and B, for the same debt but the debt is, as between the two, the debt of A only. In this form of a constructive suretyship, equity ensures that B's rights are not materially different from those of a surety by express agreement at law.[646]

589. Suretyship covers a broad spectrum from guarantees of debts to transactions involving unincorporated associations, as a means of securing contractual obligations, mortgages, leases, sale of goods, hire purchase, building contracts, performance bonds and promissory notes or bills of exchange and letters of credit.[647]

In most Australian jurisdictions, there is a statutory requirement for a contract of guarantee to be in writing and signed by the party to be charged in order to be enforceable. Section 56(1) of the Property Law Act 1974 (Qld) provides for such a

642. See *Edwards v. Lennon* (1866) 6 SCR (NSW) Eq. 18.
643. (1938) 38 SR (NSW) 512.
644. (1880) 6 App Cas 1.
645. See *Israel v. Foreshore Properties Pty Ltd* (1980) 30 ALR 631.
646. See *A M Spicer & Son Pty Ltd (in liq) v. Spicer* (1931) 47 CLR 151.
647. See K.P. McGuinness (1986) *The Law of Guarantee*.

requirement – a promise is in writing and signed by the party to be charged, or by some other person by the party lawfully authorized.[648]

Issues of undue influence and third party sureties have arisen. The actual or presumed undue influence may result from the conduct of a third party. See for example *Khan v. Khan* (2004) where a mufti influenced a Muslim woman to sign a memorandum of transfer of her house to buyers.[649]

While the relationship of husband and wife has not been seen as automatically giving rise to a presumption of undue influence, it has, 'never been divested completely of what may be called equitable presumptions of an invalidating tendency' per *Dixon J in Yerkey v. Jones*.[650]

The 'rule' in *Yerkey v. Jones* has been upheld by the High Court in *Gracia v. National Australia Bank Ltd.*[651] The joint judgment of Gaudron, McHugh, Gummow and Hayne JJ insisted that the rationale for the rule was based on the trust and confidence that is common between marriage partners rather than notions of subservience, inferior position or women or the assumed vulnerability to exploitation due to their emotional involvement.[652]

648. Similar requirements exist in other jurisdictions such as Instruments Act 1958 (Vic) s. 126; Law Reform (Statute of Frauds) Act 1962 (WA) s. 2; Mercantile Law Act 1935 (Tas) s. 6; and Law of Property Act 2000 (NT) s. 58.
649. (2004) 62 NSWLR 229.
650. (1940) 63 CLR 649, 675.
651. (1998) 194 CLR 395.
652. (1998) 194 CLR 395, 404.

Chapter 9. Pledge and Mortgage

§1. Pledge and Mortgage

590. In law a *pledge* (also *pawn*) is a bailment of personal property as a security for some debt. The term pledge is also used to denote the property which constitutes the security. Pledge is the *pignus* of Roman law from which most of the modern law on the subject is derived. It differs from a mortgage in that the pledge is in the possession of the pledgee; it also differs from mortgage in being confined to personal property. A mortgage of personal property in most cases takes the name and form of a bill of sale.

591. In Roman law certain things like apparel, furniture and instruments of tillage could not be pledged whereas there is no such restriction in English law. In the case of a pledge, a *special* property passes to the pledgee, sufficient to enable him to maintain an action against a wrongdoer, but the *general* property, that is the property subject to the pledge, remains in the pledgor.

592. As the pledge is for the benefit of both parties, the pledgee is bound to exercise only ordinary care over the pledge. The pledgee has the right of selling the pledge if the pledgor defaults payment at the stipulated time. No right is acquired by the wrongful sale of a pledge except in the case of property passing by delivery, such as money or negotiable securities. In the case of a wrongful sale by a pledgee, the pledgor cannot recover the value of the pledge without a tender of the amount due.

593. A *mortgage* can be over goods – chattel or goods mortgage – or house or land. A mortgage means that the lender (the mortgagee) has a right to take the mortgaged property and sell it to recover the money owed under the credit contract if the borrower (the mortgagor) defaults in payment or seriously breaches the contract in some other way. A mortgage may be taken over property bought with the finance or property already owned by the borrower.

594. A debtor (mortgagor) conveys an interest in property to a creditor (mortgagee) as security for the payment of a money debt. In its original form in medieval Europe a mortgagor gave the mortgagee ownership of the land on the condition that the mortgagee would return it once the mortgagor's debt was paid off. Over time, it became the practice to let the mortgagor remain in possession of the land; it then became the mortgagor's right to remain in possession of the land so long as there was no default on the debt.

595. The mortgage is a legal document by which the owner (buyer) transfers to the lender an interest in real property to secure the repayment of a debt, evidenced by a mortgage note. When the debt is repaid, the mortgage is discharged, and a satisfaction of mortgage is recorded with the Land Register Officer. Because most people cannot afford to buy real estate with cash, nearly every real estate transaction involves a mortgage.

596. Under English and Australian law, the mortgage was treated as a complete transfer of title from the borrower to the lender. The lender was entitled not only to payments of interest on the debt but also to the rents and profits of the real property. This meant that as far as the borrower was concerned, the real estate was of no value, that is, 'dead' until the debt was paid in full – hence the Norman-English name *mort* (dead), *gage* (pledge).

597. The mortgage must be executed according to the formalities required in each state jurisdiction where the property is located. It must describe the real property and be signed by all owners.

598. The mortgage note, in which the borrower promises to repay the debt, sets out the terms of the transaction: the amount of the debt, the mortgage due date, the rate of interest, amount of monthly payments, whether the loan may be repaid with larger or more frequent payments without a prepayment penalty, and whether failing to make a payment or selling the property will entitle the lender to call the entire debt due.

§2. Consumer Credit Code and Mortgages

599. In most Australian jurisdictions, uniform consumer credit legislation was introduced to commence on 1 November 1996. The Consumer Credit Code was adopted by all states and territories by legislation.[653]

600. The Consumer Credit Code applies to mortgages over land if the mortgage secures obligations under a credit contract or guarantee and the mortgagor is a natural person or strata corporation – section 8(1).

Section 6(1) of the Code relating to a credit contract states:

> A credit contract to which the Code applies is one where, at the time the credit was entered into, the debtor is a natural person ordinarily resident in the jurisdiction, or a strata corporation formed in the jurisdiction, and the credit is provided or intended to be provided wholly or predominantly for a personal, domestic or household purpose, a charge is made for providing the credit and the credit is provided in the course of business of providing credit.

601. Where the Code applies, the debtor benefits from a range of consumer protection provisions which include:

- the credit contract to be in the form of a written document: *section 12*;
- the credit provider must give the debtor a copy of the credit contract: *section 18*;

653. *Consumer Credit Act* 1995 (ACT); *Consumer Credit (New South Wales) Act* 1995 (NSW); *Consumer Credit (Northern Territory) Act* 1995 (NT); *Consumer Credit (South Australia) Act* 1995 (SA); *Consumer Credit (Tasmania) Act* 1995 (Tas); *Consumer Credit (Victoria) Act* 1995 (Vic);*Consumer Credit (Western Australia) Act* 1996 (WA).

- the credit provider must give the debtor a pre-contractual statement before entering into the credit contract containing the matters set out in section 15: *section 14*;
- the pre-contract disclosure statement must refer to matters such as the amount of credit, the annual percentage rate or rates, the calculation of the total amount of interest charges, repayments, credit fees and other charges, the default rate, if any, any commission paid by or to the credit provider and details of any insurance financed by the contract: *section 15*;
- except as provided in the Code, the credit contract must not provide for the annual percentage rate of interest to vary when the debtor is in default under the credit contract: *section 28(1)*;
- the credit contract may provide for a higher rate of interest to be charged following a default in payment but only in respect of the amount in default and only when the default continues: *section 28(2)*;
- third party mortgages are prohibited, that is to say, a mortgage must not secure obligations under a credit contract unless each mortgagor is a debtor under the contract or a guarantor under a related guarantee: *section 44*;
- the debtor has a right to pay out the credit contract at any time upon payment of specified charges: *section 75*;
- before a credit provider may take enforcement action under a mortgage against a debtor or guarantor, the debtor must be in default and the credit provider must serve a default notice giving the debtor at least thirty days to remedy the default and the default has not been remedied: *section 80*;
- acceleration clauses in a credit contract may only operate if the debtor is in default under the contract and then only if the debtor (or guarantor or mortgagor as the case may be) has been served with a default notice under section 80 which contains additional information concerning how the debtor's liability is affected by the operation of the acceleration clause: *section 85*.[654]

602. A special feature of the Code is contained in Division 3 of Part 4 relating to changes to the credit contract on grounds of hardship and unjust transactions.

654. See Duncan & Willmott, *Mortgages Law in Australia* 308–58 (2d ed., 1996).

Chapter 10. Consumer Loans and Credit

§1. Consumer Loans and Credit

603. A *loan* is a type of debt between the lender and the borrower. A lender, creditor or credit provider is someone who lends money. This can be a bank, finance company, credit union or building society; but can also be an individual who lends money. A borrower or debtor is the person to whom a loan is made. The borrower initially receives an amount of money from the lender, which they pay back, usually but not always in regular instalments, to the lender. This service is generally provided at a cost, referred to as interest on the debt.

604. Fixed term interest – only loans are available from private lenders and are often made through the officers of a solicitor. Some lending institutions will give fixed term loans with a set interest rate. The advantage here is that they offer certainty over a set term but may be unsuitable where interest rates fall. Such loans can also incur costs for refinancing at the end of the fixed term. However, fixed term loans are desirable when interest rates have risen after a loan has been taken.

605. Usually there may be a third party guarantor to a loan contract. This guarantor is a person who promises to pay the loan if the borrower cannot repay it, but who is generally not otherwise involved. They are considered third parties because they are not party to the actual loan contract between the borrower and lender.

606. In Australia consumer loans and credit is governed principally by both the respective state Credit Act and the national Consumer Credit Code. In New South Wales, for example, the *Credit Act* 1984 (NSW) regulates certain contracts which were in existence before 1 November 1996. The *Consumer Credit Code* (NSW) is part of a scheme of legislation which introduces comprehensive national regulation of consumer lending. *Credit* is defined in the Code as the deferral of the payment of debt or the incurring of deferred debt.

607. Both the Act and the Code give borrowers certain rights and remedies in respect of regulated contracts which they do not otherwise have at common law. The policy behind the Act and the Code is 'truth in lending' to ensure that borrowers are given enough information to make an informed decision as to the type of credit to get and from which lender.

I. Regulated Credit Contracts

608. In NSW credit contracts covered by the *Credit Act* 1984 (NSW) are called 'regulated credit contracts' which are divided into three categories:

- Credit sales contracts
- Loan contracts
- Continuing credit contracts

A *credit sales contract* is a sale of goods or services on credit, where the supplier of those goods or services has also provided the credit. A **loan contract** is established where the credit provider lends or postpones payment of a lump sum of money that is repayable over a fixed term by fixed repayments. These two types of credit contracts are usually for loans of less than AUD 20,000 and linked to an effective or true annual interest rate. There may be situations where the amount financed may be over AUD 20,000 but yet the contract will still be a regulated one.

A *continuing credit contract* is one where credit is available from time to time for the payment of goods or services or for cash and in which the amount of available credit increases as the amount of credit owing decreases. Examples of continuing credit contracts are the major well-known credit cards, store credit cards and overdraft facilities. However, charge cards are not regulated as no charge is made for the credit – although a charge may be imposed if the outstanding balance is not paid by the end of each month.

609. In NSW since 1 November 1996 the provision of credit by all financial institutions and other providers of personal credit including building societies, credit unions, individuals or corporations and continuing credit contracts entered into before that date are regulated by the *Consumer Credit Code.* The Code is wider in application than the Act and there is no monetary threshold to cross in order for a contract to be regulated.

II. Unregulated Credit Contracts

610. Before the commencement of the *Consumer Credit Code* all types of credit provided by credit unions, cooperative societies and building societies were excluded from the *Credit Act* 1984 (NSW). Also excluded were most personal loans for more than AUD 20,000, bank overdrafts or fully drawn advances, and rental and hiring contracts, including leases. Contracts of these types entered into after 1 November 1996 are covered by the Code. However, in general, apart from contracts regulated by the *Door-to-Door Sales Act* 1967 (NSW) and the *Pawnbrokers Act* 1902 (NSW), finance provided before 1 November 1996 which is not regulated by the *Credit Act*, is not covered by any other credit legislation.

III. Guarantors

611. The type of agreement the guarantor has entered into with the lender will determine the extent of the guarantor's liability. A guarantee from a third party needs to be distinguished from a joint debt. However, joint borrowers may be treated as guarantor and borrower if one of the joint borrowers receives no benefit under the credit contract.[655]

655. See *Permanent Trustee Co of NSW Ltd v. Hinks* (1934) 34 SR (NSW) 130.

612. There are many grounds at common law to set aside contracts of guarantee, including categories of unconscionability or unconscionable conduct, mistake, misrepresentation, undue influence and duress.

613. A number of statutes may also be used to have a guarantee set aside or varied. The *Contracts Review Act* 1980 (NSW) gives courts power to do so if the contracts are found to be unjust on one or more of the grounds specified, excluding those entered into 'in the course of or for the purpose of a trade, business or profession'. The *Fair Trading Act* 1987 (NSW) and the Competition and Consumer Act 2010 (Cth) both prohibit certain kinds of unconscionable conduct and misleading and deceptive conduct (see above). These generally do not apply to business transactions. The national Consumer Credit Code has been adopted by all Australian states and territories. The Code contains a set of general provisions about unjust contracts.

§2. Ineffective Loan Transactions and Restitution

614. Ineffective loan transactions have given rise to claims in restitution where, although unauthorized, the proceeds have been used to discharge the debts of a person on whose behalf the advances were made. Where the loans were invalid and unauthorized and hence unenforceable the law provides recoupment in equity. This was sanctioned in *Re Cork and Youghal Railway Co*[656] which involved the unauthorized borrowings by a company. Advances to the company had been secured by means of bonds which were invalid and unenforceable. The proceeds, however, of the loans were used to discharge the company's debts. It was held that the bondholders were entitled to recoup the loans in equity.

615. Banantyne v. D&C MacIver[657] applied the *Youghal* principles. In this case, an agent who was unauthorized to do so borrowed money from the plaintiff, part of which was used to discharge debts of the defendant firm. The lender claimed recoupment from the principal because the moneys had been used to discharge the principal's debts. The Court of Appeal agreed and ordered an inquiry to determine what debts had been discharged in that way.

§3. Lending Money to a Minor

616. Where loans are made to minors, the common law position is that the loan is not recoverable. The reasoning is found in the judgment in *Earle v. Peale*[658] where it was said there is no guarantee that the minor will actually spend the money

656. (1869) LR Ch. App 748.
657. [1906] 1 KB 103.
658. (1711) 1 Salk 332; 91 ER 336.

on 'necessaries' and hence the money is not recoverable. However, this is an invidious position for lenders because they cannot recover money spent by minors to buy necessaries.

617. Equity has since intervened to correct this anomaly. In *Marlow v. Pitfeild*[659] it was held that if a minor borrowed money to pay a debt for necessaries and the debt was actually paid with that money, the lender stood in the place of the person paid and was entitled to recover the loan.

618. Invalid loans such as those made not for the purchase of necessaries can be recovered if the minor agrees to repay them after attaining full age in all jurisdictions except Victoria.[660] In all other jurisdictions they become repayable on the ratification principle.

---

659. (1719) 1 P Wms 558; 24 ER 516.
660. *Supreme Court Act* 1986 (Vic) s. 50.

Chapter 11. Contracts with the Government and Other Public Sector Institutions

§1. Contracts with the Government and Other Public Sector Institutions

619. In the Australian context, contracts with the Government and other public sector institutions is complex because of the various types of 'governments' and their instrumentalities – here referred to as the Crown or the executive government. There are as many as ten such 'governments' – The Commonwealth, the six states, the two territories and Norfolk Island. Over and above this, there are public sector statutory corporations incorporated under their own specific legislation including local government bodies. In this discussion on contracts, it is therefore imperative to know which entity one is contracting with. Hence, contracts made by corporations incorporated under the *Corporations Act* 2001 (Cth), especially those substantially or wholly owned by the government is not dealt with here because of their special characteristics and the statutory rules under which these entities operate.

620. The issue of contracts with the Government and other public institutions has arisen in this age of commercialization, privatization and contracting out. Commercialization is used to mean the conduct of government work in a way that emulates the private sector and how companies there function. Privatization means the handing over of a function to a private sector company or corporation to undertake a function that was previously done by the government. Contracting out means that the government uses a contractor to carry out tasks which were formerly performed directly by public servants.

621. Contracting out as a general term raises real issues between a government's role as custodian of public resources and promoting the public good as against the need to return a 'profit' as may be found in the private sector.

622. A dilemma that often arises when discussing government contracts is to carefully note occasions when the government contracts out as a private commercial player. In such a situation the contracts assume no special rules since it is purported to be between two parties one of whom happens to be a government body. However, a conundrum arises where the contract is used for government purposes. Evidence suggests that courts would adopt a different approach in cases where government functions are involved. In *Puntoriero v. Water Administration Ministerial Corp*[661] the High Court construed an immunity provision from the legislation governing the statutory corporation. The majority held that immunity from common law liability must be interpreted narrowly when the body is engaging in commercial activities and to consider immunity more broadly where the body was undertaking a wholly governmental task or function.

661. (1999) 199 CLR 575.

I. Government Agreements

623. Whether the court will conclude that an agreement entered into by a government is intended to be binding depends in part on whether the transaction is a commercial agreement or an arrangement involving the implementation of government policy. In *Australian Woollen Mills Pty Ltd v. Commonwealth*,[662] the Commonwealth government was held not to have intended to assume a legal obligation to pay the promised subsidies to manufacturers of woollen products.

624. Another example of an agreement involving the implementation of policy is *Administration of Papua New Guinea v. Leahy*.[663] Leahy had sought the help of the Department of Agriculture in dealing with a tick infestation on his cattle property. It was agreed that officers of the Department would spray Leahy's cattle and implement other eradication measures, and Leahy would provide workers to assist them in mustering and handling the cattle. When the eradication work was not carried out properly, Leahy sought damages for breach of contract. The High Court held that no binding contract had been made. The Department was simply providing gratuitous assistance in the execution of its policy to eradicate ticks.

625. In contrast, *Placer Developments Ltd v. Commonwealth*[664] involved an agreement between the Commonwealth and Placer to form a timber company to operate in Papua New Guinea. Clause 14 of the agreement provided that, if customs duty was paid on the importation of the timber company's products into Australia, the Commonwealth would pay to the timber company a subsidy at a rate to be determined by the Commonwealth. Placer sought to enforce the agreement. The majority of the court held that clause 14 was unenforceable as an illusory promise and did not address the question of intention.

626. Seddon (2004) has likened the private vs. public roles of the government as a dilemma of the 'level playing field'. On the one hand, the government in its commercial dealings faces greater burdens and responsibilities than private operators. The operation of the common law ensures that the government observes a higher standard of conduct than do private sector market players. In addition, there are statutory standards in finance legislation and mandatory tendering requirements that may be absent in the private sector; and, a government body is subject to standards of decision-making dictated by administrative law. On the other hand, the government may be exempt from certain requirements, for example, Crown immunities and privileges could be used in a positive way as are gaps in trade practices and fair trading legislation in which government activities are exempt.

627. The general law of contract applies to all government contracts. Nick Seddon (2004: 2) is of the opinion that governments must both be more regulated as

662. (1954) 92 CLR 424.
663. (1961) 105 CLR 6.
664. (1969) 121 CLR 353.

well as less regulated. More regulated because the government is custodian of public resources and should be working towards the public good; and at the same time less regulated because it is the governing authority. This is because the government must at times be free of the constraints of contracting since there might be certain Crown immunities and privileges at play.

628. However, sometimes ordinary contract rules may be awkward when applied to government dealings. In *Airways Corporation of New Zealand Ltd v. Geyserland Airways Ltd*[665] the Corporation which was responsible for air traffic control in New Zealand sued Geyserland for fees allegedly owing for provision of services. The Corporation had sent its standard form agreement to all airline operators asking them to sign. Geyserland refused, saying that it had no intention of entering into a contract. Even so, Geyserland was obliged under statute to use the services and the Corporation was obligated to provide them. The case was decided on the application of contract formation rules – offer and non-acceptance of offer. In the event, the action for the alleged debt was unsuccessful.

§2. Government's Power to Contract

629. The power of governments to enter into contracts stems from the Crown being originally associated in the person of the sovereign. The King or the Queen had the same capacity as his or her subjects. While this notion might apply to the Crown in its various guises within the Australian Federation, it is not true of the Commonwealth. Being a creature of the Constitution, the Commonwealth's power to contract are somewhat limited because of statutory and other rules of conduct. Also unlike private bodies, the possibility that a public body acting beyond power – *ultra vires* – can and does arise.

630. There is no doubt that the sovereign can enter into contracts with the same capacity as any other person – *New South Wales v. Bardolph*[666] is the authority for the proposition. However, in this day it is more appropriate to refer to the sovereign in the guise of a corporation with defined powers – for example the Commonwealth of Australia. However, the states and territories, seemingly have unlimited capacities to enter into contracts as do statutory corporations and local government bodies.

631. The capacity of the Commonwealth to enter into contracts is a much-debated issue and has not been the subject of a ruling by the High Court. It is arguable that the Commonwealth's power to contract is not unlimited but may be restricted in practical ways.

665. [1996] 1 NZLR 116.
666. (1934) 52 CLR 455.

632. The sources of governmental power to contract are the common law, statute and the executive power. In Australia, the Commonwealth government's common law power to contract may have become subsumed with the executive power as enshrined in section 61 of the Constitution. In common law, the source of the government's power to contract can be traced to the sovereign's power to do so, and this was considered to be unlimited. Whereas in regards to statutory power, whenever Parliament passes legislation it may confer specific contract-making power on government with certain limits.

633. Academic commentators have also suggested that there may be other parts of the Constitution that give the Commonwealth the power to enter into contracts, such as the incidental power under section 51(xxxix); and the appropriation power sections 81 and 83.[667]

634. As the states and territories have no enumerated legislative powers, the implication is that there are no limits on their executive powers to enter into contracts. For instance, in *Building Construction Employees and Builders Labourers Federation of New South Wales v. Minister for Industrial Relations*,[668] the New South Wales Court of Appeal confirmed that state powers are plenary. Similarly, the South Australia Supreme Court held that the executive could validly grant an indemnity to a minister – *Xenonphon v. South Australia.*[669] In other jurisdictions executive power is made explicit in legislation such as in Queensland *Constitution Act* 2001 (Qld);[670] Western Australia *State Trading Concerns Act* 1916;[671] Australian Capital Territory *Australian Capital Territory (Self-Government Act)* (Cth);[672] and, Northern Territory *Northern Territory (Self-Government) Act* 1978 (Cth).[673]

635. In regards to statutory corporations and local governments the capacity to contract is usually dictated by a specific provision found in the legislation that establishes that corporation.

636. Given that there are possible limits to a government's power to contract, situations may arise where a state or territory government could exceed its power to contract. This may be because of a statutory provision governing the capacity to contract or that the contract may be within the Commonwealth's responsibility or that the contract could be in breach of the Constitution. If the power is lacking the effect is that the contract is void. A void contract means that the enforcement of terms, the passing of property, and the claiming of damages or a debt do not follow.

---

667. See Campbell, E., Commonwealth Contracts, 44 ALJ 14 (1970).
668. (1986) 7 NSWLR 372.
669. (2000) 78 SASR 251.
670. Section 53(10).
671. Section 4A.
672. Section 35.
673. Section 9.

§3. THE LAW OF CONTRACT

637. There is always a strong presumption that when the government enters into contracts there is an intention to create legal relations. However, there may be occasions when such a presumption cannot be assumed. This is because some government arrangements such as the payment of money in the form of grants on conditions to bodies in order to achieve a policy objective are arguably not contracts. Also some functions undertaken are uniquely governmental in nature – such as providing information – are considered not to be contracts. Uniquely, governments enter into contracts through its public servants and the issue of the law of contract and the law of agency come into play. The question of appropriation of public money and whether an appropriation is a pre-requisite for the validity of a contract is also of particular significance in government contracting.

638. In a number of instances the courts have held that there are certain government schemes and arrangements that are not enforceable as contracts. The policy behind this is that Governments should not be fettered by the laws of contract when implementing policy involving the use of public money. The reasoning therefore would be that a government is not breaking a contract because there was no contract in the first place.

639. In *Australian Woollen Mills Pty Ltd v. Commonwealth*[674] the Commonwealth implemented a wool subsidy scheme under which it undertook to pay a subsidy to wool manufacturers who bought Australian wool for local manufacturing. The scheme was later terminated and the plaintiff claimed it was entitled to certain outstanding payments on the basis of a contract. The High Court concluded that there was no offer by the Commonwealth and anything that was done by the plaintiff was not an acceptance. The Privy Council confirmed that such a scheme did not result in a contract because there was no intention to create legal relations. The arrangement was a 'non-contractual scheme'.

640. Uniquely governmental functions undertaken by governmental agencies have also been found not to result in binding contracts. In *Minister for Youth and Community Services v. Health and Research Employees' Association of Australia*[675] 'house parents' were paid by the state to provide a home for wards of the state. It was held by the court that the agreement was not legally binding. Similarly, in the provision of information relevant to land use from a local council in exchange for a fee, it was held that the provision did not give rise to a contract – *Lismore City Council v. Stewart.*[676] However, this latter case must be contrasted with *Bunbury-Harvey Regional Council v. Giacci Bros Pty Ltd*[677] where it was held that a relatively informal arrangement between the Council and the company under which the latter could dump contaminated refuse at the Council's site was a contract.

674. (1954) 92 CLR 424 (HC); (1955) 93 CLR 546 (PC).
675. (1987) 10 NSWLR 543.
676. (1989) 18 NSWLR 718.
677. [2000] WASC 223, affirmed on appeal [2001] WASCA 282.

641. Crown servants negotiate contracts on behalf of the government. The authority to do so comes from the rules on the delegation of authority. Such rules arise in legislation and instructions made under the *Financial Management and Accountability Act* 1997 (Cth) section 52. Hence, a public servant who enters into a contract does so on behalf of, and as agent of, the government. Personal liability on the contract does not arise unless the relevant legislation provides otherwise.

642. If a public servant exceeds his or her authority, the general rule is that he or she can be sued by the other party to the contract for breach of an implied warranty of authority. However, it seems that Crown servants are exempt from this rule.[678] An avenue for litigation to recover loss and damage however may be found under Schedule 2 of the Competition and Consumer Act 2010 (Cth) or under a state or territory *Fair Trading Act* for either misleading or deceptive conduct when acting 'in trade or commerce'.

643. It is not necessary that funds be appropriated for a government contract to be valid. Previously it was held that appropriation was necessary on the ground that the executive could not bind the parliament to a particular expenditure. However, since *New South Wales v. Bardolph*[679] and followed in *Vass v. Commonwealth*,[680] it is not necessary for a contract to be backed by a parliamentary appropriation of funds. *Bardolph's* case stands for the proposition that the executive power as exercised through contract justifies the expenditure of public money.

§4. Crown Privileges and Immunities

644. A government entering into contract is subject to burdens as well as some immunities of office when compared with the rules which apply in the private sector. This paradox stems from the unique and special position of the government. In respect of privileges and immunities there is no parallel with private sector entities even though the government is using a particularly private sector instrument in the form of the contract to achieve its purposes.

645. Crown proceedings and the peculiar operation of section 64 of the *Judiciary Act* 1903 (Cth) has made government contracts 'different' from those of the usual kind. Crown immunity from statute affects not just governments but also statutory bodies and local government bodies and are of relevance when entering into contracts with these bodies.

646. A Crown privilege of importance is the doctrine of executive necessity and the rule against fettering which allows the government in limited circumstances to break a contract or a particular promise. A government or government body cannot

678. See *Minister for Youth and Community Services v. Health and Research Employees' Association of Australia* (1987) 10 NSWLR 543.
679. (1934) 52 CLR 455.
680. (2000) 96 FCR 272.

be fettered by contract if there is a contest between the contract and the government's public responsibilities.

647. In Australia there are three types of legal entities: natural persons, corporations and bodies politic – referred to as 'the Crown' or 'the government'. Within the category of corporations are those incorporated under the *Corporations Act* 2001 (Cth), statutory corporations and corporations sole. Of interest here are local government bodies which are statutory corporations incorporated under local government legislation. The ten bodies politic in Australia include the Commonwealth, the six states, the two self-governing territories and Norfolk Island.

648. Identification of the legal entity is important because it is necessary to know with whom one is dealing with. This is especially so in the context of government contracting in which the status of a particular public body may not always be clear and is dependent on whether it is a corporation under a specific statute or simply a part of the government. A second reason is because of a common law rule about contracting: it is not possible for a legal person to contract with himself or herself. This may arise where a government department may attempt to contract with another that happens to be a different arm of a government department. As no contract is thus possible, the agreement must be enforced by legal instruments other than contract.

649. The Crown as a body politic enjoys certain immunities and privileges. However such privileges and immunities do not necessary flow on to statutory corporations because it will depend on the legislation that establishes the corporation and its evident purpose deduced from legislation. In general, a body set up for 'governmental' purposes will be treated as a manifestation of the Crown and thus claim relevant privileges or immunities. However, this is not definitive because of the blurring of the governmental and private functions – *Townsville Hospitals Board v. Council of the City of Townsville*[681] where a view was expressed that statutory corporations should generally not enjoy immunity.

650. There is a general rule that a contract cannot, despite its binding nature, fetter the government's ability to carry out its programs and policies. This seeming incompatibility in the rules is generally resolved in favour of the government action. In the realm of contract and future government action there appear to be five overriding principles.[682]

651. Under the principle of *executive necessity*, a government may break an otherwise perfectly valid and enforceable contract because it is necessary to do so for acceptable government reasons, for example, a change in policy.

652. A second principle is the primacy of legislation. A government cannot contract out of an *existing* statutory obligation or fetter its future exercise of a statutory

681. (1982) 149 CLR 282.
682. Seddon: 192–223.

power or discretion conferred by *existing* legislation. Here the contract is either wholly or partly ineffective.

653. The third principle is that of the rule against fettering future executive action. Hence a government cannot by contract bind its *future* freedom to govern through the use of executive power. The contract may be ineffective if at some future date action is taken that cuts across the obligations found in the contract.

In *Power Co Ltd v. Gore District Council*[683] the Court of Appeal was asked to determine whether an agreement entered into in 1927 under which electricity was supplied at a fixed rate of one penny per unit 'for all time hereafter' could be terminated by notice. The decision of this case suggests that it is always possible for a government body to obtain relief from a contract by overriding legislation. Here the special position of government has shaped the way in which contract rules were applied.

654. A fourth principle is the rule against fettering future legislative action and a final principle is that of the primacy of parliament. Under these principles, a government may legislate to override an existing contract if the obligations in the contract are proving to be burdensome or unacceptable to the government.

655. The doctrine of executive necessity might seem disturbing at first blush and has been heavily criticized. However, in a vast majority of government contracts, the doctrine may be irrelevant because of commercial and political realities. Only in extreme circumstances, such as the necessities of war where a contractual undertaking by the government was broken, has such a doctrine been used – *Rederiaktiebolaget 'Amphitrite' v. The King*.[684] Whilst heavily criticized as being 'expressed too generally' the doctrine has been accepted and recognized in Australia in *Ansett Transport Industries (Operations) Pty Ltd v. Commonwealth*.[685]

§5. The Government and Competition/Consumer Legislation

656. An ideal espoused by governments is that of competitive neutrality and that it should not enjoy any special exemption from legislation when dealing with the commercial sector. The Hilmer Report recommended that the states and territories should be bound by the competition provisions of Part IV of the Competition and Consumer Act 2010 (Cth). These recommendations were implemented by the *Competition Policy Reform Act* 1995 (Cth) which amended and added to the Competition and Consumer Act 2010 (Cth)and by complementary legislation in each state and territory.

683. [1997] 1 NZLR 537.
684. [1921] 3 KB 500.
685. (1977) 139 CLR 54.

657. Seddon 2004: Chapter 6 provides a detailed discussion of aspects of the Government and the Trade Practices and Fair Trading Legislation and identifies 'holes' in the present schemes from the perspective of government instrumentalities being exempt from the regulatory regime. The leading case is that of *JS McMillan Pty Ltd v. Commonwealth*[686] in which it was found that while the Commonwealth had engaged in misleading conduct it was not liable under the Competition and Consumer Act 2010 (Cth).[687]

§6. Tendering for Government Contracts

658. Two policy objectives of the tendering process underlie this activity: that the government obtains best value for money, and promoting reasonable access to government business in a free market. However, in Australia there is no specialized system regulating government tenders as there is in the United States and in the European Union. While the safeguards of a tailored system such as open access to government contracts and the conduct, accountability and transparency of the tendering process are absent, nevertheless, there are common law and statutory measures the permit legal challenge to the tendering process.

659. The process of tending prior to award is governed by a preliminary contract which introduces complications of its own. Ordinary contract rules applicable to tenders hold that each bid is an offer, one of which is accepted to form a contract. Most tender processes proceed along the lines of the familiar contract categories of an invitation to treat, an offer and an acceptance. Once accepted, a bilateral contract comes into existence. Hence, there can be no contractual relationship between the parties to the process before the award. The complication in the tendering process is that such a traditional path to contract may be unsuitable to the parties to a tender and so steps might need to be taken to impose some obligation on tenderers (e.g., not to withdraw for a certain period) and various rules the government party might stipulate as to how it would conduct itself. The challenge is how to make these obligations work legally.

660. Another analysis of the tendering process suggests that there may be two-contracts involved in a tender – one governing the pre-award period and the other being the award itself. The request for tender becomes both an offer for a preliminary (or pre-award) contract governing the tender process and, an invitation for bids for the main contract. By submitting a bid, a tenderer has accepted the offer for a pre-award contract and has made an offer for the main contract. Finn, J. of the Federal Court adopted and applied the two-contract analysis in *Hughes Aircraft Systems International v. Airservices Australia*.[688]

686. (1997) 147 ALR 419.
687. Section 52.
688. (1997) 146 ALR 1.

§7. Administrative Law Remedies

661. There is always the possibility of an administrative law challenge to government commercial decisions especially where the 'private' and 'public' objectives of the government collide. Acute contractual problems are raised by questioning the appropriate intervention by the courts and the role of the Ombudsman and freedom of information legislation when using administrative law remedies. Such remedies arise because administrative law provides for a review in relation to government decision-making. Examples of such decisions include the award of a contract and the administration of contracts involving the provision of services to the public. The operation of the *Administrative Decisions (Judicial Review) Act* 1997 (Cth) and judicial review under the *Judiciary Act* 1903 (Cth) may play a part in government contracting activities. However, the Federal Court has shown an increasing reluctance to permit administrative law challenges in the award of contracts by Commonwealth statutory authorities.

662. In *Australian Capital Territory Health Authority v. Berkeley Cleaning Group Pty Ltd,*[689] the Full Federal Court held that when a contract is made under a specific contract-making provision of a statute, the decision to award the contract is arguably a decision made 'under an enactment'. Here the Authority was a statutory body established under the *Health Services Ordinance* 1985 (ACT) with the power to contract. The applicant challenged both the decision that its tender was 'non-assessable' and the decision to award the contract to another. It was held that the first 'decision' came within section 6 of the *Administrative Decisions (Judicial Review) Act* 1977 (Cth) – conduct for the purpose of making a decision. The decision to award the contract was held to be one within section 5 of the Act. However, this decision of the Federal Court has since been recanted.

663. In *James Richardson Corp Pty Ltd v. Federal Airport Corporation*[690] it was argued that the decision to award a contract was not made under an enactment because the immediate source of power to make that decision arose out of the invitation to tender. Cooper, J. rejected this argument by drawing a distinction between decisions made pursuant to a power conferred by a contract or a common law power arising out of a contractual relationship as against a decision made under a statutory power to make a contract.

664. In *General Newspapers Pty Ltd v. Telstra Corp*[691] the plaintiff challenged the award of a contract by Telecom under the *Administrative Decisions (Judicial Review) Act* 1977 (Cth). The Full Federal Court held that a decision to contract, made under a statutory power to contract in the usual form for statutory corporations, was not a decision made 'under an enactment'. The legislation conferred the

---

689. (1985) 60 ALR 284.
690. (1992) 117 ALR 277.
691. (1993) 117 ALR 629.

capacity to contract but the decision to enter into a contract was made under the general law. Decisions such as these are illustrative of the view of the Courts that government contracting is a 'private' activity and not a public one.

665. The availability of administrative law remedies in the states and territories is determined by statute in the ACT, Queensland, Tasmania and Victoria; and common law in New South Wales.

666. A disgruntled contractor or potential contractor may complain to the relevant government body or department or ultimately to the Commonwealth Ombudsman if something goes wrong. The Ombudsman's jurisdiction extends to cover government departments and 'prescribed authorities' with some specific exceptions. The power to investigate a contract or tender however is limited to examining administrative mistakes or improprieties and does not extend to matters of commercial judgment or commercial disputes. In the states there are Ombudsman or Parliamentary Commissioners who can investigate complaints about the procurement practices of government, government authorities and local government. Discovery of documents may be effected through the relevant Freedom of Information legislation in the Commonwealth, states and territories.

Chapter 12. Contract of Partnership

667. Formalities to enter a partnership agreement No express formality is required to enter a partnership contract. Partnership agreements can be either oral, or in writing.[692] Partnership agreements can also be implied from conduct.[693] The existence of a partnership agreement will be determined by the intent of the parties in meeting three specific criteria established in the *Partnership Acts*:[694]

(i) that a business be carried on;[695]
(ii) that it be carried on by persons in common;[696] and
(iii) that it is carried on with a view to profit.[697]

Assuming that these three criteria are met, and the parties have the requisite intent to form a partnership, then, for the purposes of the law, a partnership will be found to exist. The partner's intention will be a significant factor in determining whether a partnership existed.[698] The intention of the parties will also be the dominant criteria in deciding the terms of the partnership agreement. The *Partnership Acts* provide for statutory criteria (such as co-ownership, sharing of gross returns, receipt of a share of profits) to assist in determining whether a partnership exists.[699] In addition to the usual form of partnership, many Australian jurisdictions also allow the establishment of limited partnerships,[700] (whereby the general partners will have unlimited liability for the debts of the organization, with the limited partner having, as the title suggests, limited liability) and incorporated limited partnerships (where the partnership is a separate legal entity from the partnership).[701]

692. Though in Tasmania, the *Mercantile Law Act* 1935 (s 6) requires that partnership agreements of longer than a year must be in writing.
693. *Re Harvey; Ex parte Chapman* (1964) 11 FLR 485.
694. Largely uniform legislation exists throughout the Australian States and Territories. *Partnership Act* 1892 (NSW); *Partnership Act* 1963 (ACT); *Partnership Act* 1997 (NT); *Partnership Act* 1891 (Qld); *Partnership Act* 1891 (Tas); *Partnership Act* 1958 (Vic); *Partnership Act* 1895 (WA); *Partnership Act* 1891 (SA).
695. As an example, see *Canny Gabriel Castle Jackson Advertising Pty Ltd v. Volume Sales (Finance) Pty Ltd* (1974) 131 CLR 321.
696. See *Kelly v. Tucker* (1907) 5 CLR 1.
697. *Customs and Excise Cmrs v. Faith Construction Ltd* [1990] 1 QB 905.
698. *Cox v. Hickman* (1860) 8 HL Cas 268; *Ex parte Delhasse; Re Megevand* (1878) 7 Ch. D 511.
699. *Partnership Act* 1892 (NSW) s. 2; *Partnership Act* 1963 (ACT) s. 7; *Partnership Act* 1997 (NT) s. 6; *Partnership Act* 1891 (Qld) s. 6; *Partnership Act* 1891 (Tas) s. 7; *Partnership Act* 1958 (Vic) s. 6; *Partnership Act* 1895 (WA) s. 8; *Partnership Act* 1891 (SA) s. 2.
700. *Partnership Act* 1892 (NSW) Pt 3; *Partnership Act* 1958 (Vic) Pt 3; *Partnership (Limited Liability) Act* 1988 (Qld); *Limited Partnerships Act* 1909 (WA); *Limited Partnerships Act* 1908 (Tas).
701. *Partnership (Venture Capital Funds) Act* 2003 (Vic); *Partnership Amendment (Venture Capital Funds) Act* 2005 (SA); *Partnership (Venture Capital Funds) Act* 2004 (ACT); *Partnership Amendment (Venture Capital Funds) Act* 2004 (NSW).

§1. Capacity

668. Generally, all persons, including corporations and children can become partners. However, the decision of *Whundo Copper Syndicate v. Ferrari*[702] demonstrates the problems in children becoming partners. In this case, the court held that the contract entered into by both the adult and child partner jointly was not binding on the infant. Nevertheless, the adult was held fully responsible. A person of unsound mind cannot enter a partnership agreement unless the person with whom they are dealing has no knowledge of the mental illness and has acted in good faith.[703] A bankrupt can enter a partnership agreement.[704] A company can enter a partnership agreement.[705] An enemy alien may not enter a partnership agreement.[706]

§2. Terms of Partnership Agreements

669. Partnership agreements will routinely cover the following topics:

(i) the names of the partners;
(ii) the subject matter of the partnership business;
(iii) the firm name, if different from the partnership agreement;
(iv) the duration of the partnership;
(v) the capital to be put into the partnership by each partner;
(vi) how each partner is to be remunerated;
(vii) how the business is to be managed;
(viii) any limitation on the authority of each partner;
(ix) any limitation on the liability of each partner;
(x) how the partnership may be terminated; and
(xi) how disputes will be settled between the partners.

§3. Unenforceable Partnerships

670. A partnership cannot consist of more than twenty persons.[707] Exceptions to this general rule include the allowance of partnerships of up to fifty actuaries, medical practitioners, patent attorneys, sharebrokers, stockbrokers or trademark attorneys; 100 Architects, pharmaceutical chemists or veterinary surgeons; 400 legal practitioners and up to 1,000 accountants in an accounting partnership firm. Partnership agreement will also be unenforceable where the contract is itself illegal or contrary to public policy (e.g., a partnership to commit a crime);[708] similarly a partnership agreement will be unenforceable where two persons enter a partnership, one

702. [1962] WAR 24.
703. *Gibbons v. Wright* (1954) 91 CLR 423.
704. Though this must be disclosed. *Bankruptcy Act* 1966 (Cth) s. 269(1)(b).
705. *Corporations Act* 2001 (Cth) s. 124. *Corporations Act* 2001 (Cth) s. 124.
706. *Stoll v. Paterson & Co Ltd* (1915) 18 WALR 42.
707. *Corporations Act* 2001 (Cth) s. 115.
708. *Foster v. Driscoll* [1929] 1 KB 470.

of whom is unable to enter the business of the firm (i.e., a partnership established between two persons to carry on a medical practice, with one person lacking the relevant qualifications).[709]

§4. Relation between the Partners

671. The *Partnership Acts* in each jurisdiction provide that each partner may take part in the partnership business.[710] However, this will routinely be excluded by the terms of the partnership contract. Each partner has fiduciary duties to protect the partnership business.[711]

§5. Relations between Partners and Third Parties

672. Given that a partnership is not a legal entity, the question arises as to how the partnership can enter into legally binding obligations with third parties. The answer is that the third party will deal with one or more of the individual partners. The question then becomes:

(i) did the individual partner(s) have the authority to contract on behalf of the partnership; and
(ii) has the contract gone beyond the authority of the contracting partner.

To resolve these questions, the *Partnership Acts*[712] provide as follows:

> Every partner is agent of the firm and his other partners for the purpose of the business of the partnership, and the acts of every partner who does any act for carrying on in the usual way business of the kind carried on by the firm of which he is a member binds the firm and his partners, unless the partner so acting has in fact no authority to act for the firm in the particular matter and the person with whom he is dealing either knows that he has no authority or does not know or believe him to be a partner.[713]

---

709. *Renowden v. Hurley* [1951] VLR 13.

710. *Partnership Act* 1892 (NSW) s. 24; *Partnership Act* 1963 (ACT) s. 29; *Partnership Act* 1997 (NT) s. 28; *Partnership Act* 1891 (Qld) s. 27; *Partnership Act* 1891 (Tas) s. 29; *Partnership Act* 1958 (Vic) s. 28; *Partnership Act* 1895 (WA) s. 34; *Partnership Act* 1891 (SA) s. 24.

711. E.g., *Kelly v. CA & L Bell Commodities Corporation Pty Ltd* (1989) 18 NSWLR 248; *Re a Firm of Solicitors* [1995] TLR 263; *Birtchnell v. Equity Trustees, Executors and Agency Co Ltd* (1929) 42 CLR 384.

712. *Partnership Act* 1892 (NSW) s. 5; *Partnership Act* 1963 (ACT) s. 9; *Partnership Act* 1997 (NT) s. 9; *Partnership Act* 1891 (Qld) s. 8; *Partnership Act* 1891 (Tas) s. 10; *Partnership Act* 1958 (Vic) s. 9; *Partnership Act* 1895 (WA) s. 26; *Partnership Act* 1891 (SA) s. 5.

713. This provision has been interpreted in a number of cases: e.g., *Goldberg v. Jenkins* (1889) 15 VLR 36; *Construction Engineering (Aust) Pty Ltd v. Hexyl Pty Ltd* (1985) 155 CLR 541.

An example of how this operates can be seen in *Mann v. D'Arcy*.[714] A partner in a firm of vegetable wholesalers bound the partnership when he entered into an agreement to buy a consignment of potatoes. It was business of a kind carried on by the partnership, and the absence of internal authority was irrelevant to the external validity of the contract.

§6. Partnership Property

673. Partnership property includes all property originally brought into the partnership, and those assets acquired since formation brought in the course of the partnership business.[715] If there is insufficient evidence to determine the intent of the partners as to whether something is partnership property, the particular asset will be considered owned by the individual partner, rather than the partnership.[716]

§7. Dissolution of the Partnership Agreement

674. Dissolution can occur in number of ways. For example, the partnership agreement may simply end because the agreed partnership has reached its duration.[717] However, it may also be terminated by the death[718] or bankruptcy of a partner,[719] by its illegality,[720] by agreement or pursuant to a clause within the partnership contract (such as the giving of notice) or by retirement. Partners are also entitled to seek court orders for the dissolution of a partnership where a partner breaches the fiduciary obligations established by the partnership agreement,[721] where the business can only be carried on at a loss,[722] where it is just and equitable

714. [1968] 1 WLR 893.
715. *Partnership Act* 1892 (NSW) s. 20; *Partnership Act* 1963 (ACT) s. 24; *Partnership Act* 1997 (NT) s. 24; *Partnership Act* 1891 (Qld) s. 23; *Partnership Act* 1891 (Tas) s. 25; *Partnership Act* 1958 (Vic) s. 24; *Partnership Act* 1895 (WA) s. 30; *Partnership Act* 1891 (SA) s. 20.
716. *Harvey v. Harvey* (1970) 120 CLR 529.
717. *Partnership Act* 1892 (NSW) s. 32; *Partnership Act* 1963 (ACT) s. 37; *Partnership Act* 1997 (NT) s. 36; *Partnership Act* 1891 (Qld) s. 35; *Partnership Act* 1891 (Tas) s. 37; *Partnership Act* 1958 (Vic) s. 36; *Partnership Act* 1895 (WA) s. 43; *Partnership Act* 1891 (SA) s. 32.
718. *Partnership Act* 1892 (NSW) s. 33; *Partnership Act* 1963 (ACT) s. 38; *Partnership Act* 1997 (NT) s. 37; *Partnership Act* 1891 (Qld) s. 36; *Partnership Act* 1891 (Tas) s. 38; *Partnership Act* 1958 (Vic) s. 37; *Partnership Act* 1895 (WA) s. 44; *Partnership Act* 1891 (SA) s. 33.
719. *Partnership Act* 1892 (NSW) s. 36; *Partnership Act* 1963 (ACT) s. 41; *Partnership Act* 1997 (NT) s. 40; *Partnership Act* 1891 (Qld) s. 39; *Partnership Act* 1891 (Tas) s. 41; *Partnership Act* 1958 (Vic) s. 40; *Partnership Act* 1895 (WA) s. 47; *Partnership Act* 1891 (SA) s. 36.
720. *Partnership Act* 1892 (NSW) s. 34; *Partnership Act* 1963 (ACT) s. 39; *Partnership Act* 1997 (NT) s. 38; *Partnership Act* 1891 (Qld) s. 37; *Partnership Act* 1891 (Tas) s. 39; *Partnership Act* 1958 (Vic) s. 38; *Partnership Act* 1895 (WA) s. 45; *Partnership Act* 1891 (SA) s. 34.
721. The statutory ground is conduct prejudicial to the partnership: *Partnership Act* 1892 (NSW) s. 35; *Partnership Act* 1963 (ACT) s. 40; *Partnership Act* 1997 (NT) s. 39; *Partnership Act* 1891 (Qld) s. 38; *Partnership Act* 1891 (Tas) s. 40; *Partnership Act* 1958 (Vic) s. 39; *Partnership Act* 1895 (WA) s. 46; *Partnership Act* 1891 (SA) s. 35.
722. *Partnership Act* 1892 (NSW) s. 35; *Partnership Act* 1963 (ACT) s. 40; *Partnership Act* 1997 (NT) s. 39; *Partnership Act* 1891 (Qld) s. 38; *Partnership Act* 1891 (Tas) s. 40; *Partnership Act* 1958 (Vic) s. 36; *Partnership Act* 1895 (WA) s. 46; *Partnership Act* 1891 (SA) s. 35.

that the partnership be wound up,[723] or where a partner becomes incapable of being a partner (e.g., a person suffers from a mental disorder).[724]

723. *Partnership Act* 1892 (NSW) s. 35; *Partnership Act* 1963 (ACT) s. 40; *Partnership Act* 1997 (NT) s. 39; *Partnership Act* 1891 (Qld) s. 38; *Partnership Act* 1891 (Tas) s. 40; *Partnership Act* 1958 (Vic) s. 36; *Partnership Act* 1895 (WA) s. 46; *Partnership Act* 1891 (SA) s. 35.

724. *Partnership Act* 1892 (NSW) s. 35; *Partnership Act* 1963 (ACT) s. 40; *Partnership Act* 1997 (NT) s. 39; *Partnership Act* 1891 (Qld) s. 38; *Guardian and Administration Act* 1995 (Tas) s. 56; *Partnership Act* 1958 (Vic) s. 39; *Partnership Act* 1895 (WA) s. 46; *Partnership Act* 1891 (SA) s. 35.

Chapter 13. Quasi-Contracts

§1. Contract and Quasi-Contract

675. A quasi-contract, a term used in the civil law, involves a situation where the law finds there to be an obligation even though the technical requirements for a contract have not been fulfilled. A contract which is implied in law is also called a quasi-contract because it is not in fact a contract; rather, it is a means for the courts to remedy situations in which one party would be unjustly enriched were he or she not required to compensate the other. For example, an unconscious patient treated by a doctor at the scene of an accident has not agreed (either expressly or by implication) to pay the doctor for emergency services, but the patient would be unjustly enriched by the doctor's services were the patient not required to compensate the doctor. The issue is whether the patient be held liable for payment? The answer will depend on the facts of the case and other circumstances.

676. In contracts there is a meeting of the mind between the parties which produces the duties and obligations. In quasi-contracts, no consent is required, and the obligation that arises is from the law or natural equity, on the facts of the case. These acts bind the parties as contracts do.

There appear to be five different classes of quasi-contracts:

(i) the voluntary and spontaneous management of the affairs of another, without authority – *negotiorum gestio* (*see infra*);
(ii) the administration of tutorship or;
(iii) the management of common property;
(iv) the acquisition of an inheritance; and
(v) the payment of a sum of money or other thing by mistake, when nothing was due.

677. *Negotiorum gestio* is discussed separately below. The assumption of tutorship or guardianship has no agreement between the tutor and minor. In the management of a common property owned by himself and others, not as partners, the manager is bound to account for profits and is entitled for the expenses sustained by virtue of the quasi-contract created by the act of managing. In the fourth class, the heir is bound to pay the legatees, who in any interpretation have no contract with him or with the deceased. Finally, in the payment of one of what is not due to him, if made through any mistake in fact, or even in law, entitles the person who made the payment to an action against the receiver of the payment. The action does not lie if the sum paid was due or by a natural obligation or if the person making the payment knew that nothing was due. Each of these have some affinity with some contract – here known as a quasi-contract.

§2. Unjust Enrichment

678. Heavily influenced by the work of the late Professor Peter Birks, the whole area of quasi-contract from the point of view of the law of restitution or unjust enrichment has been the subject of much theorizing and debate. Birks argued that the law of restitution is a separate branch of the law of obligations, distinct from tort and contract law and unified by a principle of unjust enrichment at the plaintiff's expense.

679. Yet, other scholars such as Jackman point out that much of the law of restitution has concerned cases where neither the defendant has been enriched nor has the plaintiff suffered expense. Jackman posits three distinct categories of legal thought in this area:

(i) reversal of non-voluntary transactions;
(ii) the fulfilment of non-contractual promises; and
(iii) the protection of the private legal facilities of proprietary rights and fiduciary relationships.

680. The starting point of most restitution litigation is where a plaintiff is seeking to recover a direct money payment back from the defendant through personal action. This has been characterized also as 'money had and received', 'implied contract'; and 'unjust enrichment'.

681. The scope of unjust enrichment is outlined in Lord Robert Goff and Gareth Jones (1966) *The Law of Restitution* (1st edition). The grounds for the action include: compensation for rescuers for their time and trouble; preventing a murderer from inheriting a victim's fortune; and, to unscramble a transaction that was illegal or had become frustrated.

Early cases include *Nixon v. Furphy*;[725] and *TA Sundell & Sons Pty Ltd v. Emm Yannoulatos (Overseas) Pty Ltd*[726] where the NSW Supreme Court held that restitution can be ordered of payments made in response to a threat to break a subsisting contract.

However, the High Court's decision in *Pavey & Matthews Pty Ltd v. Paul*[727] recognizes the concept of unjust enrichment as a unifying legal concept in Australia. Here the plaintiff carried out building work in consequence of an unenforceable oral agreement. Mrs. Paul had freely accepted the benefit of the plaintiff's work and was seen to have been unjustly enriched.

In a different case the High Court dealt with restitution of mistaken payments in *David Securities Pty Ltd v. Commonwealth Bank of Australia.*[728]

Also, in *Roxborough v. Rothmans of Pall Mall Australia Ltd*[729] retailers who had purchased cigarettes from a wholesaler for a price which included an amount in respect of an unconstitutional tax were held by a majority of the High Court to be entitled to restitution of that amount from the wholesaler.

It is arguable that these cases wholly support a model of unjust enrichment based on strict liability. While by itself unjust enrichment is not a cause of action in

725. (1925) 25 SR (NSW) 151.
726. (1956) 56 SR (NSW) 323.
727. (1987) 162 CLR 221.
728. (1992) 175 CLR 353.
729. (2001) 208 CLR 516.

Australia, the principle may have imposed guidelines on the types of claims brought in an action for money had and received and for a quantum meruit. Again the law of unjust enrichment is still nascent and unsettled.

§3. *NEGOTIORUM GESTIO*

682. *Negotiorum gestio,* from Roman Dutch Law, refers to a situation in which a *gestor* acts on behalf of a principal for the benefit of that principal, but without the consent of that principal, and the action is later ratified by the principal. A *gestor* is the manager of another's affairs.[730] A typical case is that of the neighbour who, in the owner's absence, orders necessary repairs to a house. Reciprocal obligations arise as a result of this action. The *gestor* is only entitled to reimbursement of expenses and not to remuneration, the underlying principle being that the *negotiorum gestio* arises from an act of generosity and friendship and is not aimed at allowing the *gestor* to make a profit out of his administration. Moreover, the *gestor* is subject to all the obligations which would have resulted had the owner given him an express agreement to do so.

683. In *Standard Bank Financial Services Ltd v. Taylam (Pty) Ltd*[731] a quasi-contractual relationship emerged where a *gestor*, acting without agreement, rendered a service to the dominus (a debtor) and in doing so acted reasonably and in the interest of the debtor. The intention here was not only to administer the affairs of the debtor but also of being compensated for doing so. An action to recover expenses will fail if the *gestor* did not intend to serve the debtor but mistakenly thought that he was administering his own affairs in making the debt payment.

684. There are two possible interpretations to the action of the *gestor*. In the first instance, the *gestor* may have acted bona fide, but in the mistaken belief that he was serving the debtor. In the second instance, he may have acted *mala fide* in his own interest. Hence the terms bona fide *gestor* and mala fide *gestor*. However, as a matter of law, neither could sue as *negotiorum gestoris* as neither had the intention to serve the debtor. However, if the debtor had been enriched at their expense, both types of *gestors* would have a right to recover from the debtor on the grounds of unjust enrichment.

Under *negotiorum gestio* when a person undertakes of his/her own accord to manage the affairs of another, the person assuming the agency contracts the tacit engagement to continue it and complete it, until the owner is in a condition to attend to him/herself. The obligations of such a person include:

- to act for the benefit of the absentee;
- to be answerable for any negligence; and
- is bound to render an account of the management.

730. See *Mt Argun; Sheriff of Cape Town and Anor v. Mt Argun, Her Owners and all persons interested in her and anor.* 2000 (4) SA 857 at 685.
731. 1979 (2) SA 383 at 388.

685. In equity, the proprietor, whose property is being managed, is obliged:

- to comply with the engagements contracted by the manager in his name;
- to indemnify the manager in all the engagements so contracted; and
- to reimburse him all useful and necessary expenses.

686. The issue here is whether Australian law recognizes a concept of *negotiorum gestio*. In the common law claimants intervening in others' affairs and seeking restitution or reimbursement of expenses are often labelled 'officious' and disallowed relief. However, this may give a misleading impression of the law. Australian law does recognize a concept of *negotiorum gestio*, which while very different to that found in German law, has parallels to versions found in other Civil law systems. Under this principle, a cause of action to recover the intervenor's expenses, and any loss suffered during the intervention is available. It also provides a defence to the intervenor's intentional torts, although negligent intervenors will remain liable for their negligence.[732]

687. For the present this civil law doctrine of *negotiorum gestio* must be discussed in a common law jurisdiction from the point of view of the basis of recovery by necessitous interveners from those who have been assisted.

In *Dorset Yacht Co Ltd v. Home Office*[733] Lord Diplock made clear that 'the priest and the Levite would have incurred no civil liability in England'. While in tort it continues to be the fact that there is no *general duty* to rescue, doubts have begun to emerge as to what constitutes 'mere' omission, as well as a growing list of exceptions to the rule in regard to 'special relationships' between parties and the variety of contexts on alleged failures to assist those in peril of one kind or another and the 'no duty affirmative action analysis'.

Examples include the late arrival of an emergency ambulance;[734] disputes about the responsibilities of other 'professional rescuers' such as coastguard, fire, and police services.[735]

688. A number of different legal responses are extant from the 'carrot' of limited legislative immunity aimed at encouraging rescuers and other volunteers – much favoured in North America, to the continental European civil law regime 'stick' of threatening criminal and sometimes civil sanctions against those who fail to go the aid of those in danger.

These different approaches reflect five different possible solutions – 'reimbursement' of expenses; 'compensation' for losses incurred; 'remuneration' and payment

---

732. See Sheehan, D., *Negotiorum Gestio: A Civilian concept in the Common Law?* 55 Intl. & Comp. L. Q. 253–280 (2006).
733. [1970] AC 1004 at 1060.
734. See *Kent v. Griffiths* [2001] QB 36.
735. See *OLL v. Secretary of State for Transport* [1977] 3 All ER 897; *Capital and Counties plc v. Hampshire CC* [1997] QB 1004; and *Costello v. CC of Northumbria Police* [1999] ICR 752 respectively.

of expenses; 'restitution' for the value of the benefits conferred; and 'reward' that reflects a profit element exceeding the other measures. These possibilities seem not to be favoured in the English common law tradition whereas civilian systems are generally in favour of these solutions.[736]

689. This area of the law (of rescue), however, is unsettled in Australia. The general principles employed for recovery include implied promise, bailment, tortious negligence, agency of necessity, unjust enrichment and salvage – each with criteria and rules that differ.

§4. Money Paid but not Due

690. A 'core' case of unjust enrichment is the accidental overpayment of money. For example, a buyer of goods tenders AUD 20 but by accident receives change as if AUD 50 was tendered. Immediate recovery of the overpayment is patently just because the buyer has received an unjustified enrichment which should be returned.

From this example, it appears that the extra money given is not due and there was an error made by the seller. The payor had made a mistake. However, a person who pays knowing that he/she is under no legal obligation to make the payment is in effect making a gift, and cannot normally claim repayment. The mistake may be one of fact or one of law.

736. See *generally* J. Kortmann, *Altruism in Private Law: Liability for Nonfeasance and* Negotiorum Gestio (Oxford U. Press 2005).

Chapter 14. Conclusion: Future Directions in Australian Contract Law

691. The early stages of this work traced the history and common law origins of Australian contract law. Thereafter, the rest of the text provided an exposition of the present state of Australian laws governing contract. This last section turns now to some likely future directions of Australian contract law.

692. In an appropriate, significant and substantial way, the future directions of Australian contract law have also been a focus of the Australian government as it seeks to ensure that contract law in Australia facilitates Australian business and social-economic policy, especially in light of other policy directions related to the twenty-first Asian Century.[737] To this end, the central government has released a Discussion Paper[738] on the future directions of contract law. The Contract Review Discussion paper makes 11 points that are relevant to future directions. This section uses those 11 points as a basic structure of a discussion about future directions and adds six additional considerations.

§1. Waves of Reform and Counter Reform

693. First, the Discussion paper notes that reviews of contract law are not new and in fact similar reviews dated back before Australian Federation. Indeed, most countries have regularly reviewed commercial laws generally as part of an overall commitment to and need for law reform generally. As society changes, so too much the laws change to ensure that they continue to serve the country's needs.[739]

§2. Accessibility

694. Contract law as a form of private law making impacts every Australian citizen. As laws have grown more complex and voluminous, there is a concern that an understanding of the law is becoming more difficult. There is need for simplification, clarity and enhanced coherence in Australia's laws so that citizens can have access to the law and use it for guidance in their business and personal lives. Such complexity is especially symptomatic of common law systems where vestiges of the historical divide between common law and equity courts and systems as well as the evolutionary growth of case law and precedent make it difficult to find and know the law less more determine how the law affects our rights and responsibilities. Another aspect of accessibility is cost. When the law is predominantly accessible to lawyers and not readily understood by citizens, the cost of justice itself becomes a

737. Australian Government, Commonwealth Attorney-General's Department: Improving *Australia* s. *Law* and Justice Framework – A discussion paper to explore the scope for reforming Australian contract law –2012 http://www.ag.gov.au/Consultations/Pages/ReviewofAustraliancontractlaw.aspx.
738. *Ibid.*
739. *Ibid.*

barrier. Australia is also a multicultural society. Many of Australia's immigrants come from cultures possessing different legal systems. If these new citizens are to understand their relationship to Australian law, it needs to be more accessible, including being easily translatable and into different languages.[740]

§3. Certainty

695. A third direction and need identified by the Discussion Paper is for certainty. When laws are vague and the status of legal standing in a particular context is unclear, then it is difficult for business or individuals to assess risk, conduct their activities or plan their affairs. This uncertainty adds to transactional costs, often results in delays, and impedes innovation.[741]

§4. Keeping Things Simple and Removing Technicality Thereby Making the Law More Accessible

696. As precedents get refined and distinctions are articulated through various judicial opinions, contract law in many areas has become increasingly complex and overly technical and riddled with unnecessary legal jargon. A future direction mooted by the Discussion Paper is for greater attention focused on the role of law as 'design' and the need to ensure that rules are simple, clear and able to give clear and useful guidance so that citizens can manage their expectations. In short, the law needs to make sense. The 'plain English' movement has been reasonably robust in Australia and is predicted to continue to grow.[742]

§5. Setting Acceptable Standards of Conduct

697. Related to the above points is the important role played by the law in setting acceptable standards. This guidance and standard setting role will be impeded unless the law is clear in terms of what is expected, for example in setting terms in contracts, for example, ensuring that citizens understand what is inappropriate in relation to engaging in unconscionable or misleading conduct related to contracting.[743]

§6. Supporting Innovation

698. The twenty-first Century is characterized by great change and fundamental transformation of most elements of and institutions in society. Contract law needs

740. *Ibid.*
741. *Ibid.*
742. *Ibid.*
743. *Ibid.*

to play a role in enabling and facilitating positive change. It needs to encourage and support innovation so that Australia's legal system will be a vital part of society's infrastructure and an important source of competitive national advantage. The rise and rise of mobile commerce, deployment of big data analytics and the never ending quest for new and improved business models need to be facilitated by laws that support such innovations. Judges, lawyers, regulators, professional groups and others that work in and with the legal profession will also have to be on top of the technology so that the law can be developed, applied, and enforced in ways that achieve the goal of greater participation of citizens in the digital economy.[744]

§7. Maximizing Participation in the Digital Economy

699. While Australia has made great strides and is among the world leaders in establishing the legal infrastructure to support e-commerce, there is no time to rest upon one's laurels and further legal reform must continue. Recent changes in Australia's privacy saws that will come into effect in 2014 is one example of the need for continual adjustment. Another is reform of consumer law so that people will be confident they will receive the same protection in an online environment as they enjoy in traditional commerce. Cybercrime is also a growing threat and security of the infrastructure plus combating such ills as identity theft will also be crucial. In this regard, special attention will have to focus upon migrants for whom English will not be their first language as well as a growing number of senior citizens.[745]

§8. Suitability for Small and Medium-Sized Businesses

700. Small and medium-sized businesses are responsible for much of the job creation in developing countries. At the same time, these smaller entities are often at the bargaining disadvantage of larger competitors. This is especially so when it comes time to contract for infrastructure like cloud computing which is dominated by a few large players and form contracts that force smaller players to comply given there have little alternative. It is thus important for contract law to continue to develop the law in relation to unconscionable conduct taking place in commercial settings. Also, contract law will have to develop go hand in hand with a rigorously enforced competition law.[746]

§9. Elasticity

701. Change today has joined death and taxes as the major certainties in life. Accordingly, legal systems need to be hard-wired to adjust to change. Regular reviews and constant adjustments in legislation need to be the norm and in the very

744. *Ibid.*
745. *Ibid.*
746. *Ibid.*

design of law making. Similarly, law needs certain 'wild-cards', doctrines that can be deployed by courts to give flexibility, elasticity to the law and soften its hard edges in order to do justice. Various rules of equity and doctrines such as estoppels and unconscionability help to fulfil this role. The law also needs to have 'gap-fillers' to fill in the gaps that often remain in the midst of the excitement of deal making. If it is clear that the parties intended to contract, the law should have the capacity to fill those gaps and thus work to meet the expectations of the parties. The notion of 'reasonableness' in price, time, etc. is perhaps the best example of this gap-filling function. It must also be acknowledged that there is always a tension and delicate balance that the law must achieve between flexibility and certainty.[747]

§10. HARMONIZATION

702. Australia's federal system of government with its multiple jurisdictions, each making their own laws gives rise to divergent legal systems, even within the same country. Yet, the economic reality is that Australia is for most purposes a national market and increasingly becoming a global one. In this context, the need to comply with multiple legal requirements, the conflicts that can arise when activities cross jurisdictional boundaries gives rise to uncertainty and adds to transactional costs. To resolve these issues and make the legal system more efficient and effective, there will be continuing movement towards the harmonization of law across state, federal and territory boundaries.[748]

§11. INTERNATIONALIZATION

703. Harmonization will also continue between countries and Australia will have to continue its efforts to align its laws with those of key trading partners. Sometimes this will take the form of Conventions. In other cases, international bodies such as the WTO, NGOs and other groups will promote dialogue and encourage harmonization. An example is the important work by bodies such as the International Chamber of Commerce with the developments of its Incoterms which are widely used in commercial transactions and procurements.[749] Another example is The Uniform Customs and Practice for Documentary Credits (UCP), a set of rules on the issuance and use of letters of credit.[750] The UCP is utilized by bankers and commercial parties in more than 175 countries in trade finance. Some 11%–15% of international trade utilizes letters of credit, totalling over a trillion dollars (US) each year.[751] In other cases still, there will be an agreement on the use of terms governing a particular sphere of economic activity in international trade. Regional cooperation will also continue, with the European Union being the most advanced

747. *Ibid.*
748. *Ibid.*
749. www.iccwbo.org.
750. *www.iccbooks.com.*
751. See generally International Chamber of Commerce: *www.iccwbo.org.*

example. As experience in international and regional harmonization grows and as the world becomes increasingly interconnected, the scope and degree of internationalization of legal systems will be further enhanced.[752]

§12. Law as Competitive Advantage

704. As suggested above, countries are increasingly seeing law not only as vital infrastructure for society but part of a nation's competitive advantage.[753] When laws promote economic innovation, certainty, and efficiency and meet the expectations of the parties, foreign investment will be attracted to Australia.[754]

§13. Dispute Resolution and Dispute Prevention

705. Contract disputes will inevitably arise from time to time. As e-commerce becomes the dominant form of commerce, dispute resolution will also increasingly adopt new and enhanced forms of online dispute resolution of those disputes. Also, we are likely to see a greater focus on good system design that emphasizes dispute prevention.[755]

§14. Legal Education

706. No one likes change, and perhaps lawyers and the legal system are among the most resistant to change. Yet, the transformative view of law and specifically of contract law will only come about if the key players of the legal system (judges, lawyers, administrators and others) receive a different focused legal education that that experienced today. The curriculum will not be based around litigation. Risk identification, risk management, design, process skills, collaboration, entrepreneurship, use of technology, emotional intelligence, and dispute prevention will have a place in this new legal environment.[756]

---

752. Australian Contract Reform Discussion Paper, above.
753. See generally, M.E. Porter, *Competitive Strategy* (Free Press 1980); M.E. Porter, *The Competitive Advantage of Nations* (Free Press 1990); M.E. Porter, *The Five Competitive Forces That Shape Strategy*, Harvard Bus. Rev.,79–93 (January 2008).
754. Siedel, George &Happio, Helena, *Using Proactive Law for Competitive Advantage*, Ross School of Business Paper No. 1148, http://papers.ssrn.com/sol3/papers.cfm?abstract_id=1664561.
755. See generally F. Tanner (2000) Conflict Prevention and Conflict Resolution: Limits of Multilateralism. www.icrc.org/eng/resources/documents/misc/57jqq2.htm; A. Nyhart, & E.A. Dauer, Preliminary Analysis of the Uses of Scientific Models in Dispute Prevention, Management and Resolution, 1986 Mo. J. Disp. Resol. 29 (1986).
756. E. Clark, *Looking Forward: Challenges Facing Legal Education in the 21st Century*, 3 Phoenix L. Rev., 461–71 (2010).

§15. Use Technology, Including Big Data Analytics

707. Technology has also played a significant role in the harmonization of contract law and practice. In law firms, the use of precedent databases for forms has helped to institutionalize best practice. Commercial publishers have also for a long time published form guides that have also led to greater consistency in the use of terms. Also on the international level, law reform and international agencies have recognized the need for harmonization and consistent use of terms by the judiciary, practitioners and others and have undertaken a range of projects aimed at disseminating information on the application of uniform tests, for example through the UNILEX database maintained by UNIDROIT, or the CLOUT system and the CISG Digest developed by UNCITRAL. Such initiatives should be expanded and further advanced in the future, with a view both to widening their coverage, supplementing each other without duplicating efforts, and enhancing their accessibility in a user-friendly manner.[757] Finally, the field of big data analytics is predicted to revolutionize social science research and provide new and more systematic insights into the actual role that contract law plays in society, especially in new environments such as a online contracting.[758]

§16. Growing Influence of 'Code'

708. Australia contract law will continue to focus on the development of 'code' which will mean less reliance on case-by-case growth and slow evolution of the law through the doctrine of precedent. A good example is Australia's comprehensive Competition and Consumer Law as well as regimes to deal with corporations and consumer credit. A second type of code development will be the growth of standards and 'soft law', i.e., codes of conduct, best practice guides and other 'persuasive' and 'educative' measures to educate citizens about what is expected of them and what rights they have under the law. As Larry Lessig demonstrates in Code and Other Laws of Cyberspace, a third type of 'code' will reside in 'software' and hardware which will determine via computer programs, the rights and responsibilities of participants in this new Information Age.[759]

757. José Angelo Estrella Faria, *Future Directions of Legal Harmonisation and Law Reform: Stormy Seas or Prosperous Voyage?*: http://www.unidroit.org/english/publications/review/articles/2009-1&2-faria-e.pdf.

758. See generally, *The Rise of Industrial Big Data* Leveraging large time-series data sets to drive innovation, competitiveness and growth – capitalizing on the big data opportunity. GE Intelligent Platforms White Paper; Leetaru, Kalev H (September 2012) A Big Data Approach to the Humanities, Arts, and Social Sciences: Wikipedia's View of the World through Supercomputing, Issue 30, Research Trends: http://www.researchtrends.com/issue-30-september-2012/a-big-data-approach-to-the-humanities-arts-and-social-sciences-summary/.

759. L. Lessig, *Code and Other Laws of Cyberspace* (Basic Books 1999).

§17. LAW AS SYSTEM

709. Increasingly, government and other architects of the legal system will adopt a 'systems' approach to law and the legal system. Drafters will take into account, more than they presently do, the role that contract law plays in the economy and society. When laws are allowed to become outdated and no longer serve their purpose, the system will not function properly. A systems view of the law will lead to a deeper understanding of the role law plays in society and the adoption of a more a holistic approach to further legal developments. This will in turn lead to a deeper understanding and practice of law as design. That design will take into account all of the features mentioned above in order to achieve a legal system that is more responsive to the needs of business, society and citizens.[760]

760. L.M. LoPuki, *A systems Approach to Law*, 82 Cornell L. Rev. 479 (1996–1997); T. Paredes, *A Systems Approach to Corporate Governance Reform, A Systems Approach to Corporate Governance Reform: Why Importing U.S. Corporate Law Isn't the Answer*, 45 Wm. & Mary L. Rev. (2004) 1055::/scholarship.law.wm.edu/wmlr/vol45/iss3/7.

Selected Bibliography

§1. Books

Astor, H. & C. Chinkin. *Dispute Resolution in Australia*. Sydney: Butterworths, 2002.

Australian Consumer Credit Law Reporter. Sydney, CCH Australia Limited (loose-leaf service).

Australian Consumer Sales and Credit Law Reporter. Sydney, CCH (loose-leaf service).

Australian Federal Tax Reporter. Sydney, CCH (loose-leaf service).

Australian Industrial and Intellectual Property. Sydney, CCH (loose-leaf service).

Australian Insolvency Management Practice. Sydney, CCH (loose-leaf service).

Australian Trade Practices Reporter. Sydney, CCH (loose-leaf service).

Barnes, J. *Who Should Know What? Social Science, Privacy and Ethics*. Harmondsworth: Penguin, 1979.

Birks, P. *Restitution: the Principle*. Sydney: Federation Press, 1992.

Carones, S. *Australian Consumer Law*. 2nd edn, ThomsonReuters, 2012.

Carter, J. & D. Harland. *Contract Law in Australia*. 4th edn, Sydney: Butterworths, 2006.

Carter, J. *Carter's Guide to Australian Contract Law*. 6th edn, Sydney: LexisNexis, 2012.

Carter, J. *Contract and the Australian Consumer Law - A Guide*. Sydney, LexisNexis, 2011.

Carter, J. *Carter's Breach of Contract*. Sydney, LexisNexis, 2011.

Cato, C. *Restitution in Australia and New Zealand*. Sydney: Cavendish Publishing (Australia) Pty Limited, 1997.

Clark, B. & B. Sweeney. *Marketing and the Law*. 4th edn, Sydney: Buttwerworths/ LexisNexis, 2011.

Clarke, P. & J. Clarke. *Contract Law: Commentaries, Cases and Perspectives*. 2nd edn, OUP, 2012.

Dal Pont, G. *Law of Agency*. 2nd edn, Sydney: LexisNexis, 2008.

Dal Pont, G. *Equity and Trusts in Australia and New Zealand*. 5th edn, LBC Information Services, 2011.

Davenport, P. & C. Harris. *Unjust Enrichment*. Sydney: Federation Press, 2007.

Davis, J. *Contract: General Principles – The Laws of Australia*. 2nd edn, Sydney: LawBook Co, 2012.

Deitrich, J. *The Third Restatement of Restitution, the Role of Unjust Enrichment and Australian Law*. Gold Coast, ePublications@Bond 2011.

Selected Bibliography

Duggan, A. *A Financier's Guide to the Law of Guarantee in Australia*. Sydney: Australian Finance Conference Limited, 1998.

Duncan & Willmott. *Mortgages Law in Australia*. 2nd edn, Sydney: Federation Press, 1996.

Edgeworth, B., C.J. Rossiter & M.A. Stone. *Sackville and Neave Property Law: Cases and Materials*. 7th edn, Chatswood, NSW: LexisNexis Butterworths, 2004.

Fisher, S. *Agency Law*. Sydney: LexisNexis/Buttterworths, 2005.

Fletcher, K.L. *Higgins and Fletcher – the Law of Partnership in Australia and New Zealand*. 8th edn, Australia: LBC Information Services, 2001.

Gibson, A. *Commercial Law: In Principle*. 3rd edn, Sydney: LawBook Co, 2005.

Gillies, P. *Concise Contract Law*. 12th edn, Sydney: Federation Press, 2004.

Gillies, S., M. Redfern & A. Terry. *Franchising Law and Practice*. Sydney: LexisNexis, 1998.

Goldring, J. et al. *Consumer Protection Law*. Sydney: Federation Press, 1998.

Gooley, J.V. & P. Radan. *Principles of Australian Contract Law*. Sydney: LexisNexis, 2006.

Graw, S. *An Introduction to the Law of Contract*. 7th edn, Pyrmont NSW: Lawbook Co., 2011.

Harland, D. 'Unconscionable and Unfair Contracts: An Australian Perspective'. In *Good Faith in Contract: Concept and Context*, edited by R. Brownsword, N. Hird and G. Howells (eds). Alderscot: Dartmouth Publishing Company, 1998.

Hird & Howells (eds). *Good Faith in Contract: Concept and Context*. Aldershot: Ashgate, 1999.

Jackman, I.M. *The Varieties of Restitution*. Sydney: Federation Press, 1998.

Latimer, P. *Australian Business Law*. 31st edn, Melbourne: CCH, 2012.

Khoury & Yamouni. *Understanding Contract Law*. 8th edn, LexisNexis, 2009.

Lewis, C. & P. Mann. *Annotated Insurance Act*. 5th edn, Sydney: Lawbook Co, 2012.

Lewison, Lord Justice, D. Hughes. *The Interpretation of Contracts in Australia*. Sydney: ThomsonReuters, 2011.

McMeel, G. *The Construction of Contracts: Interpretation, Implication and Rectification*. 2nd edn, OUP, 2011.

Mann, A.S. *Economics, Business, Ethics & Law*. Sydney: LawBook Co, 2003.

Miller, R.V. *Miller's Australian Competition & Consumer Law Annotated 35th Edition*, Sydney: Thomson, 2013.

O'Donovan, J. & J. Phillips. *The Modern Contract of Guarante*. North Ryde, NSW: LBC Information Services, 1996.

Palmer, N.E. *Bailment*. 3rd edn, Australia: Law Book Co, Australia, 2009.

Paterson, J., A. Robertson & P. Heffey. *Principles of Contract Law*. 2nd edn, Pyrmont, NSW: Lawbook Co, 2005.

Paterson, J. *Unfair Contract Terms in Australia*. Sydney: ThomsonReuters, 2011.

Paterson, J., A. Robertson & P. Heffey. *Contract: Cases and Materials*. 10th edn, Sydney: LawBook Co, 2004.

Pearson, Gail. *Understanding Australian Consumer Credit Law*. Sydney: CCH, 2013.

Peden. *Good Faith in the Performance of Contracts*. Sydney: LexisNexis, 2003.

Phillips, J. & J. O'Donovan. *The Modern Contract of Guarantee*. Sydney: Law Book Co, 1996.
Radan & Gooley. *Principles of Australian Contract Law*. 2nd edn, LexisNexis, 2009.
Seddon, N. *Government Contracts: Federal, State and Local*. 3rd edn, Leichhardt, NSW: The Federation Press, 2004.
Sneddon, N. & M.P. Ellinghouse. *Cheshire and Fifoot's Law of Contract*. 8th edn, Sydney: LexisNexis/Butterworths, 2002.
Seddon, Bigwood & Ellinghaus. *Cheshire & Fifoot Law of Contract*. LexisNexis, 10th Australian Edition, 2012.
Sneddon, N. *Government Contracts: Federal, State and Local*. 3rd edn, Sydney: Federation Press, 2004.
Traves, S.J. *Commercial Law*. Sydney: LexisNexis, 2006.
Turner, C. *Australian Commercial Law*. 28th edn, Sydney: LawBook, 2006.
Vereshack, A. *A Practical Guide to Outsourcing Agreement*. Sydney: LexisNexis/Butterworths, 2006.
Vermeesch, R.H. & K.E. Lingren. *Business Law of Australia*. 11th edn, Sydney: LexisNexis, 2005.
Willmott, L. et al. *Contract Law*. 4th edn, OUP, 2013.

§2. Articles

Aitken, L. 'Unconscionability after Wynne – Yerkey is dead – Long Live Yerkey'. *Law Society Journal* 34 (1996): 73 and *Finance Law Bulletin* 58.
Anker, K. 'Getting to the Bottom of Third Party Guarantees'. *Law Society Journal* 34 (2002): 40.
Bailey, M. 'Sexually Transmitted Debt: Criticism and Perspectives'. *Auckland University Law Review* 8 (1999): 1001.
Barron, P. 'The Exercise of Her Free Will: Women and Emotionally Transmitted Debt'. *Law in Context* 13 (1995): 23.
Baxendale, R. 'Garcia v. National Australia Bank Limited: Ensuring Equity in Surety Transactions: A Legal Debt-End?'. *Sydney Law Review* 313 (1999): 21.
Baxt, R. 'Are Banks Guarantees Safe From The Unconscionable Conduct Of The Trade Practices Act?'. *The Australian Banker* 62 (1997).
Blyth, M. 'When is a Loan Made for a Business Purpose?'. *Australian Banking* (2002): 18.
Brown, I. 'Divided Loyalties in the Law of Agency'. *LQR* 109 (1993): 206.
Burns, F. 'Undue Influence and the Elderly'. *Melbourne University Law Review* 26 (2002): 449.
Campbell, E. 'Commonwealth Contracts'. *Australian Law Journal* 44 (1970): 14.
Carlin, T. 'The Contracts Review Act 1980 (NSW) – 20 Years On'. *Sydney Law Review* 23 (2001): 125.
Collier, B. 'All Debts' Clauses in Commercial Contracts of Guarantee: Principles of Construction and Limitations on the Ambit of Clauses of this Nature'. *Monash University Law Review* 24 (1998): 7.

Duggan, A. 'Til Debt do us Part: A Note on National Australia Bank Ltd v. Garcia'. *Sydney Law Review* 220 (1997): 19.

Field, C. 'The New Face of Consumer Protection'. *Alternative Law Journal* 24 (1999): 157.

Finlay, A. 'Unconscionable Conduct and the Business Plaintiff: Has Australia Gone too Far?'. *Anglo-American Law Review* 28 (1999): 470.

Griggs, L. 'Financial Institutions and Unconscionability – The Banks are in the Wars Again'. *Competition and Consumer Law Journal* 9 (2001): 88.

Haigh, R. & S. Hepburn. 'The Bank Manager Always Rings Twice: Stereotyping in Equity After Garcia'. *Monash University Law Review* 26 (2000): 275.

Horrigan, B. 'Unconscionability Breaks New Ground – Avoiding and Litigating Unfair Client Conduct After ACCC Test Cases and Financial Services Reform'. *Deakin Law Review* 7 (2002): 73.

McLauchlan, D. 'The Uncertain Basis of the Postal Acceptance Rule?'. *Journal of Contract Law* 30 (2013): 33.

McLauchlan, D. 'Contract Interpretation: What Is It About?'. *SydLawRw* 31, no. 1 (2009): 1.

O'Connor, J. 'The Enforceability of Agreements to Negotiate in Good Faith'. *UTasLawRw* 8 (2010); *University of Tasmania Law Review* 9, no. 2 (2010): 177.

Pejovic, G. 'Civil and Common Law: Two Different Paths Leading to the Same Goal'. *Victoria University of Wellington Law Review* (2001): 79.

Phillips, J. 'Setting Aside Guarantees: Another Approach'. *Oxford University Commonwealth Law Journal* 2 (2002): 47.

Sneddon, M. 'Banking and Finance: Guarantees and the Trade Practices Act, Section 51AB'. *Australian Business Law Review* 22 (1994): 368.

Sneddon, M. 'Lenders and Independent Solicitors Certificates and Borrowers: Risk Minimisation or Sharing Loss'. *Australian Business Law Review* 14 (1996): 5.

Sneddon, M. 'Unfair Conduct in Taking Guarantees and the Role of Independent Advice'. *University of New South Wales Law Journal* 13 (1990): 302.

Zipser, B. 'Unjust Contracts and the Contracts Review Act 1980 (NSW)'. *Journal of Contract Law* 17 (2001): 76.

Robertson, Donald. 'The International Harmonisation of Australian Contract Law'. *Journal of Contract Law* 29 (2012): 1.

§3. Major Australian Business Law Journals

Australian Business Law Review. Sydney, LBC Information Services.

Australian Law Journal. Sydney, LBC Information Services.

LexisNexis Butterworths publishes a number of business law journals available online, including *Australian Journal of Corporations Law* and the *Competition and Consumer Law Journal*.

Commercial Law Quarterly, *Commercial Law Association of Australia Ltd.*

Law Reviews published by *University Law Schools and Faculties* (e.g., Canberra Law Review, University of Sydney Law Review, Adelaide Law Review, Tasmania Law Review).

LBC Information Services publishes a large number of business related titles, including *Insolvency Law Journal, Trade Practices Law Journal, Current Commercial Law. Company and Securities Law Journal.*

§4. Some Useful Australian Web Sites on Australian Law

Butterworths, LBC Information Services and CCH all provide a wider range of electronic libraries providing business law information. A standard search engine request should bring up their web site.

Clark, Julia, Australian Contract Law: <www.australiancontractlaw.com/> Library of Congress, Legal Research Guide: Australia: at <http://www.loc.gov/law/help/australia.php>.

Some of the most useful sites for Australian commercial and economic law are: <www.comlaw.gov.au>.

This is the Australian Attorney-General's legal information site and contains a wide range of legal information, including decided cases and legislation from all Australian Federal and most State and territory jurisdictions. It has two levels of searching, with Advanced providing catchword and similar detailed searching within each record according to the type of information sought. <www.aph.gov.au/library/>

This is the Australian Government entry point and allows searching through all parliamentary records and those of the House or Senate. It also holds on line papers produced in the Library's publications program, including Bills Digests, Background Papers, Current Issues Briefs, Research Notes and Research Papers.

For example, specific Intellectual Property information is held at <www.aph.gov.au/library/intguide/law/iplaw.htm>, <www.austlii.edu.au>.

The Australasian Legal Information Institute (AUSTLII) provides free internet access to Australian legal materials. AUSTLII is one of the largest sources of legal materials on the net, with over six gigabytes of raw text materials and over a million searchable documents. AUSTLII publishes *public legal information*: that is, primary legal materials (legislation, treaties and decisions of courts and tribunals); and secondary legal materials created by public bodies for purposes of public access (law reform and royal commission reports, etc.).

Selected Bibliography

Case Index (References are to Paragraph Numbers)

Case Index

Case Index

Case Index

Index

www.ingramcontent.com/pod-product-compliance
Lightning Source LLC
Chambersburg PA
CBHW071434230926
51846CB00001B/225